Women
Horror Films of
Vincent Price

Women in the Horror Films of Vincent Price

JONATHAN MALCOLM LAMPLEY

Foreword by Caroline Munro

McFarland & Company, Inc., Publishers
Jefferson, North Carolina, and London

Frontispiece: Dr. Phibes (Vincent Price) strikes a suggestive
pose with Vulnavia (Virginia North) in this publicity still
from *The Abominable Dr. Phibes* (1971).

LIBRARY OF CONGRESS CATALOGUING-IN-PUBLICATION DATA

Lampley, Jonathan Malcolm, 1967–
Women in the horror films of Vincent Price /
Jonathan Malcolm Lampley ; foreword by Caroline Munro.
      p.   cm.
Includes bibliographical references and index.
Includes filmography.

ISBN 978-0-7864-3678-1
softcover : 50# alkaline paper ∞

1. Price, Vincent, 1911–1993 — Criticism and interpretation.
2. Horror films — History and criticism.
3. Women in motion pictures.   4. Sex role in motion pictures.
I. Title.
PN2287.P72L35   2011   791.43'6164082 — dc22   2010036432

British Library cataloguing data are available

On the cover: Vincent Price and Barbara Steele in the 1961 film
The Pit and the Pendulum (AIP/Kobal Collection)

Manufactured in the United States of America

McFarland & Company, Inc., Publishers
Box 611, Jefferson, North Carolina 28640
www.mcfarlandpub.com

To my mother, Charlene Jones,
for her unyielding faith and enduring love.

TABLE OF CONTENTS

ACKNOWLEDGMENTS

No book of any significance is completed alone. The most driven authors must sometimes seek the advice and insight of other writers, and even the most astute scholar must sometimes call upon other experts in his field for the benefit of their experience and suggestions. Although many writers claim to prefer the solitude necessary for extensive composition, I daresay the vast majority agrees with me that sometimes one must step away from a project and spend time in the company of loved ones who offer sympathetic shoulders and pleasant diversions from the tasks at hand. It follows, then, that a few words of acknowledgment are appropriate when a book is finally finished.

This book is an expansion of my doctoral dissertation, which I completed at Middle Tennessee State University in 2007. I would like to again express my appreciation to Drs. Linda Badley and David Lavery for guiding me through the dissertation process; their suggestions have contributed to this expanded project as well. I am also grateful to the students, faculty, and staff of Dalton State College for their encouragement and interest in this book, especially Dr. Kris Barton, Prof. Nick Carty, Prof. Leslie Collins, Dr. Wes Davis, Prof. Jerry Drye, Dr. Kent Harrelson, Dr. Leslie Harrelson, Ms. Donna Hendrix, Dr. Clint Kinkead, Dr. Nancy Mason, Dr. Thomas Mullen, Dr. Barbara Murray, Dr. Keith Perry, Dr. Lydia Postell, Dr. Christy Price, Dr. Tony Simones, and Dr. Natalie Trice. Special thanks to Dr. Mary Nielsen, Dean of the School of Liberal Arts, and Mr. David Elrod, Director of Institutional Advancement, for their assistance with my research activities.

I would be remiss if I did not mention the support of many good friends and dear relatives, including Anthony Ambrogio, Marc Ballard, Prof. Tracy J. Barkley, Ken Beck, Bill Byrge, Mark Clark, Prof. R. Michael Darrell, Alison Egan, Andrew Egan, Dawn Gillihan, Gregory S. Greene, Dr. Johnanna Grimes, Dr. Karen Gupton, Arlena Hayden, Melody Henderson, Julian Hinson, James J. J. Janis, Lisa N. Keylon, Brenda Lampley, Jim Lampley (Senior and Junior), John Lancaster, Arthur J. Lundquist, Jim Ridley, Katherine J. Schnauffer, Brian Smith, Cindy Ruth Collins Smith, Sophia Stevenson, Gary Svehla, Sue Svehla, Steve Thornton, Prof. Michael Turner, Joshua Vance, Kate Wilson, and Laura Wilson.

Thanks also to Ronald V. Borst of Hollywood Movie Posters, from whom I acquired the images in this book except as noted below. Derek Martin (pages 8, 12, 96, and 169), Jerry Murbach of Doctor Macro's High Quality Movie Scans (cover and pages 4, 16, 20, 25, 77, and 155), and Bryan Senn (pages 9, 23, 36, 46, 51, 64, 68, 74, 87, and 100) loaned materials from their collections to illustrate the book, and John R. Barcus of Bombcat Design Company contributed his photographic skills. Special thanks go to Gary Conn, Jr., who was invaluable when it came to copying and editing images from his own and other collections (pages 142, 191, and 192). In addition to sharing materials from his private collection (pages 27, 41, and 181), Dr. Jeff Thompson read and made suggestions to the manuscript. Prof. Laurel Jenkins-Crowe also made editorial comments on the manuscript, for which I am very grateful.

FOREWORD
BY CAROLINE MUNRO

I have fond memories of working on *The Abominable Dr. Phibes* (1971) and *Dr. Phibes Rises Again* (1972). Of course, it was all done ages ago, and I've quite forgotten some details. However, I was in the papers quite a lot through modeling campaigns, so I was in the news, so to speak. I think it was a case of the studio wanting a familiar face for the part of Dr. Phibes' wife. As I recall, I was under contract with Hammer (Britain's leading producer of horror films), and they didn't want my name in other films, so that's why I was uncredited in the Phibes pictures.

Making the Phibes films was quite good in a way because I didn't have any lines to learn! Many actors would be upset because they have no lines, but I was still very young and inexperienced, so I spent a lot of time quietly watching and learning how films are made. I just sat and listened to Vincent speaking his lines, which he had memorized even though he would later be re-dubbed with the recorder effect to make his voice sound electronic and artificial. As far as the shooting itself, I was on and off the set over a couple of weeks depending on whether I was floating on the water or with that bizarre little band. I also spent two or three days shooting still pictures of Mrs. Phibes, which were used to decorate the Phibes house. We did the head shots in the studio and the rest in these wonderful, stately homes. I never got any copies of these images, so I don't know what happened to them. I would love to see them again.

The shoot itself went well. I was really quite young and didn't have a lot of experience, but as far I was concerned it went fine. My only fear was trying not to breathe during takes — I had to hold my breath, and when you are told not to flicker your eyes it's hard not to do it! I was also allergic to the flowers on the negligee, so I sometimes couldn't help sneezing, which meant we had to do another take. Overall, though, the shoot was a happy experience.

Vincent Price was absolutely fascinating to be around — witty, charming, and always a gentleman. He made you feel special even though you had a bit part. He didn't behave as if he was a big star; he was always just his charming self. He was an amazing chef and sometimes brought cakes and other treats to the set. I also liked working with Joseph Cotten on the first film; he was very quiet but a nice bloke. On the second film, Robert Quarry was quite a character and very good looking. I didn't get to know Virginia North, who played Dr. Phibes' assistant in the first one, very well, but I liked Valli Kemp (who took over the role in the sequel) a lot. Interestingly, I appeared in advertisements for Lamb's Navy Rum for about 12 years, starting in 1969 or 1970, and Valli appeared in some of the ads after the second Phibes movie.

The horror films just came about. I didn't start out to be an actress at all; I wanted to be an artist originally, but I didn't get into art school and so I got into modeling and then acting. Maybe it was my lucky thing falling into acting via modeling. Anyway, I never planned on becoming a "scream queen," and I certainly never imagined I would eventually work with Christopher Lee, Peter Cushing, and Vincent Price. It's extraordinary! I found them all to be extraordinary gentlemen, but all very different and individual. They got on so well. They all had one thing in common that I think was the key to their success: they all had such amazing imaginations. They also had such wonderful voices, and they all had great senses of humor, especially Vincent. I'm very glad that I got the opportunity to work with him and that people are still interested in those pictures even after all these years.

INTRODUCTION
Welcome to My Nightmare:
Vincent Price Considered

For generations of moviegoers, the name Vincent Price (1911–1993) has been synonymous with horror and suspense. Indeed, his reputation as the screen's greatest bogeyman remains unchallenged by any performer to emerge since his prime; only Boris Karloff and Bela Lugosi might realistically challenge Price for the title of greatest horror film star of all time, at least in terms of public consciousness, respect, and affection. Whether he was cast as the tortured or torturing (sometimes both!) protagonist in adaptations of Poe or as the scarred avenger in such classics as *House of Wax* (1953) and *The Abominable Dr. Phibes* (1971), Price's mellifluous voice, powerful screen presence, and twinkling eyes (capable of conveying madness and humor in equal measure) thrilled audiences in his heyday and continue to fascinate fans years after his death and decades after his last significant horror performance. As Mark Clark points out, "Evil never looked so good.... Price wore screen villainy like an Armani suit" (90).

Between 1960 and 1972, Vincent Price appeared in a series of Edgar Allan Poe adaptations produced under the banner of American International Pictures — the independent production company for whom he made the vast majority of his horror films. In all, Price appeared in eleven feature films at least putatively based on Poe's work; he narrated *Spirits of the Dead* (1969), a European anthology boasting Poe stories as envisioned by arthouse favorites Roger Vadim, Federico Fellini, and Louis Malle (which AIP distributed in the United States); and he starred in *An Evening of Edgar Allan Poe*, a quartet of one-man readings AIP developed as a television special. Over the course of a decade, then, Vincent Price and AIP collaborated on thirteen Poe-derived film and TV projects. While certain individual films such as *House of Wax* or *The Fly* may be more familiar "Vincent Price movies" in the minds of the general public, it is the now-legendary Poe series that really defines the actor's place in the history of horror cinema — "for better and for worse," as Lucy Chase Williams puts it (164). Indeed, the Poe cycle earns the actor a unique distinction among fantasy specialists: other thespians may be recognized for multiple performances as monster *characters* — Bela Lugosi as Count Dracula, Peter Cushing as Baron Frankenstein — yet no major "horror star" portrayed his most famous *character* as often as Vincent Price interpreted onscreen the output of horror literature's greatest *writer*.

Various articles and essays in both popular magazines and academic journals offer intriguing interpretations of specific films, but careful analyses of thematic issues in Vincent Price's body of work are virtually non-existent. It is this lack of thematic surveys that has inspired this study. *Women in the Horror Films of Vincent Price* is intended to partially fill the void that exists in horror film scholarship in particular and cinema studies in general. There are other issues of interest associated with the films, particularly the quality of Price's performances and the larger cultural context in which the actor's career needs to be placed, but the role that gender plays in the films merits special attention.

Ambivalence about gender roles and expectations is frequently the engine that propels Price's characters down the paths they pursue. Indeed, the actor's somewhat effete manner informs his characters, occasionally suggesting the exaggerated mannerisms associated with the term "camp." What Harry M. Benshoff identifies as the queer or "homo-horror approach" involving "a gay or lesbian film star (whether 'actually' homosexual or culturally perceived as such) [who] brings his/her persona to a horror film" (14) is often useful. Because the application of "queer theory" is an often misunderstood element of the larger field of gender studies, I think it is necessary to emphasize here that I am concerned with issues of gender and sexuality as they apply to characters in the films, not the performers themselves. Rumors about the sex lives of Hollywood stars are as much a consequence of celebrity as fan mail and the paparazzi (and, it must be admitted, books about Hollywood stars). It is not my intention to "out" Vincent Price or make any claims about his private life; indeed, such matters are beyond the scope of this study and my expertise, although they have been discussed elsewhere, most notably in his daughter's biography.

This shot of a debonair Vincent Price as Dr. Cross in *Shock* (1946) belies the character's homicidal but guilt-haunted nature.

Be that as it may, it is true that a wide streak of anti-intellectualism runs through American culture, particularly popular culture. To many Americans, there is something inherently "queer" (in both the term's denotative and connotative senses) about artists, scientists, and other highly creative or educated people. Regardless of their individual characters or plot elements, all horror stories share a central concern, which is the intrusion of "difference" into a "normal" environment. In light of the lingering cultural conservatism in the United States, it is hardly surprising that anxiety over difference (sexual or otherwise) often merges with anti-intellectual impulses and results in texts that purport to illustrate the consequences awaiting those who think too much or too differently from their fellow Americans. Under these circumstances, it is obvious that part of Vincent Price's appeal as a sort of "public bogeyman" is that his horror films allow audiences to confront and perhaps conquer their individual anxieties about various issues, including their assumptions about gender and sexuality.

Female characters represent fundamental concerns that horror texts frequently explore. In addition to gender ambivalence, anxiety about sexuality, romantic love, and the ramifications of challenges to existing social and cultural paradigms informs Price's thrillers. According to Steven Thornton,

> The AIP Poe films, made at the vanguard of [the women's liberation movement], reflect the tensions of the times in their compulsive, manic-tinged gender battles. ... recurring themes of premature burial, sexual repression, and passions from beyond the grave seem to reflect the frustrations of women whose voices in society were restricted by the social constraints of the time [207].

On the most fundamental level, the women in Price's films are horrific because their presence represents a transgression against the assumptions and protocols of the patriarchal communities in which the stories take place. As Barbara Creed points out in "Horror and the Monstrous-Feminine: An Imaginary Abjection,"

> In general terms, ... abjection, as a source of horror, works within patriarchal societies as a means of separating the human from the non-human and the fully constituted subject from the partially formed subject. Ritual becomes a means by which societies both renew their initial contact with the abject element and then exclude that element [36].

Women in Price's horror films, ultimately, are barometers of the "dread of difference" analyzed in Barry Keith Grant's 1996 study of gender and horror. Of course, there are instances wherein the fluidity of gender constructs among male characters equally suggests a similar dread of difference, and often such anxiety becomes an internal component that drives the Price protagonists to distraction or death.

Moreover, characters such as Madeline *House of Usher* (1960) and Sarah in *The Conqueror Worm* (1968) contribute significantly to those films' achievement of thematic fealty to the source material: the works of Edgar Allan Poe. Even when films differ substantially from Poe's fiction and poetry in the details, they nevertheless convey an accurate impression of the author's particular interest in romantic obsession, insanity, and the inevitability of death. This observation directly refutes the prevailing critical assessment of the series, which emphasizes the liberties taken with Poe's output without acknowledging the thematic connections between the films and the fiction.

Women in Vincent Price's horror films are variously depicted as villains, victims, and objects of veneration or some combination thereof. As Barbara Creed observes, "All human societies have a conception of the monstrous-feminine, of what it is about woman that is shocking, terrifying, horrific, abject" (35). It is in their depiction of women that the AIP Poe adaptations in particular illustrate the ambivalence towards the feminine that informed the mindset of many Cold War–era Americans, an ambivalence altered but not greatly different from the attitudes of the nineteenth century. While Poe himself treated women in his fiction as beings to be worshipped, his women, such as Ligeia and Madeline Usher, were often fearsome creatures. Interestingly, comparatively few of Poe's major female characters are clearly identified as victims, so the AIP films often create or modify females for Price to menace.

Frequently deemphasized in other horror film studies, the Poe series has been the subject of only one substantial article, Steven Thornton's "The Women of American International Pictures" (1996), a thoughtful piece undermined by its brevity and restricted coverage of only five films. Don G. Smith's *The Poe Cinema* (1999) is more comprehensive, but Smith discusses all cinematic adaptations of Poe, thus limiting the space available to cover the Price films. Although Ken Gelder worries that "close readings of specific horror texts" raise the question "how much significance can horror take?" (6), an area so rarely explored in depth as the AIP Poe series can surely survive an inquiry into its meaning and relevance without growing stale.

Considerable scholarship has been devoted to gender and sexuality in horror movies; most of it, however, centers on women in horror films of the so-called Modern Age of Horror Cinema (roughly the mid–1970s to the present). Innovative books such as Carol Clover's *Men, Women, and Chain Saws: Gender in the Modern Horror Film* (1992) are by chronological definition unconcerned with Price's films. It seems that women as victims (and sometimes as victimizers) in "slasher films" have proven more intriguing to academic writers. Issues of gender and sexuality in the classics of the Golden Age of Horror Cinema (roughly 1931–1948) have been explored in Rhonda J. Berenstein's *Attack of the Leading Ladies* (1996) and elsewhere, but such studies again omit Price's most significant horror movies. Ultimately the tendency of critics to focus on the early and late periods of horror film production reveals a critical void that beckons for additional interpretation and analysis of movies made during what might best be described as the Silver Age of Horror Cinema (roughly 1957–1973), the era chiefly associated with American International's Poe-Price efforts and Hammer's Gothic remakes.

Given Vincent Price's popularity, it is not surprising that he has been the subject of many brief profiles before and after his death. It is surprising, however, that full-length studies of his life and work have been less common. Price himself authored or edited several books, including works on cooking and art, but none of these have much to say about his horror films (indeed, some of these books were conceived specifically to refute his spooky public image). Price completed two volumes of memoirs —*I Like What I Know* (1959), which covered his "adventures in art," and *The Book of Joe* (1962), which discussed a favorite dog and was filled "with delightful anecdotes concerning other household pets" (Parish and Whitney 259)—yet neither provides much insight into the actor's sinister performances, many of which were not committed to film when these works were published. The actor penned a short autobiography aimed at younger readers titled *Vincent Price: His Movies, His Plays, His Life* (1978), but the book's brevity and intended audience render it practically useless as a critical source. Frankly, it appears that the actor was very reluctant to take his horror films as seriously as his fans and critics do. It has therefore fallen to other parties to produce full-length examinations of Price's cinematic career.

James Robert Parish and Steven Whitney published *Vincent Price Unmasked* in 1974, the only major biography to appear during the actor's life. Although it provides excellent factual information about its subject and is profusely illustrated, it is insubstantial as a critical study of Price's professional output, possibly because the authors were such devoted fans. Lucy Chase Williams' *The Complete Films of Vincent Price* (1995) is more comprehensive, but it too is more biographical and factual than interpretive and analytical. Williams devotes more or less equal coverage to each production, an approach which is beneficial in the sense that it exposes readers to Price's lesser-known films, especially his non-genre output, but such an all-purpose survey necessarily diminishes the opportunities to examine individual trends and themes. *Vincent Price: A Daughter's Biography* (1999), by Victoria Price, is the most carefully researched and insightful account of the actor's life, yet the biographer freely admits her relative distaste for her father's horror films. As a result, she minimizes her discussion of his most significant professional legacy.

Denis Meikle's *Vincent Price: The Art of Fear* (2003) is perhaps the best full-length survey of Price's career to appear in print thus far. An insightful critic capable of making thoughtful observations about the actor's horror and mystery films, Meikle often brilliantly incorporates material published by earlier writers and unearths a multitude of rare and unusual publicity materials to illustrate his book. Although more focused than previous surveys of Price's work, and particularly attentive to the Poe adaptations, Meikle's book is not intended to offer the close reading of individual films and themes that Price's output requires.

Vincent Price's status as a horror specialist is well served by insightful chapters in John Brosnan's *The Horror People* (1976) and Mark Clark's *Smirk, Sneer and Scream: Great Acting in Horror Cinema* (2004), but by definition such broad works must cover other performers besides Price, thereby diverting their attention from him. *Vincent Price* (1998), edited by Gary J. and Susan Svehla, contains several insightful essays on individual films, especially the ones derived from Poe. However, the fact that various authors cover individual films precludes the possibility of incorporating a single thesis or general approach to a consideration of the actor and his work. Biographical documentaries such as A&E's 1993 episode of *Biography* devoted to the actor are interesting but ultimately too brief. Price himself put little stock in such biographical projects, as suggested by his comment that "the revelation of people's personal lives, unless it has to do with their art, [tends] to be boring. When [biographies] have to do with people's art, then they're interesting" (qtd. in Svehla and Svehla, *Vincent*, back cover). All of the general studies, however, offer a framework of facts and dates upon which any serious investigation of the actor's career must rely. I am indebted to those who have gone before me, for they have paved the way for the kind of narrowly focused study I have undertaken.

The actor who "could bring an arch elegance to even the most insipid goings-on" (Skal, *Horror* 257) was born Vincent Leonard Price, Jr., in St. Louis, Missouri, on May 27, 1911, the youngest of four children born to Vincent Leonard and Marguerite Willcox Price. The family was, according to the actor, "well-to-do, not rich enough to evoke envy but successful enough to demand respect" (qtd. in Price 5). Price's father was president of the National Candy Company whose associates presented him with a plaque commemorating the birth of "the Candy Kid" on the day baby Vincent was born (Parrish and Whitney 1).

After graduating from Yale University in 1933, Price taught school briefly before

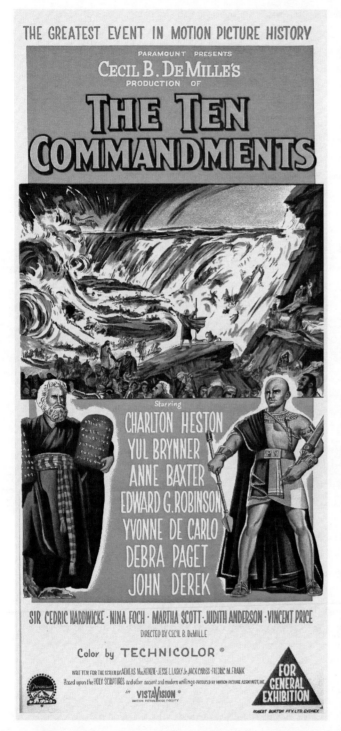

Among Price's non-genre films, *The Ten Commandments* (1956) is undoubtedly the most famous. Note Price's twelfth place billing on this rare Australian day bill.

enrolling at the Courtauld Institute of the University of London, a prestigious art school. Given the direction into horror and fantasy that his acting career would take, it is interesting that the young art lover met Florence Stoker, widow of the author of *Dracula*, during this time (Skal, *Hollywood* 232). While in England, Price decided to pursue an acting career after successful performances in *Chicago* and *Victoria Regina*. American theatrical work followed, and in 1938 Price made his cinematic debut as the romantic lead in a screwball comedy, *Service De Luxe*. Price appeared in costume dramas, historical epics, and war pictures early in his career; roles in *Tower of London* (1939, opposite Boris Karloff and Basil Rathbone) and *The Invisible Man Returns* (1940) foreshadowed the Gothic nature of his later productions.

Price's turn as a suave rake in *Laura* (1944), which remained "the best film he ever made" (Price 117), demonstrates the combination of the sensual and the sinister that made him ideal for Gothic horror productions. As tall and handsome Shelby Carpenter, the fiancé of the title character (Gene Tierney), Price was perfectly cast as a charming but ultimately unfaithful lover who turns to an older woman (Judith Anderson) for emotional and financial support when his duplicity is uncovered. Twice more the actor would be paired with Tierney (earlier both actors had performed small roles in *Hudson's Bay*, 1941): in *Leave Her to Heaven* (1945), Price plays the jilted lover of Tierney's psychotic murderess, and in *Dragonwyck* (1946), Price's drug-addled lord of the manor marries, then attempts to kill, Tierney's innocent heroine. These final pairings with Gene Tierney, with their emphasis on mental instability and Gothic iconography, provide a blueprint for the actor's horror films, for they each cast him as a more or less unstable love interest who is ultimately rejected by the Tierney character and involve a degree of sexual or romantic obsession and conflict. *Shock* (1946), Price's first top-billed screen role (Parish and Whitney 63), cemented the actor's villainous onscreen persona as a murderous psychiatrist urged to mayhem by his lovestruck mistress. This plot device alludes to the greed and ambition of Lady Macbeth in Shakespeare's play, and like *Macbeth*, *Shock* offers a female protagonist who takes on masculine traits of aggression while the male protagonist retreats to a submissive, feminine role as the somewhat reluctant instrument of his female partner's will.

House of Wax (1953), whose novel 3-D effects helped sell millions of tickets worldwide (counting revivals and taking inflation into consideration, it is probably Price's most financially successful feature), was a throwback to the sort of classic horror films popularized

by the likes of Boris Karloff and Bela Lugosi; *The Fly* (1958) was another enormous hit (although for once Price plays a sympathetic supporting character, not the titular monster). These titles are probably the most popular of Price's horror films and have inspired remakes and rip-offs of varying quality. Although Price continued to appear in non-genre films like *The Ten Commandments* (1956), his status as a horror star was fixed by 1960 thanks to his performances in *House on Haunted Hill* (1958) and *The Tingler* (1959) for William Castle and, especially, the cycle of Poe adaptations directed by Roger Corman, beginning with *House of Usher*.

Price continued to work even after the Poe series ground to a halt. He experienced a late-career renaissance in a series of darkly humorous revenge thrillers initiated by *The Abominable Dr.*

Roderick Usher (Price) fixes his ambiguous gaze upon his sister, Madeline (Myrna Fahey), in Roger Corman's seminal *House of Usher* (1960).

Phibes (1971) and its sequel, *Dr. Phibes Rises Again!* (1972). The highlight of what can be grouped as Price's "Revenge Cycle" is *Theatre of Blood* (1973), which features an all-star supporting cast of British stage luminaries and became the actor's favorite experience among his horror productions (Price 279). Unfortunately, the next film in the cycle, *Madhouse* (1974), failed with critics and audiences alike. It is a shameful waste not only of Price's talents but also those of fellow horror veterans Peter Cushing and Robert Quarry, all of whom are trapped in a confusing, illogical, slow-moving production that bungles an opportunity to provide a fitting coda to the Silver Age of Horror Cinema. Nevertheless, the Revenge Cycle films are perhaps the most interesting and respected of the actor's cinematic legacy, in part due to their foregrounding in his screen persona. Unfortunately, fatigue began to set in, as the actor explained to Stanley Wiater:

> I *was* sent some scripts. But the last ones I [made], ... like *Theatre of Blood* ... or the Dr. Phibes films, were send-ups. So everything that was sent to me after that was exactly the same story. Done in a different way or with a different plot, maybe, but significantly the same story. Or they were overly violent. ... so I didn't do them [131].

Price eschewed horror parts completely, resulting in a nearly five-year absence from the screen (television, the stage, and the lecture circuit kept him profitably employed). When he returned, he usually appeared in supporting roles in both genre and mainstream films. In 1983, Price headlined *House of the Long Shadows*, a thriller of the "Old Dark House" variety, with three other titans of terror: Christopher Lee, Peter Cushing, and John Carradine. Although flawed, the film is remarkable as the one and only film in which all four of these horror stars appear together. After winning critical approval for *The Great Mouse Detective* (1986) and *The Whales of August* (1987), Price gave his final feature performance, as the eccentric but gentle inventor of *Edward Scissorhands* (1990), for director Tim Burton, a young fan inspired by Price's Gothic thrillers to make his own fantasy-themed movies. Worn down by age and infirmity, the actor completed his final role, a brief guest appearance in the TV movie *Heart of Justice*, a few months before his death on October 25, 1993.

Vincent Price's cinematic reputation enabled him to develop a public persona that resulted in a one-man cottage industry of ghoulish profitability; the actor delivered spoken word performances of Poe for record companies, shilled numerous household products in television commercials, and lent his sardonic image to children's toys and games. A Vincent Price comic book appeared in 2008. Price's many guest appearances on TV programs (most memorably on *Batman*, *The Brady Bunch*, and *The Hollywood Squares*) further suggested his ubiquity and enhanced his standing as a cultural icon. From 1981 to 1989, Price hosted the PBS series *Mystery!* Years after his death, Price still popped up as the subject of jokes on such TV shows as *The Simpsons* (in a 1999 episode) and *Saturday Night Live* (hilariously portrayed by Bill Hader in a series of mock holiday specials).

Having already endeared himself to rock music fans by narrating a track on Alice Cooper's 1975 album *Welcome to My Nightmare*, Price cemented his standing among a new generation of admirers by performing a sort of Gothic rap on Michael Jackson's *Thriller* album (1983), one of the best-selling records of all time. In all probability, younger audiences know Price better for his participation on the title track than any of his movie

A rare lobby card prepared for the Mexican release of *The Conqueror Worm* (aka *Witchfinder General*; 1968).

or TV appearances. Following Jackson's unexpected death in 2009, sales of all his records skyrocketed; as a result, a surge in sales and downloads of the song "Thriller" has introduced Price to the so-called Millenial Generation. Other rock acts, including ZZ Top and The Misfits, have paid homage to the actor during their careers. Projects by such innovators as Alan Parsons and Lou Reed, while specifically concerned with Poe's fiction and poetry, nevertheless were composed with an awareness of Price's Poe-inspired movies.

Price's lifelong interest in the visual arts and gourmet cooking allowed him to show a different side of his personality when he lectured and demonstrated his expertise in person and on talk shows. As Rick Worland has pointed out, Price "cultivated the image of a cosmopolitan teacher of art appreciation and gourmet cuisine made accessible to the masses" (22). Price's real-life status as a Renaissance man ultimately informs his onscreen persona and vice versa; the actor has become an ambiguous figure in popular culture, a sort of Santa Claus of shudders whose impressive offscreen accomplishments somehow contradict his villainous image while simultaneously contributing to it by associating education and refinement with mental and emotional abnormality.

Almost all of Price's horror films refer to gender and sexual conflict, sometimes for comic effect. As a result, the AIP releases (especially those helmed by Corman) serve as a sort of barometer measuring changes in sex roles in American society. Thus, archetypical depictions of males as intrepid young heroes give way to more complicated visions of men as ambivalent protagonists, "bad boys" who threaten the status quo because of their disregard for societal norms, including traditional paradigms of gender and sexuality. Similarly, female roles evolve from stock characters, such as the virginal heroine or the trampy "vamp" reflective of postwar gender assumptions, into more rounded characters whose complexity indicates the radical reconception of womanhood that emerged in the 1960s.

The Price-Corman-AIP collaboration required a deep wellspring of inspiration, which the poems and short stories of Edgar Allan Poe provided in abundance. "Horror, despair, and the ever-present gaping of the grave" informed Poe's life and works (Bloom 12). Born on January 19, 1809, to itinerant actors then residing in Boston, Edgar Poe was orphaned by the age of three and taken in by John and Francis Allan of Richmond. After his foster mother died, Poe was cut out of Allan's will, left in almost unrelenting poverty for the rest of his life. Over the years, Poe edited such distinguished publications as the *Southern Literary Messenger* and *Graham's Literary Magazine*. Poe's most important poem, "The Raven," appeared in 1845, earning the critical and popular renown that continues to this day. Yet the poem's notoriety brought no financial security, and Poe struggled to survive. Tuberculosis struck his wife (and cousin), Virginia, in 1842; she succumbed to it in 1847. Crushed, Poe alleviated his pain with alcohol, laudanum, and attempts to woo other women. In October of 1849, a disheveled Poe was discovered unconscious in a Baltimore alley; he died on the seventh after uttering his last words: "Lord, help my poor soul!" (qtd. in Bloom 14).

Poe is remembered for inventing the detective story with "Murders in the Rue Morgue" and crafting satirical pieces and nonfiction articles in addition to his fiction and poetry. In "The Poetic Principle," published posthumously in 1850, Poe claimed that the love of a woman "is unquestionably the purest and truest of all poetical themes" (906), an intensely Romantic notion that is incorporated into many films adapted from his work. However, "Poe's greatest literary achievement was his renovation of the terror tale ... into what has been recognized as some of the most sophisticated creations in psychological fiction in the English language" (Fisher 78). The eminent critic Harold Bloom provides perhaps the best assessment of the author and his works:

> Chivalrous toward women, courteous and charming when not in his cups, brilliant in his work, yet one of the most deeply tormented figures of American literature, Edgar Allan Poe blazed darkly through life. He became a major influence on the French Symbolists.... His effect upon American writers is incalculable.... His stories, far from haunting us with the unknown, bring us face to face with our own devils, and through our terror we come to see a powerful, frightening side of our own consciousness [14].

Edgar Allan Poe certainly ranks high on the list of literary figures who have become integrated into popular culture, as Mark Neimeyer has demonstrated with his discussion of the T-shirts, mouse pads, coffee cups, football team, and Navy minesweeper that have been named in honor of or in allusion to Poe (205–206), but it is the cinema that "is the single most significant medium to have exploited Poe" (Neimeyer 216). Brooding, brilliant, and artistic, yet inevitably unhinged by madness and obsession, Vincent Price's Poe-derived characters became his stock-in-trade. While the actor demonstrated his versatility on television and in non-horror features, the Poesque protagonist inevitably seemed to inform his popular persona — even after the films were reduced to borrowing Poe's titles and little else, a development that especially irked their star, according to Lucy Chase Williams (218).

This study is concerned with the major horror films Vincent Price made between 1960 and 1974 — the prime years of his career and the period during which he was primarily associated with AIP. Because of their influence on his career, several key early films are included as well. Otherwise, I have chosen to exclude the minor projects that either pre-date Price's heyday as a horror icon or that followed his peak. Some of these omitted films are entertaining or interesting, but I don't feel they add much to a discussion of gender and identity (at least as far as the Price characters are concerned). The study demonstrates that while questions of gender identification and sexuality are relevant to Price's movies, the films themselves are not usually "campy" in the sense of exaggerated self-mockery that other observers have claimed. Furthermore, issues associated with sexuality, such as the number and sex of offspring, are clues that suggest the degree to which Price's characters are misaligned with conventional assumptions about gender.

Chapters 1 through 4 discuss the most significant of Price's horror and mystery films prior to the actor's association with AIP. Chapters 5 through 13 examine the six Poe adaptations directed by Roger Corman and starring Price between 1960 and 1965 except for 10 and 11. These two chapters are concerned with *Twice-Told Tales* (1963), a film made for another company that purports to be based on the work of Nathaniel Hawthorne but owes a great debt to AIP's Poe films, and *The Last Man on Earth* (1964), a radical departure from the Poe series that AIP released domestically. The cycle of Poe adaptations continued to influence Price's public persona long after the series abandoned any direct connection to Poe's material, particularly in the portrayal of female characters. The films are derived from the following works: "The Fall of the House of Usher," "The Pit and the Pendulum," "The Raven," "Morella," "The Black Cat" (combined with "The Cask of Amontillado"), "The Case of M. Valdemar" (the foregoing four stories make up the constituent episodes of *Tales of Terror*, 1962), "The Masque of the Red Death" (which also incorporates "Hop-Frog" into the plot), and "Ligeia."

"The Fall of the House of Usher" is concerned with Madeline Usher, whose brother venerates her and victimizes her (by burying her alive) but also idealizes her; this complexity is well incorporated into the 1960 production titled *House of Usher*. Poe's most familiar work, "The Raven," features the most unambiguous attitude towards a woman in any of these tales: the speaker clearly adores his lost Lenore. Interestingly, the 1963 adaptation of the film portrays Lenore as an object of worship and an agent of villainy, with emphasis on the latter. Both "Morella" and "Ligeia" are venerated and feared in roughly equal measure, while the nameless wife in "The Black Cat" and the tiny dancer Tripetta in "Hop-Frog" are clearly victims (although Tripetta is mistreated by the king, she is adored by Hop-Frog).

After a brief lull, AIP restarted the Poe franchise with a group of four films based very loosely on the author's output. Chapter 14 analyzes *The Conqueror Worm* (1968), perhaps the most critically acclaimed of the Poe-influenced productions, and traces the influence of this film and its director, Michael Reeves, on the remaining entries in the series, all of which were helmed by Gordon Hessler. Chapter 15 examines *Scream and Scream Again* (1970), one of Price's most unusual departures from period Gothic horror (and one of the most unusual horror films, period). Chapters 16 through 18 deal with the "Revenge Cycle," four black comedies that owe as much to Price's public persona as to the Gothic horror films that helped establish that persona. Chapter 19 addresses *War-Gods of the Deep* (1965), a Poe-derived production that exists outside the Corman and Reeves-Hessler "universe" but still features Price, and several other stray AIP projects, including Roger Corman's *Premature Burial* (1962) and Gordon Hessler's *Murders in the Rue Morgue* (1971), AIP Poe films that don't include Price (and suffer greatly because of his absence).

The critical models presented by such feminist and gender studies theorists as Harry M. Benshoff, Judith Butler, Barbara Creed, and Laura Mulvey have been applied to the films discussed in this work. Because her *Gender Trouble* (1990) has been so influential in establishing the theory of gender as a performative act, Butler is a crucial theorist to incorporate into any study of sexuality and gender. Similarly, Creed's theories of abjection as applied to the "monstrous-feminine," which are essential to examinations of gender in modern horror films, can also be useful tools in the analysis of the earlier style exemplified by Vincent Price's output. Benshoff's exploration of the relationship between horror and homosexuality (actual or implied) in the cinema undergirds the concept of transgressive sexualities and identities. Mulvey's exploration of the gendered gaze in narrative cinema is another fundamental theory that has not hitherto been applied to the Poe cycle.

The term "Gothic" refers to the classic iconography of Gothic literature and horror films, including such elements as aristocratic antagonists, virginal or otherwise innocent female victims, dark castles, graveyards, and preternatural manifestations. Each of the films includes some or all of the traditional Gothic trappings, echoing their presence in the source material. Many of the films included here do not feature actual supernatural demonstrations, but all more or less fit the definition of "the fantastic" offered by Tzvetan Todorov. Three conditions must be met, according to Todorov; the most important of these is the establishment of "the world of the characters as a world of living persons" that precariously balances "between a natural and a supernatural explanation of the events described" (19). In addition, any film promoted as a Poe adaptation, no matter how tenuous, is considered part of the AIP series initiated in 1960. Finally, it is assumed that Price's characters are the protagonists of the films unless specifically identified otherwise.

1

THOSE ICY EYES
Shock and *Dragonwyck* (1946)

It is true that Vincent Price was groomed to be a romantic lead when he first arrived in Hollywood. Almost from the first, however, the actor demonstrated an affinity for character roles, particularly of a villainous or horrific nature. Price's characters are more or less sympathetic in *Tower of London* (1939) and *The Invisible Man Returns* (1940), his third and fourth features, respectively; however, both films are at least borderline horror pictures and thus foreshadow the direction his career would ultimately take. By contrast, productions such as *The Song of Bernadette* (1943) and *Laura* (1944) are about as far away from the horror genre as they can be, but they feature Price in decidedly unheroic roles and underscore his innate talent for playing heavies. Yet of all the films Price made before 1953, when *House of Wax* set him on the path to horror stardom, there are two films that most clearly presage his onscreen legacy: Alfred Werker's *Shock* and Joseph L. Mankiewicz's *Dragonwyck*, both of which went into release in early 1946. Both films are thrillers that straddle the border between mystery and horror; both films feature Price in dry runs for his most notable horror film personas, the obsessed doctor and the demented aristocrat; and, not surprisingly, both films feature women as victims of Price's villainy.

Originally conceived as a second feature, *Shock* was ultimately given "A" status when it debuted in early 1946. Price stars as Richard Cross, an eminent San Francisco psychiatrist who kills his wife during an argument over his mistress, Elaine Jordan (Lynn Bari), a nurse at his private sanitarium. Unfortunately for Cross, Janet Stewart (Anabel Shaw), a veteran's wife anxiously awaiting her POW husband's return, has accidentally witnessed the crime of passion, which sends her into an almost catatonic shock. Cross arranges for Janet to be admitted to his sanitarium, where with Elaine's prodding he first tries to drive Janet mad, then conspires to kill her before she can convince either her worried husband, Paul (Frank Latimore), or an inquisitive policeman, O'Neil (Reed Hadley), that she isn't delusional. Janet really does seem on the brink of madness, particularly after an escaped psychopath, Mr. Edwards (John Davidson), wanders into her room and almost attacks her. Eventually, however, the truth comes out, and Cross is apprehended before he murders Janet—although not before he goes berserk and kills Elaine.

Perhaps the most interesting aspect of the Cross character is that he appears reluctant to commit his crimes and continually insists on his reluctance to harm others. Cross is truly wracked with doubt and guilt (and thus a precursor to many of the protagonists

Lynn Bari and Vincent Price contemplate murder in *Shock* (1946).

Price would play in the Poe adaptations), and he seems genuinely distressed that he has violated his sacred oath to first do no harm. "There's a limit beyond which even I can't go," he protests to Elaine when she urges him to use an overdose of insulin to silence Janet forever. Earlier in the film, he complains to Elaine that he shouldn't have listened to her when she told him to cover up his wife's accidental death. "Manslaughter means twenty years" is Elaine's cold retort, reminding him harshly that his life will still be ruined no matter what the circumstances of Mrs. Cross' passing. At the film's conclusion, having strangled Elaine and with his plot to poison Janet spoiled by the timely arrival of Paul and fellow shrink Dr. Harvey (Charles Trowbridge), Cross quietly returns to his office. The weary psychiatrist calmly enters a final note into his Dictaphone, and he seems relieved when O'Neil arrives moments later to arrest him, as suggested by Cross' (and the movie's) last line: "the case is closed."

Yet as reluctant as Cross seems to be when it comes time to commit murder, he ultimately kills two people and very nearly succeeds in killing a third. Significantly, all three of his victims are female. Mrs. Cross never actually appears in the movie (although we hear her voice and see her picture in a newspaper), but there is no doubt that her husband kills her in a fit of passion during the argument (the audience shares Janet's limited point-of-view from a nearby balcony). After Richard stammers that he wants a divorce, Mrs. Cross loudly says she will grant him one — but not until she tells all his friends and the local newspaper about the circumstances surrounding the marriage's termination. We see the enraged doctor pick up a large candlestick and bring it down with an unnerving crunch on his unseen wife's skull.

When Cross decides he simply can't finish Janet off, Elaine continues to berate him. Suddenly the doctor turns on his lover, dragging her behind a convenient screen where he chokes her to death. Certainly Cross strangles Elaine in a blind rage brought on by frustration, guilt, and incredible stress, but this unfortunate confluence of negative emotions doesn't completely explain why the doctor kills his girlfriend. It seems that Richard Cross has some sort of attraction-repulsion tendency towards the women in his life; weak-willed and vacillating as he is, Cross is reluctantly attracted to strong-willed women. While he desires such domineering women, he cannot fully accept their control of his life — and as a result, he must ultimately destroy them to maintain a shred of his autonomy. Cross venerates these women, but he victimizes them as well.

Considering how Dr. Cross both loves and hates the women who dominate him, it is not surprising that he is reluctant to harm Janet. "I'm your friend; I'm here to help you," he tells her while she lies bedridden with shock. While it is certainly true that Janet's testimony could prove he killed his wife, Cross doesn't fear and desire her as he does Elaine or (at one time, at any rate) Mrs. Cross. The reason for his comparative comfort around Janet is obvious: because she is a patient, Janet does not threaten Cross' autonomy. Lying helpless in a hospital bed and with her husband believing she is hallucinating, Janet is not a threat to Cross' self-image as a physician and a man. His gender assumptions are confirmed, not undermined, by Janet's appearance and behavior as a stereotypically weak and submissive woman. It is significant that Cross is almost always depicted looming over Janet; his dominance is suggested by his being physically above her while she is literally beneath him.

Just 34 when he shot the picture, Price is elegant, suave, and clean-shaven; his imposing height and handsome features are used to strong effect, suggesting at times the hero Cross might have been had he not gotten mixed up with the wrong kind of woman (a typical dilemma in *noir* thrillers such as this one). Denis Meikle asserts that "the character comes across as curiously passionless and disengaged" (22), but Price actually brings quite a bit of ambivalence and guilt to the role. Dr. Cross is obsessed with the woman he desires, Elaine; he is also tormented by his guilt over the crimes he commits, but his assaults on women suggest he is as violent and insane as the crazed Mr. Edwards. In many ways, *Shock* iforshadows the mad doctors and scientists Price would frequently portray during his later career; his next vehicle would provide practice for the Gothic protagonists Price essayed in some of his best-loved projects.

Based on Anya Seton's best-selling novel, *Dragonwyck* is the story of Miranda Wells (Gene Tierney), a nineteenth century Connecticut farm girl who journeys to upstate New York to serve as a companion and tutor for a distant cousin's daughter. The cousin in question, Nicholas Van Ryn (Price), is a wealthy "patroon," or hereditary landowner, the last of an ancient Dutch family whose existence mirrors that of a feudal lord; Dragonwyck is his ancestral mansion overlooking the Hudson River. There is an immediate attraction between Miranda and Nicholas, but he already has a wife, Johanna (Vivienne Osborne), who is unable to bear more children. Nicholas is obsessed with having a son to preserve the Van Ryn name, so he poisons Johanna with leaves from his beloved oleander plant in order to wed Miranda. At first, Nicholas and his second wife are blissfully happy; however, when their newborn son dies soon after birth, Nicholas sinks into a drug-fueled despair — "I have become what is vulgarly referred to as a drug addict," he sneeringly informs her — and eventually plots to use his favorite flower to rid himself of yet another wife. Thanks to the intervention of physician Jeff Turner (Glenn Langan), who has loved Miranda from afar, Nicholas' mad plan fails, and the last master of Dragonwyck is shot to death.

Dragonwyck is not an out-and-out horror film, but it is unquestionably a Gothic thriller and presents Price with an intriguing dress rehearsal for the Poe adaptations he would make in the 1960s. In fact, one of author Seton's inspirations for the Van Ryn character was Poe's melancholy poem "Alone," and in the novel Van Ryn briefly befriends Poe himself, who recommends laudanum to Nicholas, but these sequences never made it into the film's script (Meikle 25). Nevertheless, there is a clear link between Nicholas Van Ryn and such future Price protagonists as Roderick Usher and Verden Fell.

As in most of the Poe films, Price plays the last male descendant of an ancient and aristocratic family; and, as in most of the Poe films, Price's character is obsessed with a beautiful young woman. One significant difference between *Dragonwyck* and the Poe cycle is that here the Price character is clearly obsessed with the matter of preserving his family name, a concern never explicitly articulated in the latter productions. Price's characters are fixated on their wives or other females in the Poe adaptations, but there is also a degree of veneration present in their obsessive behavior that suggests abstention from, and perhaps abhorrence to, conventional sexual relations, which is evidenced by the near total absence of children within the households of Usher, Medina, et al. In *Dragonwyck*, however, Nicholas Van Ryn is completely dedicated to siring a male heir — a mission that can only be accomplished by sexual congress with a woman. So great is Van Ryn's zeal to reproduce that when it appears his wives cannot give him a son, he loses his mind and develops homicidal tendencies.

Van Ryn's descent into madness and drug addiction suggests another connection to the likes of *House of Usher* and *Pit and the Pendulum*: an overwhelming sense of guilt on the part of the Price character. For all of his aristocratic sense of entitlement, Nicholas Van Ryn cannot be totally unaware of the fact that it is not the fault of his wives that they have not provided him with the male heir he so desperately seeks. Indeed, perhaps Nicholas subconsciously fears it is as much his fault as Johanna's that their only child is a daughter — and since a child's sex is determined by its father's chromosomes (an unknown fact during the film's 1840s setting), it is technically true that any "blame" for the birth of a daughter rests upon Nicholas, not his first wife. Nicholas is aware of his role in Johanna's death and his attempt to kill Miranda; therefore, at least on a subconscious level he suffers guilt from the knowledge of his murderous deeds. When Dr. Turner tells Nicholas that the baby boy has a defective heart and cannot live, Van Ryn refuses to accept the news, an unreasonable reaction that surely results from guilt over his deadly but futile efforts as much as it does from his grief and frustration. Significantly, Van Ryn ignores Turner's diagnosis that Miranda is perfectly healthy and therefore able to bear children in the future, which suggests Nicholas' mental and moral degeneration is already irreversible.

This mental and moral decay is an ironic twist of fate, for Nicholas Van Ryn also recalls another Gothic/Romantic protagonist, Victor Frankenstein, in his amoral rationalism. Nicholas' hubris leads him to ridicule Miranda's simple country piety; when she asks if he believes in God, he proudly responds, "I believe in myself" and insists, "I will not live according to printed mottoes like directions on a medicine bottle." Yet for all his protests about his intelligence and disdain for religion, Nicholas still rages against God after the baby dies (why wonder about God's motives if God doesn't matter — or exist at all?), and he demonstrates a Romantic susceptibility to the influence of beauty (at one point he tells Miranda, "Your tribulations seem to become you. I cannot remember you more beautiful than you are now") and to nature (during a storm, Nicholas remarks that in his native Catskills, "the lightning seems to set the mountains on fire, and they roar back at it"). To the more or less pious audiences of 1946, it is doubtful that any of Nicholas' maliciousness would be more unforgivable than his rejection of Miranda's Christianity; filmmaker Mankiewicz definitely emphasizes Nicholas' secular tendencies by having the character make his first onscreen appearance while Miranda and her father, Ephraim (Walter Huston), are reading a Bible passage that includes the phrase, "I will not know a wicked person."

Another trait that Nicholas shares with the protagonists of the Poe cycle is his stubborn affiliation to an obsolete way of life. Mankiewicz makes the point much more aggressively than does Roger Corman, but both directors concern themselves with characters who vainly attempt to preserve an old-fashioned aristocratic existence within the confines of a putatively democratic society. The hegemony that characters like Nicholas Van Ryn and Roderick Usher have enjoyed by virtue of their birthrights is contrary to the egalitarian principles embraced by most of their fellow Americans, and because they resist progress, they are doomed to madness and death.

One of the major subplots of *Dragonwyck* is Van Ryn's insistence that his tenants pay tribute because the land they farm belongs to him. Van Ryn rejects any suggestion that the farmers ought to own their farms, for the land has belonged to his family since 1630. Dr. Turner enters the storyline because he supports the rights of the tenants to own property, but Nicholas firmly defends his paternalistic lifestyle. "I will never relinquish my position," he tells Turner. Elsewhere, Miranda's father expresses astonishment that none of Nicholas' tenants own their own land. Eventually much of his property is taken from him by the state and turned over to the erstwhile tenants, a factor that contributes to Nicholas' mental deterioration. When Turner leads a group of farmers and local authorities to arrest Van Ryn for Joanna's murder, the demented squire resists, forcing Turner to shoot him. As Van Ryn dies, his former tenants doff their headgear, inspiring Nicholas' arrogant last words: "That's right — take off your hats in the presence of the patroon!" So much attention is devoted to the conflict between Van Ryn and the farmers that the conclusion is inevitable: Nicholas Van Ryn is villainous as much because he rejects the traditional American values of piety and democracy as because he kills the women who fail to bear him a suitable heir.

It is interesting to note the standing of women in *Dragonwyck* as a reflection of the film's 1840s setting. Although intelligent and kind as well as beautiful, Miranda continually finds herself under the thumb of a patriarchal society. As the film opens, the letter from Van Ryn arrives for Miranda's mother (Anne Revere), informing her that she may recommend one of her daughters to come to Dragonwyck. Miranda is excited by the opportunity, but her mother immediately defers to Ephraim, the head of the household. When Miranda tells her father that the invitation could be a good opportunity for her, he curtly rejects her, saying, "Your opinion is of no consequence whatsoever." Eventually Ephraim reluctantly agrees to let his daughter go to Dragonwyck, and later (and with even greater reluctance) he consents to her marriage to Nicholas. In spite of Nicholas' wealth and fine manners, he is just as dominant in Miranda's life as her father. Throughout the movie, Miranda is threatened not just by Nicholas' madness, but also by his absolute control of her life. Her attraction to Nicholas — whom the screenplay takes great pains to establish is not a blood relation, probably to stave off the appearance of an incestuous relationship — is replaced by dread. "He watches me all the time through those icy eyes of his," she tells Turner, a statement that references both Nicholas' insanity and his status within the patriarchy.

Miranda is not the only woman victimized by Nicholas, however. Johanna inspires

a great deal of pity, for she seems to both love and dread her husband. Fully aware of his disappointment that they have no male children, Johanna has become both bratty and obsequious towards her husband, whining about sweets he has promised to bring her from New York City one minute and fawning pathetically over the slightest kindness he demonstrates towards her the next. In effect, Johanna is reduced to a child-like state, her childishness a result of her oppression by both Nicholas and the society in which they dwell. Johanna deals with her misery by becoming obsessed with food; while not as obese as depicted in Seyton's novel, the cinematic Johanna is plump and matronly in comparison to Miranda.

Perhaps the saddest case is the victimization of little Katrine Van Ryn (Connie Marshall, an excellent child performer). The

Nicholas Van Ryn (Price) admires cousin (and future wife) Miranda (Gene Tierney) in *Dragonwyck* (1946).

offspring of Nicholas and Johanna is introduced as a lonely and pitiful child, acutely aware that her father is disappointed in the fact that she is not a boy. Katrine's melancholy seems to lift when Miranda pays attention to her, although she insists that she doesn't love her parents, much to Miranda's chagrin. Katrine also suffers from the Van Ryn curse, which is to hear the phantom harpsichord playing of her long-dead ancestor, Azilde, something only those of Van Ryn blood can hear. These manifestations seem to be genuinely supernatural in nature, as both Katrine and Nicholas experience them; however, it is possible — and perhaps more tragic — to think that Katrine has inherited her father's obsessive and melancholy nature.

As gloomy as things at Dragonwyck appear to be, the film ends optimistically. With Nicholas' death, Miranda (or possibly Katrine, who has been shipped off to boarding school following the marriage of Miranda and Nicholas) inherits Dragonwyck and the remaining property. However, Miranda opts not to remain in the Hudson Valley; as the film ends, she is leaving for her family's farm back in Connecticut, but not before inviting the kindly (if somewhat dull) Dr. Turner to call on her there. The implication is that Miranda has found true love with a "normal" man — someone who is not an aristocrat and who embraces such progressive American values as Christianity and individual property rights. Presumably Miranda and Turner will eventually marry, which prompts an unanswered question: will Turner prove to be any more mindful and supportive of Miranda's rights and individuality than her father or her first husband were? It is a provocative question that inspires the mind long after *Dragonwyck* fades out.

2

THAT LOOK OF HORROR
House of Wax (1953)

There is little doubt that *House of Wax* (1953) was the single most influential assignment in Vincent Price's cinematic career. Although his daughter's claim that the film was Price's "first role in a pure example of the horror genre" (Price 159) is perhaps debatable given his earlier performances as the Invisible Man, *House of Wax* was certainly a major box office success in 1953; taking subsequent re-releases into account, it is easily the single most profitable of Price's horror titles. Even more significantly, the film established a connection in the public consciousness between the actor and scary movies that would ultimately define him within the boundaries of popular culture. By the end of 1953, Price wasn't yet a horror star, but he had taken a long stride in that direction.

It is unlikely that Price's participation was a substantial factor in the film's initial success. Gothic horror was ripe for a comeback, having been more or less moribund on the screen since the end of World War II, and audiences flocked to a style of entertainment so out of fashion that it suddenly seemed fresh again. Even more importantly, *House of Wax* was shot in 3-D; more than any other element, the novelty factor propelled the film to the top of the box office charts. However, the film's enduring popularity is unquestionably due to the fact that Vincent Price is in it — the once-amazing 3-D effects having largely been lost on the generations of TV and video viewers unable to appreciate such trickery when the film is shown "flat."

A remake of Warner Bros.' 1933 chiller *Mystery of the Wax Museum*, *House of Wax* tells the story of Henry Jarrod (Price), an eccentric sculptor at the dawn of the 20th century whose more pragmatic business partner, Matthew Burke (Roy Roberts), wants to burn down their failing waxworks in order to collect the insurance money. Jarrod is stunned during their subsequent scuffle, and Burke leaves the sculptor to the flames. Jarrod survives, but he is horribly disfigured and driven insane by the experience. Hiding behind an improbably expressive waxen facial mask, Jarrod reappears, this time as proprietor of the house of horrors Burke wanted to promote in the first place.

Audiences flock to Jarrod's gruesome tableaux, commenting on how lifelike the figures appear, never guessing that the remarkable verisimilitude comes at a terrible cost: Jarrod has been killing people, including his former partner, and covering them in wax. Only Sue Allen (Phyllis Kirk), whose fiancée Scott Andrews (Paul Picerni) has become one of Jarrod's unwitting assistants, suspects the truth. Sue recognizes her missing roommate, Cathy Gray (Carolyn Jones), as the basis for Joan of Arc. In turn, Jarrod decides that Sue would be perfect as the secret ingredient in his masterpiece, Marie Antoinette. Sue tries to convince Scott and the police of the terrible truth while evading Jarrod's clutches, and eventually the sculptor is undone, plunging into a vat of boiling wax.

House of Wax boasts a screenplay by Crane Wilbur, an aging former silent film star, sometime director, and Broadway playwright (among his most successful plays was *The Monster*, which in 1925 became a cinematic vehicle for Lon Chaney). Wilbur made his professional debut around the time *House of Wax* is set, and in *The Monster* and other plays he experimented with the traditions and expectations of the "mystery thriller" genre. Consequently, Wilbur was an excellent choice to update the screenplay of *Mystery of the Wax Museum* by taking what in 1933 was a contemporary story and setting it 30 years earlier. Wilbur subsequently collaborated with Price on *The Mad Magician* (1954), directed by John Brahm, and *The Bat* (1959), which Wilbur himself

Vincent Price as the horribly burned Henry Jarrod in *House of Wax* (1953), the actor's first major horror hit and (adjusted for inflation) his highest-grossing starring vehicle. Gordon and George Bau created the truly gruesome makeup.

directed (in fact, it was his final credited directing job).

The first of Wilbur's three collaborations with Price remains the best. *The Mad Magician* and *The Bat* are minor projects; the former is a blatant rip-off of *House of Wax* (it was even released in 3-D, although unlike its predecessor it was shot in black-and-white) featuring Price as Don Gallico, the titular insane illusionist, who also seeks revenge on a crooked business associate *a la* Henry Jarrod; and the latter is a slow-moving, talky throwback to the sort of "old dark house" thrillers Wilbur specialized in decades earlier. Furthermore, *The Bat* was promoted as a horror film to cash in on Price's presence, but it's merely a crime mystery (and not a very good one at that). Although it certainly has its admirers, *The Bat* ranks among the most disappointing of the star's films, for it wastes him in the thankless red herring role of Dr. Malcolm Wells, a murderous physician who turns out not to be the titular master criminal. Whatever magic Crane Wilbur brought to *House of Wax*, it was evidently a formula that could not be repeated.

Compared to some of the more outrageous 3-D productions of the period, *House of Wax* is relatively restrained in its use of stunt shots, a circumstance the film's star attributed to the fact that director Andre de Toth had only one eye and therefore could not fully appreciate the 3-D process (Price 159). Certainly de Toth emphasizes mood and characterization over spectacle, a decision that imbues the action sequences with more power. Working with playwright Wilbur, de Toth offers three particularly interesting characters: Jarrod, Sue, and Cathy.

The contrast between kindly Jarrod and the roguish Burke symbolizes the larger conflict between art and commerce, for without financial backing Jarrod cannot display his creations to the world, and without a product to sell Burke has no channel for his investments. Price interprets Henry Jarrod as an odd but harmless artist, bestowing the character with aesthetic sensibilities that are ultimately perverted by the professor's descent into homicidal madness. Ironically, Jarrod must ultimately embrace Burke's position, devising a profitable but crass Chamber of Horrors to earn the funds necessary to pursue his aesthetic vision.

Although the element of gender ambivalence that can be identified in later Price characterizations is far less pronounced in *House of Wax*, it is already present. Because he is an artist and aesthete, Professor Jarrod is interested in beauty and grace, qualities often associated with the feminine. Furthermore, Jarrod truly loves his waxen effigies, which he sometimes refers to as his "children" or his "people." These references associate Jarrod with the female ability to create life. As he explains to a visitor, "To you they are wax, but to me, their creator, they live and breathe." It is ironic that Jarrod must pollute his commitment to life by killing people to amplify the verisimilitude of his creations — both Burke and Cathy, for example, wind up sheathed in wax as a result of Jarrod's mad quest.

Even in the Chamber of Horrors, the insane artist cannot abandon his need to create beauty. Interestingly, Jarrod must recruit other artists to complete his sculptures, for his hands are severely burned and therefore useless as instruments of creation. In addition to Scott, Jarrod employs two shifty assistants, the alcoholic Leon (Ned Young) and the brutish Igor (Charles Buchinksi, soon to change his name and achieve superstar status as Charles Bronson), who proves particularly adept at sculpting faces. It is perhaps a symbol of the artist's mania that he takes on two such disreputable characters; ultimately Leon betrays his employer to the police, who torment the drunken ex-con with a bottle of whiskey. "The whole place is a morgue," Leon admits when he confesses the secret of the wax museum. Igor is useful as muscle and contributes one of the more effective 3-D shocks in the picture when at one point he confronts Scott by appearing to leap into the scene from the audience.

Jarrod must resort to such desperate characters because he can no longer give form to his artistic visions. This loss of creative ability — a symbol of castration — is a key element to Jarrod's mental state and functions as a manifestation of his madness and as an explanation of his fanatical need to imbue his later creations with an even greater degree of realism than his original figures. It is absolutely critical to Jarrod's deranged mind that his "people" truly live and exhibit the sort of physical beauty he can no longer provide himself. As he complains to the terrified Sue during the film's climax, "That look of horror spoils your lovely face! What if it should show, even through the wax?"

The character of Sue Allen is the real "hero" of the film, even if her boyfriend and a skeptical police officer, Lt. Brennan (Frank Lovejoy), perform most of the physical action. Intelligent, polite, and chaste, Sue presages the virginal Final Girl identified by Carol Clover in the modern slasher film. "Doesn't seem proper, all those girls showing off their — talents," she primly remarks to Scott after he takes her to a mildly suggestive burlesque show. Her purity and intelligence allow Sue to see what others do not — namely, that Jarrod is a monster. It is Sue who recognizes the uncanny resemblance between the Joan of Arc figure and Cathy, and it is Sue who goes to the police with her bizarre story about being pursued by a monstrous stranger. "Leave it to a skirt to dream up a crazy idea like that" is the judgment of one dull-witted policeman regarding Sue's suspicions about Jarrod.

House of Wax benefits from a number of well-staged shock scenes, including the sudden drop of Burke's strangled body — which Jarrod has cleverly disguised as a suicide — on a rope down an elevator shaft. When Sue smashes Jarrod's waxen mask, the hideously scarred makeup by Gordon Bau is truly gruesome. Yet the film's most memorable sequence is probably Jarrod's initial pursuit of Sue through the streets of New York. There is something profoundly disturbing about the image of Jarrod, his scarred visage hidden beneath

Vincent Price and Phyllis Kirk in *House of Wax* (1953).

an enormous slouch hat and swirling cloak, skittering (spider-like on his damaged legs) unsteadily yet implacably through the foggy streets towards his prey. Sue's function as a symbol of purity and goodness sharply contrasts with the troll-like Jarrod, who has become a sort of catch-all symbol representing all things evil and insane.

While Jarrod and Sue are the most important characters in the narrative, it is the doomed Cathy with whom the audience most closely identifies. The performance is a minor triumph for Carolyn Jones, herself destined, like Price, to become an icon for her work in the horror genre: she gained pop culture immortality as Morticia on TV's *The Addams Family* in 1964. Ostensibly Cathy is just another victim, a stereotypical "dumb blonde." Yet the character is far from a mere cipher, for Jones imbues Cathy with a great deal of charm and self-awareness. Cathy is truly concerned with her friend's well-being, and her good nature inspires genuine sympathy when she meets her unfortunate end.

Clearly spawned from a working class background, Cathy survives by finding prosperous men to support her — a situation that suggests she is a prostitute, or very nearly so. "All I got is all I got," she tells Sue to explain her lifestyle, a line delivered humorously yet with the realization that Cathy's options in late Victorian America are decidedly limited. However, she is truly interested in settling down and establishing a life more in life with the expectations of her time and place, finally persuading her reluctant suitor, Matthew Burke, to marry her. "Why not? It might be fun!" Burke half-heartedly exclaims when Cathy convinces him to get married. The dynamics in Cathy's relationship with Burke imply the larger concerns of single women within the context of the film's setting, for both Cathy and Sue are presented as being highly vulnerable to the social and economic conditions of the period.

Moreover, the film frequently reveals significant evidence of casual misogyny throughout its running time, evidence that suggests as much about the attitudes of Fifties Hollywood as turn-of-the-century New York. Sue is at the mercy of larger economic forces, trying to get a job in order to pay the rent — which, significantly, Cathy provides at one point, her own finances improved (temporarily, at least) by her relationship with Burke. While Cathy seems genuinely fond of Burke, she does acknowledge his rough and potentially disrespectful nature when she comments that he is "a real gentleman, except when he's had a couple of drinks in him." Elsewhere, a morgue attendant complains that it's "just like a woman" to "always have to have the last word." These and other lines, usually delivered in a humorous context, nevertheless convey an impression of assumed female inferiority. It is little wonder that Sue and Cathy are victimized when they are at the mercy of social and economic forces almost entirely controlled by men.

Yet the most relevant suggestion of misogyny in the film and the most important commentary on gender issues is represented by Professor Jarrod's insane scheme. Ultimately his plan involves the literal objectification of women; he murders them to preserve their beauty, to make them things, not humans. As much as he desires to create beauty, he can do so only by killing. This fact underscores the irony in Jarrod's claim that "once in his lifetime, every artist feels the hand of God and creates something that comes to life." While he murders men when necessary, Jarrod's greatest creations are female: Joan of Arc and Marie Antoinette (interestingly enough, these figures represent famous women in his-

Vincent Price and Paul Picerni on a promotional tour for *House of Wax* (1953).

tory whose chief claims to fame are the circumstances surrounding their deaths — which, incidentally, result from the decisions of men). In his obsession to perfect these particular statues, Jarrod makes his greatest exertions, believing success will justify all of his previous trials. "Everything I ever loved has been taken away from me," he tells Sue, "but not you, my Marie Antoinette, for I will give you eternal life!" Only by destroying female life can Jarrod preserve the female beauty he prizes above all else.

Jarrod's obsessive desire to venerate the female form by killing women is more than a mere plot twist in *House of Wax*; it is also a suggestion of the shape of things to come. The deranged artist is the first of many Price characters to embrace murder and mayhem as a result of real or perceived wrongs inflicted by others or society itself. Inevitably these characters wind up threatening women in the films. In many of Price's horror films, particularly the Poe series, the protagonist is an insane aesthete who harbors ambivalent and often violent notions about women. The particulars of the characterization change from film to film, but the initial model is Professor Henry Jarrod. The introduction of the female-obsessed, aesthetically inclined protagonist is yet another reason why *House of Wax* remains the single most important film in Price's career.

3

BRAIN SAYS STRANGE THINGS NOW
The Fly (1958) and *Return of the Fly* (1959)

In the wake of *House of Wax*, Vincent Price was firmly associated with screen villainy. However, he had yet to become a bona fide horror star in the tradition of Karloff and Lugosi. The transformation from mere heavy to legendary boogeyman would not be complete until Price became associated with Roger Corman and the Poe series in 1960. Between *House of Wax* and *House of Usher*, though, Price appeared in a transitional film that remains one of his most famous credits: Kurt Neumann's *The Fly* (1958), which Michael Weldon considers "a brilliant, sick, absurd hit" (249). Price's participation in this sci-fi classic underscored his association with horror and fantasy films in the minds of Hollywood producers and movie audiences alike; indeed, if only one title could be cited to exemplify Price's career, either *The Fly* or *House of Wax* would be it — with the other a close second. Ironically, the second major step in Price's conversion into a horror specialist presents the actor with his most unambiguously sympathetic characterization among all of his horror films. More than fifty years after the film's release, Price is often associated with the titular monstrosity, but in fact he plays the de facto hero of the piece.

Famously adapted by *Shogun* author James Clavell from George Langelaan's short story of the same name, *The Fly* is the story of the unfortunate Delambre family, particularly wife Helene (Patricia Owens), who seems to have murdered her beloved husband, Andre (David Hedison, here billed as Al Hedison), by crushing his head and arm in an industrial press. Vincent Price appears in the supporting role of Francois Delambre, Andre's brother (and the narrator of Langelaan's tale), who, along with police inspector Charas (Herbert Marshall), attempts to figure out why so devoted a wife would kill her spouse. The bulk of the story plays out in flashback, as Helene explains to her brother-in-law that Andre had developed an amazing transmitter capable of disintegrating and re-integrating matter across long distances. Unfortunately the overzealous scientist attempted to transmit himself, failing to notice that an ordinary housefly had wandered into the booth with him. Horribly mutated into a fly-headed monster, complete with one hideous fly-arm, Andre sent his wife to find the human-headed insect in a desperate attempt to re-transmit himself and hopefully return to normal. When Helene failed to find the mutated fly, Andre begged her to help him commit suicide before his personality was consumed by the fly's bestial brain.

Naturally Francois and Charas are skeptical about Helene's story. However, her little boy, Philippe (Charles Herbert), tells Francois that the white-headed fly is trapped in a nearby spider web. Francois and Charas rush to investigate, where they witness the other victim of Andre's accident about to be eaten by the web's hungry creator. As a tiny voice screams "help me," Charas smashes the web and everything in it with a handy rock. Now convinced that Helene is telling the truth, the men conspire to cover up the truth lest they, too, are hauled off to prison or an asylum.

The Fly has become one of the most beloved of the landmark science fiction films of the Fifties, although not entirely because of its merits, not the least of which is its beautiful appearance thanks to a masterful use of CinemaScope. Whereas other sci-fi productions of the era such as *The War of the Worlds* and *Invasion of the Body Snatchers* retain their classic status thanks to the thoughtfulness of their screenplays or the majesty of their special effects, *The Fly* is remembered in large measure because of its camp appeal. The plethora of fly-inspired puns is simply too great to be accidental, and much of Clavell's romantic and scientific dialogue is so painfully corny that the screenwriter had to have penned the lines with his tongue firmly stuck in his cheek. Yet this sardonic streak is a sign of Clavell's fealty to Langelaan, whose own dry humor laces the horror of his story as exemplified by Francois' rhetorical question, "Have you ever tried to explain to a sleepy police officer that your sister-in-law has just phoned to say that she has killed your brother with a steam hammer?" (248).

Serious lapses in the film's logic are so obvious that it is hard to imagine Clavell and producer-director Neumann were unaware of them during production. For example, what makes Andre so sure that running himself back through the transmitter with the fly will work? Why wouldn't their atoms become even more hopelessly entangled? (This probability would be exploited decades later for comic effect on TV's *The Simpsons* in a pointed parody of *The Fly*.) Furthermore, why does Helene agree to so completely destroy her hapless husband and all evidence of his experiments when Andre's body, notes, and equipment are the only evidence she has to avoid incarceration or execution? Finally, and most infamously, if Andre retains his human brain, how does the fly with his head have the ability to speak and express terror at its impending doom?

It seems impossible that such a confused storyline would endear the film to audiences then or now, but the film was a smash hit upon first release, was followed by a pair of sequels, and was successfully remade (perhaps re-imagined is a more accurate term) by David Cronenberg in 1986. An absurdist sensibility pervades *The Fly* and is one of the reasons why this film continues to fascinate viewers after more than half a century. Fuzzy logic and goofy dialogue certainly imbue the production with camp appeal, but there is something more than draws fans like—well, like flies, actually.

The gender roles portrayed in *The Fly* are interesting to consider, although much of the film's campy reputation can probably be traced to the stereotypes these roles promote. Initially Helene's shockingly violent acts seem incredible because as a Fifties housewife she is assumed to be incapable of such transgressions against the social order. "Helene was always so gentle," an incredulous Francois tells the inspector. Her gentle nature is referenced frequently, as when Helen tells Andre, "No more experiments with animals" after his attempt to transmit the family cat ends in disaster. Before her husband's accident,

Helene won't even allow Philippe to catch flies, scolding him for doing so. When in the wake of Andre's transformation Helene tells Philippe to help her find the white-headed fly, the boy is exasperated by her unexplained change of heart. "You know how women are" is the pat explanation he offers to his uncle, Francois, a wry line borrowed from the original story (Langelaan 253). Such sexual stereotyping is also displayed by Helene early in the narrative which she half-jokingly complains to her brother-in-law that Andre spends too much time in the lab. When Francois responds by saying his brother must be working on something important, Helene retorts with mock exasperation, "How you men stick together!"

The fact that Andre and Helene have a strong, healthy marriage is worth noting here. Much dramatic conflict stems from this fact, for it is the family unit itself that is under siege in *The Fly*, not merely the laws of science and nature. The affection the Delambres maintain for each other is clear when Andre observes, "You're in an unscientific mood tonight" as his wife comes on to him following a night at the ballet. When Andre is finally ready to show off his invention, it is his wife to whom he calls excitedly. "Helene, you're the first to see a miracle," Andre boasts, little realizing his home-grown miracle will destroy him and thus the traditional family organization. Indeed, the matter disintegrator Andre invents ultimately becomes a symbol for the disintegration of the family the modern world threatens, and Helene herself complains about the rapid pace of modern life thanks to the overabundance of new scientific discoveries. When a mentally disintegrating Andre destroys his invention and his notes ("brain says strange things now" he scrawls on a chalkboard), his destructive acts symbolize his inability to reclaim the life his transmitter has irrevocably altered.

One of the film's most interesting aspects is that it is largely a female-centered project, a comparative rarity among science fiction films of the period. Second-billed Owens is the real star here, and her comparatively restrained performance is remarkable given the hysterical nature of the storyline. Helene's character is significant because she is the one who tells the story; moreover, she is the person who must endure the possibility of spending the rest of her life in a mental institution or prison, assuming she is not executed for murder, her reputation forever rendered infamous, her only child condemned to believe his mother killed his father. As terrible as his fate might be, Andre Delambre will be remembered as a victim, not a monster.

The depiction of Helene and of her relationship with her family members — significantly, all of them male — bears some scrutiny here. Helene is initially portrayed as an apparently insane woman; when she admits to Francois that she is merely pretending to be mad in order to protect herself and Philippe from the scandal of a murder trial, she reveals herself to be far more cunning than the more typical helpless female of Fifties fantasy cinema. Over the course of her flashback, Helene initially appears to be cut from the same cloth as her sisters in science fiction: beautiful, loving, patient, and passive. Yet once her husband suffers his accident, it is Helene who must become the active partner, for the cloth Andre drapes himself with is too flimsy a disguise to prevent detection should he assume leadership of the fly-finding mission.

Andre hides in his basement laboratory, vainly seeking some solution among his notes and equipment, but Helene must search the house and grounds for the elusive fly

Francois Delambre (Vincent Price) comforts his brother's wife, Helene (Patricia Owens), in *The Fly* (1958). It is Helene who is the true protagonist of the film — an unusual plot device for an Eisenhower-era science fiction film.

while also attempting to maintain an atmosphere of normality for Philippe and the maid, Emma (Katherine Freeman). Thus to a great extent the roles of husband and wife are reversed; now it is Andre who is passive, helpless to contribute manfully to solving the problem his own recklessness has created. Helene is jolted out of her domestic tranquility and must assume the husbandly duty of solving problems and preserving the family unit. Tragically, Helene is unable to catch the human-headed fly in time; therefore, it is she, not Andre, who must bear the awful responsibility of destroying the results of Andre's experiment. An extra dash of horror is included when Helene must raise the press after pulping Andre's head because the disfigured fly-arm has been missed and must also be crushed into paste. "I'm glad the thing is dead," Helene later tells the inspector, obviously relieved that her active role in the horrific affair is finally over. In a very literal sense, *The Fly* is about a woman who must clean up the mess made by a man.

It is also significant that there is no real villain in *The Fly*, a film more concerned with the tragedy of fate rather than the machinations of evildoers. Andre Delambre is presented as the very opposite of the stereotypical mad scientist; according to his brother, Andre "had a keen sense of humor, loved children and animals and could not bear to see anyone suffer" (Langelaan 255). As played by Al Hedison, the scientist is handsome, witty, and genuinely convinced that his invention is "the most important discovery since man first sawed off the end of a tree trunk and found the wheel," as he tells his wife in another line paraphrased from Langelaan (259). Although distracted by his work, Andre is still a family man, a situation that forecasts the emphasis on the Delambre family as a modern clan of Frankensteins that will become explicit in *Return of the Fly* (1959) and *The Curse of the Fly* (1965). Francois is a concerned relative and Charas a dedicated policeman, so there is no malice displayed in their skepticism pertaining to Helene's story. In fact, it is Francois and Charas who arrange a cover-up story to make it appear that Andre committed suicide unassisted, a decision these middle-aged male authority figures reach partially in order to protect a woman who would otherwise face harsh treatment at the hands of other male authority figures. Even the spider that captures and starts to devour the human-headed fly acts out of instinct, not malice, a fact that underscores the fatalistic tone of the film.

Price's performance in *The Fly* is atypical and certainly at odds with the image of screen villain that would soon haunt the rest of his career. There is none of the actor's patented evildoing here, for Francois is a heroic figure, a loving family man genuinely distressed by the tragedy unleashed on his brother and sister-in-law. As the older brother of the Delambre clan, he holds the privileged status of family patriarch, yet he obviously shares the Delambre wealth, which is necessary for Andre to continue his experiments. Inspector Charas points out that Francois is in love with Helene, a fact to which the aging businessman readily admits. Had *The Fly* been made a few years later, it is likely that, with Price in the role, Francois would be a tyrannical patriarch and might even engineer his brother's "accident" in order to make Helene available to his advances. As it is, Francois can only ruefully admit his sister-in-law never even noticed him because of her great love for Andre. While Francois does not lust after Helene in a villainous manner, his unrequited love foreshadows later Price characterizations, particularly in the Poe adaptations, where love for unavailable women often degenerates into obsession.

Other elements of Price's performance foreshadow characters to come. For example, Francois is depicted relaxing in his study, which is lavishly decorated with works of fine art (it is interesting to speculate whether or not noted connoisseur Price had any influence on the selection of the paintings used to decorate the set), a testament to the character's wealth and aesthetic preferences. Francois wears an elegant red smoking jacket in this scene, further evidence of the good taste that even Price's bad men possess. When Helene informs Francois that she has killed Andre, Francois contacts Inspector Charas directly, calling the police officer at the private men's club to which they both belong. Although a minor plot element, this attempt to go around the usual channels of police procedure — necessary to maintain discretion to forestall a public scandal that would certainly embarrass the Delambre family business — suggests the privilege associated with Francois' wealth and influence. In many films to come, such privilege will enable Price's less noble characters to pursue evil or insane agendas without influence from the police and other public guardians.

The financial success of *The Fly* inspired 20th Century–Fox to prepare an immediate sequel, *Return of the Fly* (1959). The sequel was released barely one year after the original, yet it involves a storyline that must take place at least 15 years later. The film opens with Helene's funeral, at which an obnoxious reporter attempts to stir up news by baiting Francois (Price, the only actor to return from the original) and a now-adult Philippe (Bret Halsey). The cover-up planned by Francois and Inspector Charas has obviously failed, for Philippe demands to know why his mother was "accused" of his father's death. "If I tell you, Philippe, it will haunt you for the rest of your life," is Francois' grim reply.

It doesn't take too much effort on Philippe's part to convince his uncle to tell the truth and reveal the location of Andre's long-abandoned laboratory. Like the children of Henry Frankenstein in the long-running Universal series, Philippe decides he must preserve his father's legacy by recreating his experiments; and, as with the Frankenstein descendents, tragedy quickly follows the rash decision. Philippe believes he has perfected his father's invention, but he has taken on an English assistant, Alan Hines (David Frankham), who turns out to be a desperate criminal wanted by Scotland Yard. Hines intends to steal Philippe's plans and use a portly undertaker, Max (Dan Seymour), to negotiate some industrial espionage with the Delambres' business rivals; however, Philippe discovers the plot and attempts to stop his erstwhile assistant. Alan overpowers Philippe and places him in the transmitter, tossing in a stray fly for grim good measure.

Soon a new fly-man is on the loose, seeking revenge on the criminals who betrayed him. Eventually Philippe kills Max and Alan, then returns home to his housekeeper-girlfriend Cecile (Danielle De Metz) and long-suffering uncle. Because the human-headed fly has been caught, Francois is able to reverse the transformation, and a restored Philippe seems destined to enjoy a happy life with Cecile.

Return of the Fly is inferior in every way to *The Fly*, in part due to the absence of original director Kurt Neumann, who had died between the production of the two films. Although the sequel is shot in CinemaScope, it is not in color, a budget-conscious decision that immediately signals the studio's lack of care for the follow-up. The special effects are especially weak, particularly the unconvincing double exposures that attempt to convey the mixture of humans and animals. Most laughable of all is Philippe's oversized fly-head, clearly a cheaply-constructed mask that graces the long-suffering noggins of the stuntmen (Ed Wolff and Joe Becker) condemned to wear it during the monster sequences. (One slight improvement, however, is the addition of an additional fly leg to replace one of Philippe's own, which makes a disturbing scraping sound as Philippe drags it behind him while stalking his prey.)

All these cost-cutting decisions might be forgiven if the screenplay by writer-director Edward L. Bernds weren't so laughable. It's bad enough that Philippe immediately sets out to avenge himself on Alan and Max without first trying to reverse the transformation; even worse is the fact that Philippe heads straight to Max's funeral parlor, *even though there is no way for Philippe to know that Max is involved in the matter*! Although Price does his best with the lines written for him, nobody can wonder aloud "What if Philippe does not have the mind of a human, but the murderous brain of a fly?" and not sound foolish. Such dialogue opens the film up to charges of intentional silliness, or at least an inability to handle the inherently absurd elements of the story with any degree of sophistication.

Indeed, the potential for camp in *Return of the Fly* far exceeds that of *The Fly*, as demonstrated by the unease with which Price reacts to the buzzing of yet another fly in the film's closing shot. Evidently Bernds' initial script contained substantially more character development and less emphasis on the sensational aspects of the storyline, but these elements were largely eliminated during subsequent revisions and at the time of production. Price himself complained about the decisions that compromised the film:

> The script was one of those rare cases when the sequel proved to be better than the original. When I first read it, I was very excited about the possibilities. Then the producers, in obvious bad judgment, proceeded to put in a lot of gimmicks in the belief that films need gimmicks to be popular. In the end, they lessened and nearly ruined the dramatic effect that could have made a truly superior picture [qtd in Parish and Whitney 96].

Return of the Fly offers little of value to an in-depth study of Price's career; although now top-billed, Price is given relatively little to do in the film, existing primarily to give actual star Brett Halsey ominous warnings about tampering with the laws of nature (a sentiment specifically refuted by Price's final speech at the end of *The Fly*). Furthermore, the presence of women in this film is so limited and inconsequential — Cecile is around for no other apparent reason than the clichéd scene of a monster scaring a pretty girl, and the other female characters are glorified extras — that without its connection to *The Fly* (and Price's participation) the sequel would be entirely inappropriate for inclusion in a study of this nature. Other than the sympathetic nature of Price's role and the fact that the film expands on the theme of a family cursed by excessive scientific curiosity — a theme further developed in the 1965 follow-up *Curse of the Fly*, in which Price does not appear at all — there is little buzz about *Return of the Fly*.

4

ARSENIC ON THE ROCKS
House on Haunted Hill (1958) and *The Tingler* (1959)

Few among Hollywood's most notorious hucksters have demonstrated the remarkable sense of showmanship perfected by William Castle (1914–1977), the so-called "King of the Gimmicks." A veteran of Columbia's B-unit, Castle went out on his own as an independent producer-director in the late Fifties; he quickly discovered a knack for gimmicky promotions, such as insuring patrons through Lloyd's of London against death by fright to publicize *Macabre* (1958) or offering audiences the opportunity to vote thumbs up or down to decide the fate of *Mr. Sardonicus* (1961), for which the thrifty Castle filmed only the "thumbs down" ending. Castle's reputation as a specialist in low-budget "gimmick" pictures cost him the opportunity to direct his most prestigious picture, *Rosemary's Baby* (1968), although he did produce the classic horror film for Roman Polanski. A bargain-basement Hitchcock, Castle emulated the master by appearing as himself in films and publicity materials to promote his movies; his image and gimmicks made quite an impression on Baby Boomer film fans, and Joe Dante's valentine to the period, *Matinee* (1993), features a very Castle-like main character played by John Goodman.

Of all Castle's directorial efforts, two stand out in particular: *House on Haunted Hill* (1958) and *The Tingler* (1959), both starring Vincent Price. Both productions remain cult favorites thanks to the combination of Castle's gimmicks and Price's full-blooded barnstorming. Appearing as they did in the wake of *The Fly* (1958), Price's two Castle projects further confirmed his standing as a horror specialist and paved the way for Roger Corman's *House of Usher* (1960) to cement the actor's status as a horror icon. Yet while the Poe cycle initiated by Corman would ultimately associate Price with period Gothic horror, both of the actor's collaborations with Castle would boast contemporary settings and subjects, largely eschewing the Gothic iconography that would help define Price's screen persona during the Sixties.

According to Castle, the star of *House on Haunted Hill* "had to be someone special — elegant, fey, with an offbeat personality" (145). The filmmaker claimed a chance meeting with Price in a coffee shop led to the actor's participation in the film, with Price responding to Castle's pitch by describing the story of murder and deception as "charming" (Castle 146). No doubt much of the affection the film still enjoys stems from its star's acidic delivery of screenwriter Robb White's dialogue. Price's gleaming eye and the repressed malice with which he delivers the choicest lines to his unfaithful wife are wickedly funny and suggest the dark sense of humor that won the actor praise — and sometimes condemnation — in later performances.

Price stars as Frederick Loren, an eccentric millionaire who invites five guests to spend the night in an allegedly haunted house. If his guests will stay until morning, Loren promises them $10,000 apiece — provided they survive the experience. The guests include lovely young Nora Manning (Carolyn Craig), one of the anonymous minions who make up Loren's enormous work force; Dr. David Trent (Alan Marshal), a seemingly well-grounded psychiatrist; Ruth Bridgers (Julie Mitchum, older sibling of Robert), a newspaper columnist with a gambling problem; Lance Schroeder (Richard Long), a handsome test pilot; and the alcoholic owner of the house, Watson Pritchard (Elisha Cook). Loren claims that the party is for his wife, Annabelle (Carol Ohmart), although she seems reluctant to participate. Loren arms his guests with pistols — or "party favors," as he puts it — and Pritchard explains that over the course of a century the house has been the site of seven murders, including that of his own brother, which is how the drunken little man came to inherit the place.

Over the course of the evening, various strange phenomena occur, such as a ceiling that drips blood and a severed head that appears and disappears with vexing regularity.

Carol Ohmart and friend in *House on Haunted Hill* (1958).

Annabelle is found hanging from the ceiling, apparently murdered. Pritchard insists that the ghosts have chosen Nora as their focus, and with each shock she suffers, Nora becomes increasingly hysterical. Nora becomes convinced that Loren is out to kill her, and at the film's climax she shoots her host and employer — or so it seems. It turns out that Annabelle and Trent have been conducting an illicit affair, and it is Trent who has been trying to scare Nora into killing Loren. Trent goes to throw Loren's body in a convenient acid bath, but it is Trent and Annabelle who wind up in the vitriol courtesy of Loren, who has thoughtfully loaded most of the pistols with blanks. As the film concludes, Loren explains to his guests that he knew all along about his wife's infidelity and the plan that she and her lover had concocted for him. The entire "ghost party" has been an elaborate ruse to trap the lovers, and Loren announces his willingness to let the law decide his fate.

In terms of logical coherence, *House on Haunted Hill* is a mess. Loren's exposition at the end fails to explain how Annabelle and Trent are able to fake her death and otherwise arrange various spooky happenings; furthermore, there is no explanation offered for how the conspirators know that Nora is hypersensitive enough to be driven to shoot a man. For that matter, none of the so-called "logical explanation" at the film's finale confirms whether or not the house is truly haunted (the film fades out with Cook's Pritchard announcing to the audience that the ghosts are "coming for me now, and soon they'll come for you"). Nevertheless, the picture works despite its gaping plot holes thanks to Castle's sense of atmosphere, White's catty dialogue, and Price's sinister performance.

From the beginning, Castle manages to imbue the picture with a Gothic feel in spite of its modern setting. The moody black-and-white photography by Carl E. Guthrie helps immeasurably, as does Von Dexter's ominous score (enhanced by the "House on Haunted Hill" theme contributed by Richard Kayne and Richard Loring). Art director David Milton and set decorator Morris Hoffman provide the house's interior rooms with an oppressive sense of decay and neglect and truly convey the notion of an ancient haunted house. Interestingly, the faux Victorian look of the interior sets doesn't jibe with the house's Art Deco exterior — no surprise, since the exteriors were shot at a modern structure designed by Frank Lloyd Wright.

Yet what would be a mere error of continuity in most other movies somehow make sense here, as if the disparity between the house's interior and exterior appearances symbolizes the other contrasts abounding within the storyline. Lance and Nora look like the typical horror movie hero and heroine, but Lance does nothing particularly heroic during the film's running time, and Nora's instability contributes mightily to the chaotic proceedings. Dr. Trent appears to be the voice of reason and logic, yet it is he whose illicit passion for Annabelle has driven him to devise an insanely convoluted murder plot. Ruth and Pritchard initially seem like the most mild-mannered of the guests, yet they are the ones with the most obvious compulsive behavior problems (gambling and alcohol addictions) and the greatest desperation for Loren's lucrative financial offer.

The sense of uneasy contrasts that pervades *House on Haunted Hill* is most obviously depicted in the relationship between Loren and Annabelle. Frederick Loren isn't the first wealthy man to marry a significantly younger woman, and when required to do so in front of their guests, the Lorens manage to display a reasonably believable veneer of graciousness and hospitality. However, in private their relationship is every bit as corrosive as the acid bubbling in the basement. Both parties delight in tormenting each other with sarcastic comments, and Price's interaction with Ohmart is delicious.

"She's so amusing," Loren observes repeatedly in a soft yet bitter tone that fully conveys his true opinion of Annabelle. Price's ironic delivery milks the statement for its full worth; that same delivery informs other lines, including his query to Annabelle, "Do you remember the fun we had when you tried to poison me?" Annabelle's protest of innocence drips with equal venom, inspiring Loren to quip that she served him "arsenic on the rocks." Price adopts an almost legitimately desperate tone when Loren asks, "Would you go away for a million dollars — tax free?" Annabelle, however, simply shakes her head in response, her smile triumphant and devilish. When her husband observes that she "wants it all," there is a note of real vituperation in her voice when she responds, "I deserve it all!"

It is clear that the relationship between Loren and his wife has deteriorated to a truly toxic point, and one is forced to wonder why they don't just get a divorce (White's script explains that Loren's many earlier wives either disappeared or died under mysterious circumstances). Loren and Annabelle clearly share characteristics of pride, greed, intelligence, and determination; perhaps it was the recognition of these shared qualities that brought them together in the first place and now results in the bitterest irony of all: as much as the millionaire and his spouse despise each other, they are more alike than either could ever admit. Loren's wealth and power could bring him almost any woman he chooses, and Annabelle could easily find herself another rich husband with her sultry looks (Ohmart herself was a real-life beauty queen — Miss Utah of 1946, in fact). Yet could anybody else offer them the intellectual and emotional challenges that the Lorens offer each other? It is this element of what might be termed "toxic co-dependency" that contributes a fatal spiciness to their relationship and hints at a sadomasochistic connection.

It is a further irony that Frederick and Annabelle can't be truly happy together or apart. While Annabelle professes to love Trent, who boasts about the perfect plan that he has designed, it is obvious that she would inherit Loren's money if he did actually perish — meaning that she would have the ultimate power in the relationship with Trent. If she were truly wealthy and in charge of her life, would Annabelle still be interested in the bespectacled, rather nondescript shrink? It seems doubtful, particularly given the obvious and almost feral hunger in Mrs. Loren's eyes when she asks the studly Lance to protect her from her husband. "He would kill me if he could!" she claims, but once it is known that she has been plotting to kill Frederick all along, it is unnecessary for her to plead with Lance so plaintively. Yet as handsome as Lance may be, he offers neither wealth nor wit, nothing but his physical beauty with which to hold Annabelle's interest. Even if her murderous scheme had succeeded, Annabelle would still be unfulfilled without a partner to match her own devious nature.

That Loren feels the same kinship with his wicked wife is indicated as well. His wealth and prestige might appear to give the millionaire access to all manner of beautiful women, but clearly he requires the psychosexual stimulation that only a woman as ruthless as he is can provide. That there are sadomasochistic elements in their relationship is suggested by such bits of business as Loren's strong-arm tactics to assure Annabelle's presence at the party. "Are you ready, dear?" he asks with mock concern while pulling his wife's hair, ultimately forcing her to attend the gathering. That Annabelle has responded to Loren's cruelty by cuckolding him repeatedly is made clear when the couple discusses Lance: "Don't you want to console him," Loren asks in his falsely solicitous manner, "as you do most men — in your fashion?" The ambiguity of the actor's delivery of this line, which hints at a mix of anger, humiliation, regret, and perhaps even sexual stimulation, is used brilliantly. Finally, Loren delivers a brief eulogy to his dead wife and her lover: "It's a pity that you didn't know when you started your game of murder that I was playing, too." Price wisely chooses to imbue his delivery with a tinge of genuine regret as well as a note of triumph. Loren has won the game of treachery and deceit, and his wealth and influence may well protect him from the full legal ramifications of his involvement in two people's deaths (to say nothing of the mental anguish he has visited upon Nora and the other guests); however, his money cannot bring back to life the one woman who has challenged his own twisted imagination and intellect.

The contributions of the newspaper columnist to the plot are very small; Ruth Bridgers exists in *House on Haunted Hill* to provide the film with one more red herring and potential victim. Therefore, it is Loren's interaction with Nora that provides the film's second most important conflict to the storyline. Much of the film's running time is devoted to showing Nora's increasing hysteria and suspicion of Loren, a necessary element to throw viewers off the scent of the real killers. Regardless of Loren's ultimate motives, the way he reacts to Nora is crucial to establishing the film's atmosphere of menace.

From the first the audience is primed to identify with and care about Nora. "Isn't she pretty?" Loren asks rhetorically during the voice-over introduction of the party guests. Once again, Price's delivery implies some threat directed at the nominal heroine of the film — a threat that, ultimately, is nonexistent. That Nora is young and hardworking — the sole support for her impoverished family — further commends her to the viewer's affection. A sociopolitical conflict is thus established: the poor working girl already being exploited for her labor by the wealthy millionaire appears to be Loren's literal victim as well.

As the horrors of the house are unleashed, Nora's behavior becomes increasingly erratic. She suffers a great shock when the caretaker's witchlike wife suddenly passes her in a darkened room (perhaps the film's most unnerving moment). Later the caretaker himself spooks Nora, grabbing her from behind and hissing, "Come with us before he kills you!" The vagueness of the pronoun "he" in this context is particularly significant; who is the "he" who intends to kill Nora — Loren or Marshal? For that matter, why do the caretakers think anybody intends to kill anybody else?

Nora discovers a severed head in her suitcase and flees her room. She asks Pritchard about the legend of dismembered murder victims in the house before finally inviting the partygoers to see for themselves what's in her room: "Would you all like to see one of those heads?" Of course, the head has vanished by the time the crowd gathers upstairs, suggesting Nora is hallucinating or lying. Distraught and embarrassed, Nora angrily dismisses the group from her quarters.

After discovering Annabelle's hanging corpse, Nora is attacked in her room by the same rope that seems to have killed Mrs. Loren. A ghostly image of Annabelle appears, further driving the terrified young woman into hysterics. Almost incoherent with fear, Nora winds up in the basement, where she unwittingly fires blanks at her employer. Soon Loren has completed his deadly game with Annabelle and Trent, and he explains the situation to his guests (and the audience).

Significantly, Loren makes no apology to Nora, nor does he appear to have any shame or guilt about involving this innocent person in his bizarre scheme. Such nonchalance indicates the lack of regard Loren has for his employee; he seems to take no personal responsibility for her welfare, recognizing no difference between the role she's played in his plan and the anonymous and subservient role she plays as one of his countless workers. This lack of regard on Loren's part may be an oversight on the part of Castle and White, who are clearly anxious to wrap up the picture. Intentional or not, however, Loren's attitude at the film's conclusion says much about his true nature. At first glance, it appears that for once Price's character is not really the villain of the piece; however, Frederick Loren is clearly an unpleasant fellow and inspires none of the sympathy or understanding that distinguishes so many of the Price protagonists in the horror films to follow.

The immediate financial success of *House on Haunted Hill* assured a follow-up vehicle, and Castle returned to Columbia (this time with his own independent unit) to make it. Price returned as the film's star, further associating him as a horror specialist in the public's mind. Castle once again called on Rob White to provide the screenplay and Von Dexter to contribute the atmospheric score, this time for a film so bizarre it makes their previous effort look as logical as a mathematician's proofs. Once again, however, it is the tone of casual surrealism that makes a Castle-Price collaboration so effective.

The Tingler features Price as Dr. Warren Chapin, a part-time researcher and full-time pathologist whose specialty is the study of fear. Chapin is convinced that "there's a force in all of us that science knows nothing about, a force of fear," and he is desperate to prove his theories. Working with his young assistant, David (Darryl Hickman), Chapin has discovered that the sensation of being frightened creates a microscopic organism in people's spines, and he believes that the organism grows in proportion to the degree of fear victims' experiences. Chapin believes that only screaming breaks the tension and prevents "the Tingler" (as he calls it) from causing death by crushing the spine. Chapin uses LSD as part of an experiment on himself, inducing terrible hallucinations while vainly attempting to repress his own screams; he even shoots his unfaithful wife, Isabel (Patricia Cutts), with a pistol loaded with blanks, causing her to faint and allowing him to x-ray her spine for evidence of the Tingler. Yet none of these unorthodox activities are enough; Chapin theorizes that he needs a subject who cannot scream and thus cannot destroy the Tingler in order for him to prove the organism exists.

Conveniently enough, the doctor has befriended Ollie Higgins (Philip Coolidge), a mild-mannered chap whose wife, Martha (Judith Evelyn), is a deaf-mute with a pathological aversion to the sight of blood. After Chapin treats Martha for shock, she wakes up in the middle of the night to find the lights flickering and a deformed maniac stalking her through the apartment she and her husband share over the revival house they run

WHEN THE SCREEN SCREAMS YOU'LL SCREAM TOO ...IF YOU VALUE YOUR LIFE!

PERCEPTO!
newest and most startling gimmick on the screen!...

COLUMBIA PICTURES presents

The Tingler

starring

VINCENT PRICE

with JUDITH EVELYN

DARRYL HICKMAN · PATRICIA CUTTS

Written by ROBB WHITE

Produced and Directed by WILLIAM CASTLE

A WILLIAM CASTLE PRODUCTION

GUARANTEED

'The Tingler' will break loose in the theatre while you are in the audience. As you enter the theatre you will receive instructions ... how to guard yourself against attack by THE TINGLER!

Promotional material for William Castle's delightfully illogical *The Tingler* (1959).

(showing only silent movies, in deference to Martha's afflictions). Confronted with these and other horrors, including a bathtub full of blood (the black-and-white film's only color sequence), Martha dies of fright. Chapin performs an impromptu autopsy, removing the vaguely insectioid Tingler from Martha's spine. Eventually Chapin figures out that Ollie intentionally scared his wife to death, and during their confrontation the Tingler gets loose in the movie theater. Ultimately the creature is subdued, and Ollie prepares to make his getaway — only to be confronted by a repeat of the ghoulish phenomena he used to kill his wife. When Martha herself rises from the dead and stalks Ollie, he dies of fright.

The Tingler is an odd little film, and its narrative is so illogical that it seems even more dreamlike than *House on Haunted Hill.* Unlike the earlier effort, though, there is a specific event in the film that could be construed as an explanation for the bizarre events that follow: Dr. Chapin's experimental use of LSD. "From the articles I've read, this is a very interesting drug," Chapin tells David in an understatement modern audiences find unintentionally hilarious. In all probability, neither Castle nor White nor anybody else associated with the film's production cared how preposterous the plot might be; the film-makers just wanted to make a scary movie. Nevertheless, the fact that Chapin takes a powerful hallucinogen suggests that the implausible events that follow are all in his mind.

If Chapin is just imagining the rest of the story, the narrative inconsistencies resolve themselves pretty easily. The inclusion of a possibly unreliable narrator alludes to the works of Poe and provides an unconscious hint of the shape of things to come in Price's career.

As in *House on Haunted Hill*, three significant female characters are depicted in *The Tingler*, and as in the previous film, two of the three women demonstrate characteristics of both villainy and victimization (the innocent Nora character is mirrored in *The Tingler* by Isabel's younger sister, Lucy, who is in love with David; Pamela Lincoln plays the part). Once again the Price character is saddled with an unfaithful wife, but in this case it is she who has the money. Isabel is very wealthy and is financing Chapin's unorthodox experiments — a fact she never fails to bring up during their frequent arguments. The couple's arguments are as vicious as those of the Lorens, and White's script includes some savage witticisms that would have been perfectly suited to *House on Haunted Hill*. "There's a word for you," Isabel remarks to Chapin. "There are several for you" is the doctor's reply. During a confrontation in the laboratory, Chapin points out a stray cat to be used in an experiment to Isabel and mockingly wonders, "Have you two met in the same alley, perhaps?"

Like Annabelle Loren, Isabel Chapin cuckolds her husband — openly so. "That was quite a charming little scene out there," Chapin remarks after observing the conclusion of one of Isabel's assignations. "Don't tell me you've abandoned corpses for peeping out of windows" is her reply, an icy retort that associates Chapin with necrophilia and voyeurism. It is possible that Isabel is simply trying to annoy and humiliate her husband with her taunts, but the remark does pose a question: What has gone wrong with the Chapin marriage? The Chapins demonstrate none of the sadomasochistic attraction that is hinted at in the Loren marriage in *House on Haunted Hill*, although like the Lorens, the Chapins are, significantly, childless. Is Warren Chapin sexually twisted? It is an intriguing notion that would explain much about the character dynamics in *The Tingler*; the hypothesis certainly adds telling weight to one of Price's otherwise thrown away lines. "It's not all her fault," Chapin mutters to his sister-in-law when they discuss Isabel's indiscretions, thereby suggestion that the fault is his own.

One of the central conflicts between Chapin and his wife is Isabel's refusal to share her inheritance with Lucy. Isabel claims that she disapproves of Lucy's relationship with David, but her objections to the romance seem to be nothing more than justification for her own greed. Chapin seems genuinely fond of his sister-in-law and seems sincere in his desire to help her; in fact, during the experiment in which he threatens his wife with a pistol, Chapin demands that Isabel share her fortune with Lucy. Whether or not Isabel does so is not clearly established in the film; her last significant act is to unleash the Tingler on her husband, whom she has drugged with sedatives, a murderous act that fails only because Lucy returns from a date with David and screams at the sight of the monstrosity. Although Isabel has previously been victimized by her husband's unethical and unorthodox fear experiments — and perhaps by his personal proclivities as well — her attempt to murder him underscore her ultimately villainous nature.

Martha Higgins is obviously victimized in *The Tingler* — but, as it turns out, by her husband, not Price's character. Ollie explains to Chapin that he simply couldn't take living with his wife any longer, and not just because of her deafness; she demonstrates a number of unattractive qualities, including various nervous tics and a degree of genuine paranoia — for example, she won't let Dr. Chapin remain in the room while she deposits the theater's receipts into a safe. There is little doubt that Martha is a relatively unpleasant person to be around, but of course that's no reason for her to be frightened to death in such a cruel way. Nevertheless, she is villainous as well, though her actions are not directed toward Chapin; her unexplained resurrection occurs so she can avenge her murder at Ollie's hands. It is a testament to the performance of Judith Evelyn, whom Price apparently suggested for the role (Meikle 57), that Martha comes across as a believably complex human being, by turns pathetic, annoying, and terrifying.

No discussion of Price's collaborations with William Castle would be complete without some mention of the master showman's gimmicks. For *House on Haunted Hill*, Castle devised "Emergo," a process that attempted to go 3-D one better. At the film's climax, Annabelle is confronted with a skeleton, apparently all that remains of Loren, which eventually chases her into the acid bath. Castle cuts to a shot of Price, who is using some sort of reel to manipulate the fake skeleton. During the film's original release, Castle startled

William Castle, Vincent Price, and an unidentified bogeyman enjoy a snack in this publicity still for *The Tingler* (1959).

audiences by arranging for skeletons to seemingly emerge from the film thanks to some trick wires. The effect may well have been amusing fifty years ago, but watching *House on Haunted Hill* on TV or video today, the shot of Price operating the skeleton reel doesn't quite make sense.

Similarly, Castle devised a new process for *The Tingler*, which he called "Percepto." Realizing his cross between a crustacean and an insect would not provide enough figurative shocks on its own — although he did predict that viewers "wouldn't be eating lobster for the next five years!" (Castle 150) — the filmmaker decided that a literal shock would be necessary. Percepto involved wiring theater seats with small electric buzzers so that at a certain point theater employees could zing unsuspecting patrons. According to Castle, "In the final count, I think we must have buzzed 20,000,000 behinds" (153). Certainly Castle's sense of timing was impeccable, for the buzzers were supposed to be activated during the scene wherein the Tingler gets loose in the movie theater. It is still delightful to watch the movie on DVD and see the shadow of the Tingler wander across the screen as the film appears to break, then hear Price urge audiences to "scream for your lives," speaking to viewers of *The Tingler* as much as to the onscreen patrons of silent cinema (where the movie they're watching, incidentally, is the 1921 version of *Tol'able David*).

There is little doubt that Emergo and Percepto were the primary reasons why 50s audiences flocked to see *House on Haunted Hill* and *The Tingler*. In the wake of their success, William Castle had to promote his later films with even more outlandish gimmicks — yet as well regarded as these efforts may be, none are as beloved by modern fans as Castle's two projects starring Price. Castle and screenwriter Robb White can be credited with devising memorable plots, dangerously ambiguous female characters, and deliciously quotable dialogue as well. However, there is no doubt that the films endure because of the charisma and sense of menace suffused with fun that Vincent Price brings to the proceedings. The actor's appeal has proven far more durable than the passing delights offered by plastic skeletons and hidden joy buzzers.

5

A History of
Savage Degradations
House of Usher (1960)

Vincent Price's series of Poe-based movies started with *House of Usher* (1960), "one of the best Gothic horror films America has ever made" (McCarty 57). The idea for a series of Poe adaptations originated with independent filmmaker Roger Corman, American International Pictures' most prolific producer during the 1950s, who was so adept at making films quickly and cheaply that "if anyone can be said to have kept drive-in pictures in business in the late 1950s, and early 1960s, it was Corman" (Lampley, Beck, and Clark 231). Founded in 1954, American International Pictures was the brainchild of Samuel Z. Arkoff and James H. Nicholson, film distributors who realized that a fortune could be made by producing low-budget product for drive-in theaters. Teenagers made up most of the market for AIP releases; according to David J. Skal, nearly three quarters of the moviegoing public were between the ages of twelve and twenty-five by 1958 (*Horror* 255).

Born in Detroit on April 5, 1926, Roger Corman grew up in Los Angeles. In 1954, Corman co-wrote and helped produce his first movie, *Highway Dragnet*, for Allied Artists; produced his first science fiction film, *The Monster from the Ocean Floor*, for distributor Robert Lippert; and finally co-wrote and produced *The Fast and the Furious* for a newly formed production company, American Releasing Corporation, which soon became American International Pictures. Although Corman would never produce exclusively for AIP, the company distributed his most famous — in some cases, perhaps, infamous — low-budget projects, including such archetypal titles as *It Conquered the World* (1956), *A Bucket of Blood* (1959), and *The Little Shop of Horrors* (1960), the latter probably the most famous of Corman's cult films and the inspiration for the popular 1982 stage musical, itself filmed in 1986.

After *House of Usher* in 1960, Corman found himself at the helm of eight more Gothic horror films, most of which were inspired, directly or indirectly, by the works of Poe. Tiring of period horror films, the filmmaker explored the world of motorcycle gangs with *The Wild Angels* (1966) and shot a key drama about the Counterculture, *The Trip* (1967), both for AIP. Corman's *The St. Valentine's Day Massacre* (1967), which Gary Morris praises as one of the director's "most controlled, resonant productions" that works "both as a straight, 'torn-from-the-headlines' gangster film, and as a highly stylized philosophical drama that casts Fate as alternately indifferent and malign" (57), was distributed by 20th Century–Fox, one of Hollywood's oldest and most prestigious studios.

By this time, the specialist was beginning to enjoy serious critical attention, particularly from European critics. Corman began his career with no significant technical training or experience, literally learning how to make his frugal movies on the job. With each project, Corman improved his understanding of film language and eventually became adept at devising interesting angles, such as placing his camera inside a fireplace in *The Haunted Palace* or shooting from within an open grave in *Premature Burial*, which allowed him to achieve impressive visual and stylistic flourishes on a fraction of the budgets allotted to typical Hollywood projects.

The repetition of Poesque and Freudian themes, plus his continued fascination with misfits and rebels, so impressed critics at the 1970 Edinburgh Film Festival that a full-length appreciation—*Roger Corman: The Millenic Vision*—followed; according to Gary Morris, the monograph is "unquestionably the most important and substantial criticism of Corman in English" (153). The director eventually developed his own theories of filmmaking, derived largely from the *auteur* theory and informed by his legendary thriftiness:

> On most films, the director is the dominant creative force. But it is not always that way .... More times than the critics think, the most important person is the producer. Sometimes the most important person is the writer, and occasionally, the most important person will be the star. But, in general, the most dominant creative force is the director [qtd. in Wiater 46].

Vincent Price as Roderick, master of the guilt-haunted *House of Usher* (1960).

While Corman unquestionably practices his *auteur* theories in the Poe cycle, he and his screenwriters also tailor the protagonists to fit Vincent Price's onscreen persona. Although the notion that these characters are tortured and haunted by lost love, encroaching madness, and the weight of family history is derived from Poe and fine-tuned by Corman, each of these characters remains intelligent, articulate, and more or less artistic and aesthetically aware. Their sophistication and charm ironically underscore their eventual descent into insanity and malevolence. These traits are all derived from Price's public image as an aesthete, which is why he was Corman's first (and apparently only) choice to play Roderick Usher and other leads in the series (Smith 107).

Corman left AIP for good in 1970 and decided to start his own distributing firm. Under the aegis of New World Pictures, the freshly minted mogul approved and financed exploitation fare for the drive-in circuit. Corman sold New World in 1983 for a reported 16.5 million dollars (Gray 155); soon, however, he set up yet another company, Concorde-New Horizons Pictures. In 1990, he briefly returned to the director's chair for *Frankenstein Unbound*, based on the science fiction novel by Brian Aldiss. The film's box office failure, coupled with advancing age, convinced "the King of the B's" to retire from directing for good.

If Roger Corman had never made a single Poe film, his standing as a director would be confirmed by *The Little Shop of Horrors*, *The St. Valentine's Day Massacre*, his counterculture movies, and *The Intruder* (1961), a powerful exploration of race relations that failed to find popular or critical favor at the time of its release — and whose failure became "the biggest disappointment of [his] career" (Corman 103). His ability to make coherent films cheaply and quickly set a standard that independent filmmakers continue to emulate. Yet Corman's greatest contribution to motion pictures may be his legendary "unofficial film school." Such actors as Jack Nicholson, Bruce Dern, Peter Fonda, and Pam Grier earned early credits on Corman projects. Significant directors, including Francis Ford Coppola, Peter Bogdanovich, Martin Scorsese, Ron Howard, and James Cameron, worked for Corman in the infancy of their careers.

Ultimately, Roger Corman is probably less important as an exploiter of popular tastes than as a symbol of the independent filmmaker and as the mentor for three generations of younger creators who have gone on to outpace him in terms of both commercial and critical significance. In recognition of his accomplishments, Corman received an honorary Oscar from the Academy of Motion Picture Arts and Sciences in November 2009. There seems little doubt that Corman's career and influence disproves the prediction his former employer, Samuel Z. Arkoff, made in 1970: "When you come right down to it, I don't think there are any of us in the film industry who are making anything today that will be of more than passing historical interest fifty years from now" (qtd. in Brosnan 135).

The Poe cycle represents Corman's first attempt to improve the quality of the films he made. At the end of the Fifties, the developing producer was ready to do something different from the cheap fare that James H. Nicholson and Samuel Z. Arkoff had hitherto marketed. When AIP offered him $200,000 to make two more cheap thrillers, Corman countered with a proposition for something new:

> A longtime admirer of the works of Edgar Allan Poe, Corman envisioned a lavish Gothic adaptation in rich color and widescreen.... Not only were the author's works in the public domain, but their exploitation possibilities and Corman's reputation for turning a modest investment into box-office gold were an irresistible mixture. By the time the negotiations were completed, Corman had scored CinemaScope, color, and a $270,000 budget [Nollen 139].

Choosing his childhood favorite Poe tale, "The Fall of the House of Usher," Corman began developing the project, which he would both produce and direct. Veteran science fiction writer Richard Matheson (b. 1923) penned the script, which he later claimed was "pure Poe" and the best of the series that eventually developed (qtd. in Brosnan 128). Now hailed as "dean emeritus of American fantasists" (Lampley, Beck, and Clark 228), Richard Matheson won early acclaim for his novels *I Am Legend* (1954) and *The Shrinking Man* (1956), the latter of which he adapted for Universal in 1957. He adapted the vampire-laden *I Am Legend* for AIP as *The Last Man on Earth* (1964), with Vincent Price as the lead. In time, Matheson would win further acclaim as the author of several classic episodes of *The Twilight Zone*; his associations with a young Steven Spielberg (1971's *Duel*) and *Dark Shadows* creator Dan Curtis (1972's *The Night Stalker*) would become landmarks of television horror. By the time Matheson began his association with Corman and AIP, he was well on his way to becoming the most important author of science fiction and horror scripts of the Sixties and Seventies.

Whatever Matheson contributed to the screenplay, ultimately *House of Usher* (the abbreviated release title, although some publicity materials and prints of the film are titled *The Fall of the House of Usher*; many of Corman's Gothic productions feature similar variant titles) is primarily the artistic vision of Roger Corman, whose Freudian reading of Poe's story dictated the visual and psychological style of the film:

> The house can be seen as a woman's body with its openings — windows, doors, arches .... The corridor becomes a woman's vagina. The deeper you go into the dark hallways, then, the deeper you are delving into, say, an adolescent boy's first sexual stirrings.... Put together correctly, the classic horror sequence is the equivalent of the sexual act [80].

Corman also uses the house and the forlorn, blasted grounds that surround it as a symbol of what he terms protagonist Roderick Usher's "fevered and deranged mind" (81). Similarly, Corman followed the Gothic tradition of utilizing an old house or "haunted castle" to establish "an atmosphere conducive to the anxieties in the protagonist and ... other characters in general" (Fisher 75). The film benefits immensely from the production design of Daniel Haller, the art director who gave physical form to the crumbling house of horrors "luridly visualized" by Roger Corman (Kendrick 7). As a result of these symbolic underpinnings, *House of Usher* literalizes a madman's disordered psyche, twisted and tormented by his perverse simultaneous attraction and repulsion toward his own sister, Madeline (Myrna Fahey). To achieve this effect, Corman deliberately eschewed natural light and realistic sets, confining his production almost exclusively to studio soundstages. The film's only location footage, shot amid the aftermath of a forest fire in Los Angeles' Griffith Park (according to Corman's DVD commentary), provides the scarred earth and devastated trees necessary to convey the "singularly dreary tract of country" and "sense of insufferable gloom" described by Poe (231) and representative of Roderick's mental condition.

Complementing these physical production decisions is a significant shift in focus and motivation. Corman and Matheson completely alter the reason why nominal hero Philip Winthrop (Mark Damon) — the unnamed narrator of Poe's original story — has come to the house of Usher. In the story, Roderick summons his childhood friend "with a view of attempting, by the cheerfulness of [his] society, some alleviation of [Roderick's] malady" (Poe 232). The narrator is surprised to discover his mysterious host has a sister, the terminally ill Madeline. Yet in the film it is *Madeline* whom Philip has come to see, not Roderick. Philip explains that he met and fell in love with Madeline during her visit to Boston at some recent point, and he intends to marry her and take her away from her ancestral home.

Roderick initially refuses to allow Philip to see Madeline, claiming she is too ill for visitors. Soon, however, it is revealed that Roderick believes his family to be cursed; he wants the Usher line to finally die out, and the notion of his sister marrying and producing children terrifies him. "If you knew the nightmare you were picturing for me, sir," Roderick mutters sadly. Philip cannot bring himself to believe his beloved is anything but the lively, beautiful girl he fell in love with — even when he finally reunites with Madeline, who is almost as pale and eccentric as her brother.

Although Roderick mentions "the Usher curse" as the source of his family's misfortune, there does not seem to be a truly supernatural cause; a more scientific, if no less sensational, explanation is offered: the Ushers suffer from hereditary insanity. "Three-fourths go mad," Roderick explains while guiding Philip through a bizarre family portrait gallery (the incongruously abstract paintings were provided by avant-garde artist Burt Schoenberg) depicting the various murderers, thieves, harlots, and "merchants of flesh" from whom Roderick and Madeline have descended. Here Corman and Matheson once again depart sharply from Poe, who notes the Ushers have always distinguished themselves through "a peculiar sensibility of temperament, displaying itself ... in many works of exalted art, and ... repeated deeds of munificent yet unobtrusive charity" (232).

In any case, it quickly becomes obvious that Roderick's objections to his sister's marriage are not entirely based on the family's haunted past. Roderick's love for his sister exceeds the normal familial limits; initially depicted as more paternal than fraternal, Roderick's concern for Madeline is really a psychosexual obsession. The film's suggestion of an excessive intimacy between Roderick and Madeline is more explicit than Poe's; the author's closest reference to incest is the narrator's acknowledgment that "sympathies of a scarcely intelligible nature had always existed between [the Ushers]" (240). The screenplay further underscores the ambivalence of Roderick's strange compound of brotherly concern and forbidden desire for Madeline and the consequences of an incestuous union, associating his sister with "female genitalia as a monstrous sign" that threatens "to give birth to equally horrific offspring" (Creed 56). Though subtle, the indications of Roderick's forbidden desire are present throughout *House of Usher*.

Much of the credit for the film's success goes to Vincent Price, whose performance avoids the self-conscious histrionics and audience winking that undermine some of his later characterizations and contribute mightily to his reputation as a "camp" performer. Poe describes Roderick as a person with "a countenance not easily to be forgotten," including luminous eyes, thin lips, a strong chin, and "hair of a more than web-like softness and tenuity" (234) — a description well embodied by the film's star — who paints strange scenes and endures a "morbid condition of the auditory nerve which render[s] all music intolerable to the sufferer, with the exception of certain effects of stringed instruments" (237). Allegedly, Price himself suggested dyeing his hair white to suggest Roderick's hypersensitivity and rapidly deteriorating mind and body (Nollen 141). Price makes the most of his distinctive voice, subtly lowering it when Roderick seems threatening (as in the portrait gallery, where he tells Philip that "the history of the Ushers is a history of savage degradations"), making it higher and raspy when describing his cruelly heightened morbidity of the senses ("I can hear the scratch of rat claws in the stone walls!" he hisses to Philip), and smooth and comforting when addressing his beloved Madeline. "Don't you know I love you more than anything in the world? Can't you see it's my love for you that makes me act as I do?" he pleads tenderly, the true nature of his affection almost — but not quite — masked by Price's sincere delivery.

Price also conveys Roderick's unhealthy obsessions through the use of his expressive eyes. The actor alters his glance continuously throughout the picture, conveying Usher's intelligence and commanding presence when protesting Winthrop's marital plans, then squinting as if recoiling from a blow when Winthrop raises his protesting voice to a painful volume. When he addresses Madeline directly, Roderick's eyes soften; yet when he spies her kissing Philip passionately, his eyes blaze, suggesting jealously, panic, and heartbreak simultaneously.

In addition to his voice and his eyes, Price accomplishes much with gestures — or the lack of them. Sometimes the actor seems particularly motionless, his arms at his sides, but tensed, as if expecting a physical altercation. At other times, Roderick is depicted making deliberate and controlled moves within his limited personal space — the scenes of Roderick plucking the strings of his lute, producing an odd and unsettling tune, for example — that imply his growing frustration with his inability to dictate the minions of his crumbling world. Most significantly, Roderick strokes Madeline's hair and gently guides her to her room. These fatherly gestures are replaced with more sinister, sensual contact with his sister during a dream sequence in which Philip sees himself overwhelmed by Usher ancestors as a triumphant Roderick carries Madeline away in what appears to be a marital embrace.

Price's ability to convey so much information and such conflicting emotions is especially crucial given the fact that any explicit mention of incest was taboo for movies in 1960. His performance, frankly, far outshines those of his young co-stars, Damon and Fahey, neither of whom seems particularly comfortable with delivering their faux Victorian dialogue, much less conveying the complex and provocative emotional conflicts inherent in the story. Yet even this obvious deficiency in acting experience (and, perhaps, ability) contributes mightily to the emotional tensions in *House of Usher*, for there is something about Price's professionalism and polish that underscores the innocence of the young lovers whose union he opposes. It is almost as if the older actor's experience and worldliness imbue Roderick Usher with suggestions of emotional ruin brought upon by his greater knowledge of the world outside the family mansion. Damon and Fahey, by contrast, give less credible performances that nevertheless telegraph the inability of their characters to fully comprehend the extent of their hideous plight.

As with so many of Price's screen villains, Roderick Usher is a man out of touch with the world around him, a relic of a bygone era when the patriarchal social system allowed the older brother in an orphaned family to control his younger, female, relatives. S. S. Prawer asserts that horror films succeed because "the terror they induce in us, and articulate for us, is not infrequently terror at the order we have created or help to uphold

Madeline (Myrna Fahey) avenges herself upon her domineering brother (Price) at the climax of *House of Usher* (1960).

as well as the anarchic desires that oppose such order" (270). In the context of *House of Usher*, Prawer's theory indicts Roderick for his responsibility in upholding a sexist and increasingly obsolete social system. "You cannot order my life, Roderick," Madeline protests at one point, yet this is precisely what personal inclination, buttressed by nineteenth century cultural norms, inspires Roderick to do.

In a major thematic departure from the original story (in which her most autonomous act is to break out of her tomb), Madeline aspires to a degree of freedom and independence impossible to reach within the confines of the Usher home. Times are changing, a new world order — a new life — awaits Madeline, and Roderick cannot stand to lose her in the process. The madness he fears she will unleash on the world — "most of all does this evil reside in her," he warns Philip — is of less concern than the madness that will consume him if the house of Usher is left without its mistress. It appears that Philip is the hero of *House of Usher*, come to rescue Madeline from the madness and death that will be her lot if she doesn't escape her brother's clutches (it is interesting to speculate about just how Philip and Madeline met; on what pretext was she allowed to visit Boston in the first place?). Certainly the necessity of a virile young hero was a given in most 1960s-era horror films (and most films of other genres as well). However, a careful reading of the film reveals some intriguing issues in the relationship between Philip and Madeline, issues that suggest more ironic similarities between Roderick and Philip than either character would readily admit.

While Philip Winthrop is young, dashing, and apparently sincere in his love for Madeline, he is not completely liberated from the hegemony that so restricts Madeline's opportunities. He constantly pleads with her to leave with him, and he repeatedly protests his genuine concern for her to Madeline, Roderick, and even the Usher butler, Bristol (Harry Ellerbe). Yet once Philip believes matters are finally working out in his favor, he begins to demonstrate some of the very same assumptions that permeate Roderick's attitude towards Madeline. Knowing that his bride-to-be is wasting away and not eating, Philip brings her breakfast in bed — a thin and unappetizing gruel, apparently the only sustenance her weak system can take. Cajoling her to eat something, Philip seems half-serious when he admonishes her, saying, "I'll have no scrawny women in my house." There is no ambiguity about a later statement: when Madeline continues to predict her imminent demise, Philip sternly rebukes her, finally declaring, "I forbid you to ever say that again!" Clearly, Philip Winthrop is operating under the same assumptions about the roles of women in society that — in an exaggerated and perverted sense — Roderick Usher embraces. It is telling that for the most part, Philip and Roderick argue over Madeline's future, yet she is never given the opportunity to contribute to the debate. The doomed Miss Usher gets no vote in her fate; Philip begs her to run away with him rather than participate in a family decision-making process.

Madeline's lack of freedom and self-determination manifests itself in other ways. Philip learns from Bristol that the last of the Usher women is prone to spells of sleepwalking. Specifically, she unconsciously makes her way to the crypt in the basement of the mansion because "she is obsessed with thoughts of death," as the old butler puts it. Obsession with death is not merely a symptom of Madeline's mental erosion; it is subconsciously an obsession with freedom, a desire on Madeline's part to liberate herself from the oppressions of her family, her history, and even the conventions of society itself. Cataleptic seizures manifest themselves, apparently in response to the incredible levels of emotional stress to which Madeline is exposed.

It is a cataleptic spell, interestingly, that leads to the film's climax. Madeline is discovered in the crypt, apparently having collapsed while wandering in her sleep. The three men in the house hastily arrange a funeral service — during which Roderick notices a slight movement of his sibling's hand. Thus, Roderick willingly buries Madeline alive, a deception Philip discovers only when Bristol inadvertently confesses (this is another deliberate and significant departure from the short story, in which Roderick seems to accidentally inter his sister). The terrified suitor rushes to Madeline's coffin, only to find it empty. Roderick has spirited her away, claiming she is truly dead this time when Philip confronts him. However, Madeline is not dead yet; unfortunately, the experience of being literally buried alive, combined with her figurative burial under oppressive cultural and familial norms, has shattered the fragile remnants of her sanity.

Madeline attacks her brother, strangling him with a final burst of manic energy. As they grapple, the house catches fire; the noisy and ominous fissure in the wall (here as in

Poe's story a symbol of a cracked and crumbling mind) finally gives way, and Philip barely escapes with his life. As the ruins of the house sink into a brackish lake, a title card repeats the last line of Poe's tale: "The deep and dark tarn closed sullenly and silently over the fragments of the house of Usher" (245). Corman provides a final shot of Roderick and Madeline, lying dead in an embrace that "evokes both physical violence and the tumult of repressed sexual passion" in the ruins of "the house [that] has symbolized their inbred world throughout the film" (Silver and Ursini, *More* 51). The shot seems customized from Allen Tate's vision of the literary Madeline as "the unquiet spirit of the vampire [who] in falling prone upon her brother ... takes the position of the vampire suffocating its victim in a sexual embrace" (qtd. in Bloom 30). In her final insane moments, Madeline has finally accepted her place in the tiny universe of her brother in spite of the bizarre nature of his interest in her. The Usher siblings will remain together for eternity, precisely as the fatalistic Roderick — and possibly Madeline herself — has always wished it to be.

Whether his unnatural love was requited or not, Roderick is finally united with his beloved Madeline, and in a grotesque parody of marriage. Winthrop, tellingly, lives on — but without the object of his affection. In the end, there simply is no room for him in Madeline's life — or afterlife. The Usher line is extinct, and Winthrop has lost the woman he loves. Is he doomed to mourn her forever? Will he be transformed by his terrifying experiences and dreadful loss into a typical Poe protagonist, obsessed with the life (and death) of the fiancée he will never again see? These questions haunt the viewer long after the bleak and fatalistic conclusion of *House of Usher*.

6

THE RAZOR EDGE OF DESTINY
Pit and the Pendulum (1961)

The critical and (especially) financial success of *House of Usher* guaranteed a follow-up vehicle, and after briefly considering other projects, Roger Corman choose "The Pit and the Pendulum" as the sophomore entry in his Poe cycle. The resulting project is "a claustrophobic film that investigates a small group of characters caught in a nightmare of murder, torture, madness, incest, and hallucinatory images" (Silver and Ursini, *Roger* 150). This investigation follows a familiar pattern in the cycle, as the Corman-helmed productions foreground sexual anxieties such as gender role reversal and female sexual aggression that Poe only suggests, often in a romanticized fashion, in the source material. Ultimately the film successfully illustrates the physical and mental degradation and death that inevitably result from a potent brew of such intense psychosexual impulses, which are further complicated by suggestions of gender ambivalence on the part of Vincent Price's character, Nicholas Medina.

Originally published in 1842, "The Pit and the Pendulum" is one of Poe's most famous tales. The anonymous narrator of the story relates the bizarre torments visited upon him by the monks of the Spanish Inquisition, which include being plunged into total darkness and exposed to a yawning well, or pit; being confined to "a species of low framework of wood" (Poe 251), from which he is forced to watch a razor-sharp pendulum slowly descend upon his person; and finally being oppressed by heated walls, which begin to close in on him, inexorably pushing him towards the abysmal pit. At the last moment, having expressed "the agony of [his] soul ... in one, loud, long, and final scream of despair" (Poe 257), the narrator is personally rescued by General Lasalle, Napoleon's cavalry commander.

The difficulties of transforming this brief, essentially one-man tale into a feature-length motion picture were immediately apparent to Roger Corman and Richard Matheson. Having previously expanded "The Fall of the House of Usher" with great success, Matheson seized upon the notion of "[imposing] a plot from an old suspense mystery on [Poe's] basic premise"—an admission of liberal "borrowing" from the plot of Price's earlier horror classic, *House on Haunted Hill*, according to Denis Meikle (78). Whether or not Matheson consciously referred to the 1958 William Castle production, it is significant that both films feature adulterous lovers conspiring against the woman's husband, played in both cases by Vincent Price.

Barbara Steele, one of horror cinema's greatest "scream queens," as Elizabeth Medina in *Pit and the Pendulum* (1961).

The adulterous conspiracy plot twist is far from the only alteration to Poe's storyline found in Matheson's script. Whereas the original story apparently takes place in 1808, the year Napoleon captured Toledo from Spain, *Pit and the Pendulum* (note the omission of the initial article) is definitely set in 1546 — just after the Spanish Inquisition's most significant period of operation, Meikle notes (76). Furthermore, Poe's unnamed narrator is identified as Francis Barnard (John Kerr), an Englishman who journeys to Spain to investigate the circumstances surrounding the death of his sister, Elizabeth. Arriving at Castillo Medina, Barnard is greeted by Catherine (Luana Anders), loyal sister of troubled Nicholas, who still grieves for his dead wife.

Nicholas Medina, "a tortured, unbalanced, and greatly wronged man," abruptly appears when Francis and Catherine investigate "terrifying clacks of immense clockwork and chains" emanating from the castle dungeon (Miller 167–168). Initially Nicholas explains that Elizabeth died from an unknown illness — "something in her blood," he claims — but soon Francis learns the truth: Elizabeth died of fright, according to family physician Dr. Leon (Antony Carbone). Barnard also discovers that Catherine and Nicholas' father, Sebastian (also played by Price in flashbacks), was one of the Inquisition's chief torturers — a talent he put to malevolent use on his unfaithful wife, Isabella, who had been conducting an affair with Sebastian's brother, Bartoleme. Operating in his personal basement torture chamber, Sebastian beat his brother to death and buried his wife alive, not realizing that young Nicholas was secretly watching the entire gruesome business. As a result of his mother's horrible demise, Nicholas has grown up with an acute fear of premature burial.

Soon the guilt-ridden Nicholas finds his slender grasp on sanity slipping; he begins to hear Elizabeth calling to him, and the entire household is disturbed by the unmistakable sound of the late Donna Medina's harpsichord. Nicholas insists on breaking into his late wife's tomb, where to his horror he discovers that she had been buried alive, "her tortured face frozen in a rictus of terror, her bulging eyes, her clawlike fingers, the skin stretched tight and gray" in what Stephen King calls "the most important moment in the post–1960 horror film" (135). Eventually, Elizabeth's ghostly voice — "a terrifying mixture of malicious coaxing and playful seduction," according to Mark A. Miller (167) — leads Nicholas beneath the house to the family crypt, where he witnesses his wife slowly emerge from her coffin. Elizabeth (Barbara Steele) pursues Nicholas to the torture chamber, where he stumbles to his apparent death. Dr. Leon arrives and embraces Elizabeth; they have been conducting their affair in secret, and their plan to drive Nicholas mad has resulted in his unanticipated demise.

Nicholas is not really dead, but his mind is finally unhinged. Moreover, Nicholas now thinks he is his father, and Nicholas/Sebastian avenges himself by tossing Leon in the torture chamber's pit and locking a gagged Elizabeth in an iron maiden. Price engages in a particularly effective bit of acting in these scenes, gradually adopting the mannerisms of Sebastian, "a sadistic cripple, wild-eyed and wicked, and quite, quite mad" (Meikle 81). When Francis confronts him, Nicholas confines his brother-in-law to a platform over the pit, above which the titular pendulum begins to swing. Ultimately Catherine and a servant free Francis, and Nicholas plunges to his death in the pit. As the survivors depart,

Catherine remarks that the torture chamber will be permanently sealed; Corman's camera zooms in on the terrified eyes of Elizabeth, now doomed to slow starvation in the iron maiden.

Many elements of *Pit and the Pendulum* are clearly borrowed from *House of Usher*. Like the Usher mansion, Castillo Medina is a Gothic pile, ancient even in the film's period setting. Similarly, the Medina family crypt, as well as the torture chamber, is located beneath the house, and the protagonist is another young man who makes a perilous journey in what turns out to be a vain effort to "save" an ostensibly "innocent" young woman. Both films incorporate Freudian principles by requiring characters to descend into basement crypts; these downward movements symbolize the exploration of the unconscious and the investigation of emotions long thought "dead." In addition, these trips to the basement suggest the "downward spiral" that the primary characters must inevitably follow to their ultimate doom.

Once again, the Price character is a "guilt-ridden, sexually tormented aesthete" (Morris 100) whose grip on sanity is tenuous at best. Like Roderick Usher, Nicholas Medina lives with his only surviving relative, a female sibling. Most importantly, both *House of Usher* and *Pit and the Pendulum* emphasize catalepsy and premature burial to generate chills as well as plot twists, although in the latter film the cataleptic seizure upon which so much depends is faked.

Although at first glance Corman and Matheson may seem to borrow too liberally from themselves, they actually expand their exploration of certain concepts embedded in Poe's fiction. Nicholas Medina is at least as dedicated to Elizabeth as Roderick Usher is to Madeline. "I worshipped her," Nicholas tells Francis at one point, a statement that becomes tragically ironic once Elizabeth's infidelity comes to light. Nicholas demonstrates an even more ambivalent degree of desire suffused with dread toward Elizabeth than Roderick demonstrates toward Madeline.

Elements of Price's performance symbolize certain ambiguities pertaining to established concepts of gender. These ambiguities are somewhat exaggerated and foreshadow the actor's reputation as a specialist in "camp." Judith Butler has described "a sedimentation of gender norms" that is parodied by cross-dressing and other examples of "gender parody"; ultimately these parodies challenge the "social fictions" that compose traditional assumptions of sex roles (2500). In this context, Price's early interpretation of Nicholas as emotionally unstable and physically weak seems campy because it appears to feminize the actor. Furthermore, Nicholas' sickly demeanor, which Price communicates through languid gestures and a plaintive, slightly whiny voice tone, implies a lack of masculine vigor that may serve as the initial source of conflict between Nicholas and his wife. If Nicholas has displayed "feminine" weakness prior to Elizabeth's faked death, then it is logical to presume she compensates for this shortcoming by becoming more sexually aggressive, assuming the "masculine" traits that Nicholas has consciously or unconsciously eschewed. Elizabeth's aggression, which culminates in the plot of murderous deception she crafts with the doctor, is the final result of this transference of gender roles. Eventually, the unstable personas of Nicholas and Elizabeth Medina symbolize Butler's assertion that gender "is also a norm that can never be fully internalized" and is "impossible to embody" (2501).

The sexual ambiguities and obsessions suggested in *Pit and the Pendulum* are considerably more explicit and complex than those hinted at in *House of Usher*. References to aberrant impulses and fetishes abound in the 1961 production; on the most basic level, the film's focus on torture and pain recalls the nomenclature of sadomasochism. Sebastian's cruel delight in torturing his wife and brother — to say nothing of his victims in the Inquisition — strongly suggests sexual arousal. It is said that Sebastian punished Isabella after "accusing her of vile debaucheries with his brother," but the precise nature of these sexually motivated activities is left unnamed, no doubt in deference to the social decorum prevalent in the less liberated early Sixties. Under the circumstances, though, it seems likely that Isabella and Bartolome engaged in an affair that involved a significant amount of sadomasochistic activity.

Nicholas' fascination with his father's predilections involves not just horror and guilt about his family but ambivalence about his own emotional responses to torture, which partially explains the "air of definite guilt" that emanates from him. Nicholas' ultimate revenge on Leon and Elizabeth occurs after he has assumed the personality of his father, but this transformation also suggests that Nicholas has finally overcome his ambivalence about his sexuality and is now truly a sadist. Corman and Matheson obviously want audiences to respond to the irony inherent in Nicholas' repetition of his father's wicked deeds, but there is another irony in play as well: Nicholas Medina has embraced sadomasochism as an expression of personal power, and he no longer resists the challenge to "normal" sexual desire that he has clung to in his desperate attempt to maintain his sanity. In a sense, Nicholas' acceptance of his father's persona represents "a monstrous parody of a 'real-life' coming-out process" similar to that found in later works such as Joel Schumacher's 1987 vampire movie *The Lost Boys* (Benthoff 253).

In her influential essay "When the Woman Looks," Linda Williams notes that "in the classic horror film, the woman's look at the monster offers at least a potentially subversive recognition of the power and potency of a nonphallic sexuality" (24). This idea is certainly manifested in Elizabeth's growing interest in her late father-in-law's collection of torture devices. Nicholas describes the "haunted fascination" Elizabeth developed before she died, "as if the aura of pain and suffering which surrounded [the devices] was leading her to sickness and to death." Elizabeth thus demonstrates sadomasochistic tendencies, which is significant given that sadomasochists are stimulated by pain and the psychological ramifications of power exchange rather than ordinary genital couplings.

Elizabeth's unusual preferences are further illustrated by the speech with which she teases the apparently deceased Nicholas. "I have you exactly as I want you — helpless," she purrs. "Is it not ironic, oh my husband? Your wife an adulteress, your mother an adulteress, your uncle an adulterer, your closest friend an adulterer — do you not find that amusing, dear Nicholas?" Elizabeth's mocking sincerity recalls the verbal torments of a dominatrix or a dominant "hot wife" — a woman who openly engages in extramarital sex, often with the more or less willing consent of her cuckolded husband. Such sexual hegemony suggests both an exaggeration and a reversal of traditional gender roles, although ultimately these roles are reaffirmed. Elizabeth's dominant tendencies identify her as the "masculine" partner in the relationship. By the same token, Nicholas' physical and emotional indecisiveness make him ineffective and submissive, coding him as the more "feminine" partner. Yet this reversal of gender assumptions does not last; it is violently and fatally suppressed when Nicholas' personality is replaced by his father, resulting in a brutal re-assertion of psychosexual norms.

The casting of Barbara Steele (b. 1937) in the role of Elizabeth Medina is crucial to the success of the film and the potency of its sexual imagery; the performer's "wicked sensuality" is one of the "superior qualities" of the production, according to Don G. Smith (120). Prior to shooting the Poe adaptation, Steele headlined *Black Sunday* (1960), an excellent Italian vampire film that AIP distributed in the United States. By joining the cast of *Pit and the Pendulum*, Steele solidified her position as the premier "scream queen" of her generation; the appellation ultimately proved to be a mixed blessing for the actress, but her work in a number of Italian horror films remains the inspiration for a small but rabidly devoted cult following. Steele largely retired from acting after her marriage (ironically to a screenwriter named James *Poe*), but she later became a TV producer, working frequently for former horror specialist Dan Curtis, in whose short-lived revival of *Dark Shadows* (1991) Steele briefly returned to performing.

The actress is in fine form in *Pit and the Pendulum*. Thanks to her striking features and piercing eyes, Steele perfectly embodies both the dread and the desire necessary to imply alluring and transgressive sexuality. It is easy to believe that this dark beauty could be a predatory force of evil, a sexual libertine, or a wanton member of the living dead. Yet in spite of her "bad girl" mien, the actress also conveys a subtle sense of innocence — an unusual duality previously developed by *Black Sunday* director Mario Bava, who cast her as both villain (ancient vampire-witch) and victim (innocent descendant of said vampire-witch), and later exploited by countless lesser talents desperate to make the most out of her physical attributes. The aforementioned final shot of Steele's terrified, doomed eyes is arguably the most frightening image in the entire movie, and the intensity of her gaze, whether suggesting lust, cunning, or fear, dovetails nicely with the rich tones of Price's voice to make the couple believably sinister, psychotic, and sexually ambivalent. Speaking of actors' voices, Elizabeth's wicked yet alluring voice is not Steele's own; according to Lucy Chase Williams, Steele's "voice had to be dubbed prior to the film's release" because director Corman thought her accent was too "working class" compared to the other actors (166). Be that as it may, "whoever did dub Steele's voice was perfect" (Miller 167).

Regardless of how dominant she eventually becomes, Elizabeth's existence is defined by her husband. It is Nicholas' wealth and aristocratic heritage that place the couple in the upper strata of society; her material comfort and status, then, are predicated on his status regardless of the degree of her putative superiority in the relationship. As Gary Morris observes, "This is Nicholas' world, and his wife embodies Nicholas' impulse toward self-destruction"— an acknowledgment that his obsessions ultimately define both of their lives (106).

As potentially disturbing as sadomasochism might be to conventional sensibilities, it is marginally less upsetting than the shadow of incest that falls upon *Pit and the Pendulum*. As Alain Silver and James Ursini point out, Nicholas suffers from a "traumatic oedipal memory" as a result of seeing his father torture and kill his mother; his final descent into the torture chamber is "a way of reliving his oedipal childhood trauma" and thus "is the key to understanding the film as well as the character of Nicholas" (*Roger* 153). It is no coincidence that Nicholas has taken a bride who resembles his mother — tall, brunette, and cruelly beautiful. For most of his life, Nicholas has been haunted by his mother's adultery and horrific demise; his conflicting emotions have coalesced into an attraction-repulsion towards the late Isabella that compels him to choose Elizabeth — ultimately another unfaithful wife — to join him in his tragic castle. In a sense, the dread and desire Nicholas feels for Elizabeth mirror the conflicted feelings he has towards his mother.

Furthermore, the affair conducted between Isabella and Bartolome — siblings-in-law — is itself symbolically incestuous; although technically they are not related by blood, their legal connection identifies them as family in the eyes of society. This fact suggests another meaning inherent in Sebastian's statement about Isabella and Bartolome's engaging in "vile debaucheries"; incest is far more repugnant to conventional sensibilities than sado-masochism. So strict is the social taboo against incest that it finally gives the deranged Sebastian a comparatively rational justification for the murders he commits: Sebastian kills primarily for revenge, certainly, but he also kills out of a desire to restore and reaffirm the hegemony of traditional sexual expression, itself defined and controlled by the Catholic church, which is symbolized by Sebastian's affiliation with the Inquisition.

It makes little difference whether the ghosts that haunt Castillo Medina are supernatural or psychological in origin when Nicholas (Vincent Price) attacks his faithless wife (Barbara Steele) in *Pit and the Pendulum* (1961).

It appears the entire Medina household suffers from a sexual obsession with other family members except for Catherine — who, tellingly, has returned to her ancestral home only recently as the film opens, and then for the express purpose of looking after her brother in his period of mourning. In the absence of a husband or children, it must be assumed that she has never married. Why, then, did she leave in the first place? The character functions as a symbol for conventional sexuality; she represents a nominal "heroine" in the film, and therefore she cannot be depicted as a regular inhabitant of Castillo Medina. It is logical to assume that if Catherine remained long in the castle, she would eventually become as psychosexually disturbed as her brother. That this idea occurred to Corman is strongly suggested by additional sequences shot a few years later for the film's television broadcast on the ABC network. These scenes portray Catherine, again played by Luana Anders, "in a madhouse, telling the horrifying story, with the original film presented as her flashback," according to Mark A. Miller (171). Prolonged exposure to the very atmosphere of the castle has driven Catherine insane.

Although Elizabeth's apparent ghostliness is soundly disproven, and regardless of the fact that all the sordid events are given natural (albeit bizarre) explanations, there is nevertheless a subtle evocation of the supernatural throughout *Pit and the Pendulum*. Corman and Matheson go to considerable lengths to establish the psychological issues that are the root cause of the film's conflicts, but suggestions of preternatural phenomena nevertheless manifest themselves. Early on, Nicholas describes the instruments of torture as "my birthright — and my curse," a line that literally links the dysfunctional Medina clan to a supernatural agency. "If Elizabeth Medina walks the corridors of this castle, it's her spirit, not herself," Leon remarks; he makes this statement to help drive Nicholas mad, but the line still recalls the very real belief in ghosts prevalent in the sixteenth century. Finally, the transformation in personality that Nicholas experiences when he "becomes" Sebastian is so rapid and complete that it implies a spiritual possession as well as a psychological development. The notion that the spirits of the dead threaten to assume the personalities of the living makes sense given the decades of pain, misery, and horror associated with the "haunted" house of Medina and is reiterated later in some of Corman's other Poe adaptations, including *The Haunted Palace* and *The Tomb of Ligeia*.

Much has been made of Corman's techniques to portray the aura of madness and dread that emanates from the film. He opens the film with a lengthy pre-credit sequence that consists of a "Panavision vista of paints on glass" that finally "projects a surreal, otherworldly quality upon the real coastline" that sets the first actual scene (Miller 164). Corman makes frequent use of colored filters during flashback scenes, using blue filters for more erotic moments and red filters for depictions of violence. Corman also exploits the talents of art director Daniel Haller to the fullest; Haller built immense sets "to create an aura of depth and menace" and "painted murals along the walls" of the torture chamber, giving sumptuous visual symbols that allowed the producer-director to convey "color, vitality, and dynamic tension" (Corman 83).

Perhaps the greatest thematic achievement in *Pit and the Pendulum* is the film's depiction of a fatalistic worldview well aligned with Poe's own. Corman and Matheson constantly reiterate the sense of unavoidable destiny that foreshadows the Medina tragedy. The film compellingly demonstrates "the repetition of time," which as Alain Silver and James Ursini point out is "a favorite Corman theme" (*Roger* 153). In this context, "though Barnard may look to be an innocent victim of Nicholas' insane delusions, he can be thought of as a true successor to Bartolome by threatening to steal away one of the Medina women," thereby contributing to the notion of inevitable and repetitive destiny (Thornton

220). Nicholas' final speech to Francis, trapped beneath the descending pendulum, is particularly noteworthy:

> Do you know where you are, Bartolome? You are about to enter hell. In hell, Bartolome, IN HELL! ... The razor edge of destiny ... Thus the condition of man: bound on an island from which he can never have hope to escape, surrounded by the waiting pit of Hell, subject to the inexorable pendulum of fate, which must destroy him finally.

As Mark A. Miller notes, "This melancholy metaphor is unmistakably the epitaph for Edgar Allan Poe" (170). It is a chilling bit of dialogue that concisely summons up the tremendous forces, psychological, supernatural, and otherwise, that haunt the characters in *Pit and the Pendulum*—and by extension, the world beyond Castillo Medina.

7

DEDICATED TO YOUR DESTRUCTION
Tales of Terror (1962)

Having briefly departed the Poe series by sitting out of *Premature Burial* (1962), Vincent Price returned in not one but three roles for *Tales of Terror* (1962). With this film, director Roger Corman and screenwriter Richard Matheson strayed from the tradition of fleshing out Poe's short stories into feature length, experimenting with the anthology format in order to convey both horror and humor and to achieve a greater degree of fidelity to the stories. The episodic nature of *Tales of Terror* recalls *Dead of Night* (1945), the classic British portmanteau that provided the blueprint for such films and presages the group of horrific anthologies produced by the British-based Amicus company, of which *Dr. Terror's House of Horrors* (1964) was the first.

Tales of Terror opens with "Morella," the least faithful Poe adaptation in the movie. In the story Morella is an expert in the black arts; her arcane knowledge allows her spirit to live on after death, eventually possessing the body of the daughter she delivers even as she expires. Although her husband, Locke, expresses "feelings of deep yet most singular affection" for his wife, he "never [speaks] of passion, nor thought of love" in regard to her — suggesting a psychological seduction on Morella's part (667). Locke lovingly raises his daughter, but he doesn't christen her until she turns ten, at which point he is mysteriously compelled to name her Morella. The child immediately dies, and as Locke places her in the family vault, he discovers "no traces of the first, in the charnel where I laid the second, Morella" (671).

Price portrays Locke, a drunken widower wasting away in his crumbling mansion by the sea. To this desolate place comes Lenora (Maggie Pierce), the daughter whom Locke sent away years before. Initially Locke blames Lenora for the death of his wife, Morella, who died giving birth to Lenora. "Morella, my beloved wife, your murderer has returned," he murmurs to his deceased wife's portrait. However, Lenora is dying of an unspecified illness, and she hopes to effect a reunion with her father before she passes. Locke immediately agrees to the reconciliation, but soon Lenora falls ill and dies. At the point of death her body is possessed by the spirit of Morella (Leona Gage), whose features superimpose themselves over her daughter's face. Morella/Lenora then strangles Locke, and during their struggle a fire breaks out, consuming the house and everyone in it. In death, both Morella and Lenora — whose body has aged and deteriorated as her soul is supplanted by her mother — are depicted with wicked grins of triumph upon their lips.

Lenora (Maggie Pierce) confronts her estranged father, Locke (Vincent Price), in the "Morella" segment of *Tales of Terror* (1962).

"Morella" is the weakest of the three segments of *Tales of Terror*. Denis Meikle dismisses it accurately: "Price turns in one of his more intense performances for a pasta of pre-digested ingredients and a storyline into which even Matheson could barely be bothered to breathe life or logic" (87). Ultimately what Matheson incorporates into the episode is largely swiped from Poe's similarly themed but superior tale, "Ligeia," which itself would be adapted for Corman by Robert Towne a few years later. Locke constantly bemoans the loss of his wife and expresses hatred for his only child, yet he instantly changes his mind when he learns she is terminally ill, expressing sorrow and a strong desire to reconcile. Even more nonsensical is Morella's treatment of Locke when she returns from the dead: why does she murder the man who has loved her so faithfully for a quarter century after her death? No mention is made of her magical expertise, so no explanation for her supernatural abilities is given. Locke has even robbed Morella's grave and keeps her mummified corpse in his bedroom — but Lenora's reaction to this blatant touch of necrophilia is mild, to say the least.

It is easy and convenient to dismiss "Morella" as lazy scripting on Matheson's part; nevertheless, the changes he makes to the storyline are rich with symbolism. Morella's ability to possess Lenora's soul represents a perversion of the notion that parents achieve a degree of immortality through their children. The natural order is compromised when the dead live on, and the fact that the wicked mother would plot to overwrite her daughter's personality — her soul — with her own is unnerving. In the nineteenth century, childbirth was an especially serious danger to women's health; many women died delivering babies, and the lack of effective birth control methods meant that most fertile women were either pregnant or nursing during the vast majority of their childbearing years. Morella's willingness to "become" her own daughter can thus be seen as a bizarre retribution for losing her own life through the process of bringing Lenora into the world. Moreover, Morella's assumption of control over Lenora symbolizes the conflict inherent in relationships in which an overbearing mother dominates her daughter's adult life (and specifically echoes the relationship between Eleanor Vance and her domineering mother in Shirley Jackson's *The Haunting of Hill House* [1959], which had recently been published when Matheson penned his "Morella" script).

Morella's desire for revenge against Locke seems exceptionally misdirected given his decades of fidelity to her memory; what motivates the attack on the faithful husband? Considering that Morella died in childbirth, it is likely she blames her husband for impregnating her. As a husband at this time, Locke would be well within his legal and cultural "rights" to demand coitus with his wife, regardless of whether she wanted to engage in sexual relations or not. Many an inattentive or inconsiderate husband has learned to cherish his late wife's memory after her death, and Locke's devotion could easily be inspired, in part, by guilt associated with his role in Morella's death.

Similarly, Locke may have killed Morella deliberately. Certainly there is evidence in Poe's story that Locke may have played a part in Morella's death. Before her final illness emerges, his wife's strange interests and personality "oppress [him] as a spell"; furthermore, he muses,

> Shall I then say that I longed with an earnest and consuming desire for the moment of Morella's decease? I did; but the fragile spirit clung to its tenement of clay for many days — for many weeks and irksome months — until my tortured nerves obtained the mastery over my mind, and I grew furious through delay, and, with the heart of a fiend, cursed the days, and the hours, and the bitter moments, which seemed to lengthen and lengthen as her gentle life declined — like shadows in the dying of the day [668].

It is conceivable, then, that Locke sped his wife on her way to the great beyond; doubtless he suffered terribly under the pressure and stress of caring for his slowly dying spouse. In any case, the ambiguity of his feelings is hinted at in the film version. Furthermore, "Morella" follows a motif established in *House of Usher*, developed in *Pit and the Pendulum*, and revised to meet plot requirements in *The Raven* and *The Tomb of Ligeia* wherein a woman's posthumous revenge symbolizes an awareness of gender inequity not emphasized by Poe. The redressing of real or perceived wrongs acknowledges the dawn of the sexual revolution and is accomplished with such aggression that the victims cannot avoid becoming signifiers of villainy; the vengeance of Morella and the other Poe females must be explicit in order to underscore its relevance to a mass audience composed, in great measure, of teenagers and young adults.

Ultimately, Locke himself is an ambiguous protagonist in the "Morella" segment.

The fact that he keeps his wife's withered body in his bed strongly suggests necrophilia, and the fact that his daughter "becomes" his beloved wife implies a degree of incestuous attraction between Locke and Lenora. One cannot help but wonder what the nature of their life together would be if Locke and his daughter had remained together in solitude for many years. It is significant that Price shaved off his trademark moustache for this episode, giving him a younger, more virile appearance than is customary in his horror performances (or indeed almost any of his work in the postwar era). This visual allusion to Price's early cinematic career as a romantic lead is key to an understanding of the Locke character and his motivations. In this context, Morella's thirst for revenge can be explained by her desire to avenge her mistreatment at Locke's hands and as a means of protecting Lenora as well from the tragedy of incest.

Notions of incest are also suggested by Lenora's explanation of how her life has turned out since her rejection by her father. Lenora explains that she has had many failed relationships with men, including a marriage that has apparently ended in divorce — or desertion on Lenora's part. "I cannot give, you see," Lenora cryptically explains — without ever quite specifying what it is she cannot give. Since she apparently has no children, she may be infertile. It is also possible that Lenora may never have consummated her marriage. She feels she cannot maintain a romantic relationship with a man without reaching some understanding of her father and his motivations. The father is the most significant signifier of the concept of the male to children, especially female children, so in a sense Lenora cannot "give" herself to another man without first learning how to do so from Locke. The ramifications of this emotional incest, particularly in light of Lenora's terminal illness (which will prevent her from applying any lesson she learns from her father to a future romantic arrangement), are as perverse to cultural norms as Morella's excessive lust for life is to the natural order.

The exact nature of Lenora's illness is never stated, but it is possible that she suffers from venereal disease. Perhaps instead of withholding physical affection from men, she has been wanton in her sexual activity in a vain attempt to replace the relationship she never enjoyed with her father. Such promiscuity could easily lead to syphilis or other sexually transmitted diseases for which there was no cure in the nineteenth century. Infidelity compounded with syphilitic infection would certainly justify any divorce proceedings initiated by Lenora's husband. Of course, it is also possible that it is the husband, not Lenora, who engaged in extramarital sexual activity and thus introduced the disease that is now killing her. Maggie Pierce's nuanced performance, including restrained gestures and a slightly quavering voice, suggests a character consumed with anxiety about the emotions and impulses she fails to completely repress — in effect becoming a distaff version of the unreliable Poe narrators Locke represents. As a result, a duality between father and daughter is established that mirrors the more explicit duality between mother and daughter. The ambiguities in the Locke family dynamic, whether implicit or plainly stated, contribute what psychological interest there is to the uneven "Morella" segment.

Sandwiched between two straight adaptations of Poe in *Tales of Terror* is the comic episode "The Black Cat," which incorporates "The Cask of Amontillado" for good measure. Neither of these tales would be included in an accounting of Poe's more humorous works, but Richard Matheson's script picks up on traces of dark comedy in the stories and amplifies them considerably. Although by 1962 Vincent Price was firmly established as a "horror star," he had always demonstrated an affinity for lighter fare going back to his first film, *Service de Luxe* (1938), and further manifested in such films as *Champagne for Caesar* (1950) and *His Kind of Woman* (1951), all harbingers of the humor the actor would later bring to many of his film and television assignments. For "The Black Cat," Price was teamed with another specialist in sinister roles who also evidenced superb comic sensibilities: Peter Lorre. Both actors had appeared in *The Story of Mankind* five years earlier, but "The Black Cat" marked the first time they physically appeared together in a movie; it would also represent, in the words of Paul Castiglia, the birth of "the horror genre's all time classic comedy scream team!" (185).

In "The Black Cat," Poe presents yet another nameless narrator who insists upon his sanity even while confessing to crimes so foul they must surely be the result of madness. Claiming to be a mild-mannered person undone by alcohol, the narrator relates how his drunkenness leads him to disfigure a beloved cat and abuse his devoted wife before finally killing her. Similarly, "The Cask of Amontillado" is the confession of another murderer, Montresor, who avenges some unnamed slight at the hands of wine expert Fortunato by entombing the living victim within the walls of the catacombs. The confessional nature of the stories, coupled with their shared notion of victims buried within walls, make them appropriate choices for the amalgamation of plots envisioned by Corman and Matheson. The infusion of black comedy and the addition of a love triangle that recognizes gender issues of the 1960s are the most inspired of Matheson's contributions to this compound of two stories.

Lorre stars as Montresor Herringbone, an alcoholic whose perpetual inebriation has kept him unemployed for years. Only his long-suffering wife, Annabel (Joyce Jameson), has prevented the family from total financial collapse thanks to her sewing talents. When Montresor stumbles into a convention of wine merchants, he is ridiculed until he trumps respected oenologist Fortunato Lucresi (Vincent Price) in a wine-tasting contest. Thoroughly humiliated, Fortunato nevertheless escorts the drunken Montresor to his home, where Fortunato and Annabel fall in love (or something reasonably similar) at first sight. Eventually Montresor discovers that his wife is cuckolding him with his new friend; Montresor avenges himself by murdering his wife and entombing her and the still-living Fortunato behind a brick wall. Montessori's crime is discovered, however, when investigating police officers hear a strange cry from behind the freshly mortared wall and tear it down — as in Poe's story, a black cat has been inadvertently entombed alive with the doomed lovers; Montresor has "walled the monster up within the tomb" (230).

Much of the humor in "The Black Cat" is due to the contrast in delivery between the two stars. Price's performance remains somewhat overdone throughout the episode, but Lorre, after playing his drunken scenes broadly, reverts to the subtle sardonic persona that he chilled audiences with in such classics as *The Man Who Knew Too Much* (1934) and *The Maltese Falcon* (1941). Both actors demonstrate a flair for slapstick in the film's funniest sequence, the wine-tasting contest. Price's Fortunato demonstrates traditional (albeit exaggerated) techniques, and Lorre's Montresor is content to simply swig his wine —

yet he still correctly identifies both vintage and year! As Price put it to interviewer Lawrence French:

> Peter and I played two drunks, but before we did it they brought in this very famous wine taster to show us how it was done. We enjoyed that enormously; we got very drunk in the afternoons.... I did it exactly the way [the wine taster] showed us, but added just a little bit more, and Peter was doing it the way they didn't do it, which made for a very funny scene [qtd. in Castiglia 189].

The wine-tasting contest allows the actors to mine farcical gold through unsubtle jabs at gender stereotypes. Price plays Fortunato as a fop, a dandy — as an aristocratic and possibly homosexual hedonist — as demonstrated by his prissy manners and campy technique. Lorre, despite his diminutive height, high-pitched voice, and lascivious leer (all elements the actor used to during his career to establish sexually transgressive characters, which typecast him as a "creep"), comes across as stereotypically heterosexual, gleefully eschewing the "sissified" manner and technique of Price by simply gulping each sample crudely yet identifying the wines accurately.

The way the main characters interact with Annabel is also a study in contrasts. Although the episode is played for laughs, there is no doubt that Montresor treats his wife

Montressor (Peter Lorre) and Fortunato (Price) prepare for the wine-tasting contest in "The Black Cat," the second segment of *Tales of Terror* (1962).

with particular sadism. The threat of physical violence permeates Lorre's scenes with Jameson, a fine comic actress who never loses sight of the real danger that threatens Annabel. Montresor hounds his wife, bellowing at her to "give me my money!" Having been out of work for seventeen years, Montresor has no money of his own — it is Annabel's sewing money that he claims as rightfully his, and given the Victorian-era setting, he is doing so with the full consent of the law and social custom. Montresor's exploitation of Annabel is further underscored later, when in a drunken spree he comments to a bartender that "she gives me what is rightfully mine" — a comment that acknowledges Montresor's fiscal and sexual command of his wife.

Fortunato, on the other hand, treats Annabel with a reverence as exaggerated as Montresor's sadism. The oenologist woos the object of his affection with excessive romantic gestures, even referring to his friend's wife as "heart of my heart" in a line that, as Mark Clark notes, "Price delivers with sickening earnestness" (94). The lovers share a fondness for cats, as evidenced when Fortunato spots Annabel's feline pet — like her, despised and abused by Montresor — and lovingly strokes the animal, commenting, "I have several of my own at home." Ultimately, Fortunato's attractiveness to Annabel seems to stem from their feminine alignment; he is as dainty and fragile as she is, and they relate to each other through their appreciation of art, poetry, and other "feminine" interests. Fortunato and Annabel are aesthetic beings, linked by their intuitive and artistic natures. Montresor, of course, is too brutish — too manly — to appreciate the more artistic elements in life. Or so it seems.

Montresor's ability to expertly recognize fine wines is not merely a coincidence of his profound alcoholism. Somewhere along the way, the cruel drunk has developed an aesthetic appreciation for the grape — and, given his choice of a lovely bride and a well-appointed home even in the midst of poverty, Montresor apparently maintains other powers of observation and appreciation, albeit diminished by what Poe calls "the Fiend Intemperance" ("Black" 224) and a compulsion to evidence his masculinity (indeed, this compulsion may be the source of frustration that drives him to drink). When Montresor realizes that his wife and friend have betrayed him, he remains sober enough to plot his horrific revenge. Lorre's delivery of such lines as "I am genuinely dedicated to your destruction" is truly disturbing as he addresses the appropriately panicky Price. By giving Montresor a specific motive for his revenge, "The Black Cat" departs from Poe's story "The Cask of Amontillado" completely, since Poe never reveals the insult that inspires Montresor's fiendish plot. As Poe's Montresor explains, "I must not only punish, but punish with impunity. A wrong is unredressed when retribution overtakes its redresser. It is equally unredressed when the avenger fails to make himself felt as such to him who has done the wrong" (274). As in the story, the cinematic Fortunato (and Annabel, a character totally absent from "The Cask of Amontillado") fatally underestimates Montresor, although since the movie incorporates "The Black Cat," Lorre's avenger ultimately faces justice. Before Montresor meets his fate, however, his comic cruelties delight and disturb in roughly equal measure, resulting in an entertaining and thoughtful episode.

"The Case of M. Valdemar" closely follows the general outline of Poe's story, which is essentially a case study of an experiment to determine what the moment of death is like. However, the episode substitutes a villainous hypnotist, Carmichael (Basil Rathbone), for the benign but anonymous narrator of the story. Even more significant is the addition of a female protagonist, an element wholly absent in the source material. The addition of a wife opens the way for two romantic and sexual triangles involving the Price character and his female partner.

Price essays the role of Ernest Valdemar, a dying man whose terminal suffering has been eased by the mesmerist's ministrations. Valdemar consents to be placed in a sort of hypnotic trance at the moment of his death, assuming the experiment will delay his final passing only briefly. Yet Carmichael manages to keep Valdemar in an *indefinite* state of suspended animation, becoming increasingly obsessed with his ability to forestall death. Months pass, during which time the voice of Valdemar's tormented soul occasionally moans for relief. When Carmichael attempts to rape Helene (Debra Paget), Valdemar's wife, the semi-dead man lurches from his perennial deathbed and strangles Carmichael, dissolving into "a nearly liquid mass of loathsome — of detestable putrescence" (Poe 103) as he finally expires.

"The Case of M. Valdemar" presents a rare opportunity for Price to portray a completely sympathetic character, a kindly old man who suffers the hellish fate of being imprisoned in a perpetual state of non-death. Even when Valdemar finally rises up and kills Carmichael, he does so more to protect his beloved wife than to exact well-deserved vengeance upon his tormentor. Corman and Matheson are careful to underscore the thoughtfulness and consideration of the character, an especially important task given that he is caught in the middle of two unusual relationship triangles. Valdemar repeatedly tells Helene how much he loves her and expresses his appreciation for her devotion several times during the episode. Most significantly, Valdemar has recognized the attraction between Helene and his young physician, Elliot James (David Frankham). Unlike the typical jealous or homicidal Price husband, Valdemar fully endorses the relationship between his wife and his doctor; he informs Helene that his dying wish is that she marry Dr. James.

It is clear from the text that Helene and James have not acted on their feelings out of the love and respect that they both demonstrate for Valdemar; for his part, Valdemar knows his wife will be happy and properly cared for by the doctor. Thus the three-way relationship is a sort of chaste *ménage a trois* rather than the conflicted triangle presented in *House of Usher* or "The Black Cat" episode. It is not insignificant that Dr. James is an honorable man with firm ethics, for he will win not only the hand of Valdemar's widow but a fortune as well. Thus Carmichael's villainy is further compounded when he reveals his desire for Helene and her inheritance.

The threat to Helene's property is not present in Poe's story; for that matter, neither Helene nor Dr. James appears in the tale, in which Valdemar is portrayed as a bachelor, and the nameless mesmerist who narrates the case is portrayed as a sincere and honorable friend of Valdemar who is genuinely concerned with his patient's well being and initiates the hypnotic experiment at Valdemar's request (91). Yet the idea of a female protagonist being menaced by a threat to her property is a common element in the Gothic tale, which Donald E. Westlake glibly defines as a story "about a girl who gets a house" (qtd. in Fisher 73). As James J. J. Janis points out in his survey of the role of women in horror,

In almost every instance ..., the heroine is set upon by villains preternatural, outré, or mysterious who seek to deny her birthrights, her honor, her freedom, her happiness, and frequently her life ... to take away her right of choice. If she gets the house, then she has attained freedom. If not, then she loses all [56].

Yet while Carmichael is certainly an evil scoundrel and Valdemar and James are clearly good men, there is an undeniable and unsettling subtext of sexism to the story. It is fairly obvious that what Helene wants for herself is of comparatively little importance in the scenario; although she is in love with the physician, ultimately her desires are secondary to those of her husband and the men who vie to become her next spouse. Although a specific year is not established in the episode, the set and costume designs indicate a setting circa 1845, the year Poe composed the original story. Therefore, Helene exists in a time during which the rights of women were sharply curtailed; in most American communities they could not vote, pursue most professions, or retain ownership of property if they married (unless specifically protected by a "marriage contract" equivalent to a modern prenuptial agreement). Under the circumstances, Valdemar's ostensibly benign wishes are announced in the context of a rigid patriarchy that upholds his right to direct his wife's destiny long after his death.

Helene is as much a property as a person, as much a commodity as Valdemar's mansion and fortune (ironically, Valdemar is himself a commodity in terms of his importance to Carmichael's experiments). Though Carmichael's lascivious designs on Mrs. Valdemar are telegraphed early in the episode — he stares at her with a crafty expression mingled with lust — it is also her wealth he covets. As a loving wife, Helene agrees to marry Carmichael on condition that he release her husband's tortured spirit, but even this reasonable request is refused as the lecherous hypnotist attempts to force himself upon her. It is true that Valdemar is inspired to throw off Carmichael's psychic yoke at the sight of Helene's distress, but it is also true that Valdemar must kill Carmichael to protect his final wishes for his wife and his property. As in so many of Poe's stories, a character's will becomes a psychic force capable of bestowing supernatural abilities.

It is also significant that Valdemar and Helene are apparently childless. The absence of heirs to the Valdemar name helps clear the way for Carmichael to gain control of Valdemar's estate. The lack of offspring also suggests the possibility that Valdemar and Helene are not sexually active; indeed, sexual congress is certainly no longer possible for the old man when the story begins and may not have been for a considerable period of time prior. Given Valdemar's almost worshipful objectification of Helene, it is even possible that the marriage has *never* been consummated, which implies her virginity remains intact. If this is the case, Carmichael's intentions are all the more monstrous, for he desires Helene's innocence as well as her rightful fortune.

Whether Helene is a virgin or not, the vigorous young doctor is clearly intended to represent a more appropriate match than either the kindly Valdemar or the wicked Carmichael. The passing of both older men clears the way for Helene to marry Dr. James — and presumably to reproduce with him. Having children with Helene and benefiting from her considerable inheritance is a high honor, a privilege Valdemar intends to grant to an appropriately worthy (male) successor. Furthermore, the acquisition of Valdemar's possessions — including his wife — represents a transformation of sorts: Valdemar in effect "becomes" the man who replaces him in the house and in Helene's bed, thus allowing the old man to live on in the more idealized form of a younger, more virile husband to the young woman. Carmichael's heinous designs, therefore, threaten to supplant not only Dr. James, but the unusual concept of life after death that Valdemar's wishes represent.

In the end, then, "The Case of M. Valdemar" is an intriguing compound of conflicting wills, both legal and psychological, that incorporates the ironies inherent in a paternalistic system that is undoubtedly sexist even when it seeks to protect women. It is a story of psychological horror that touches on the very real dread that loss of property and material wealth would inspire in anyone, especially a young woman in the nineteenth century. Don G. Smith accurately notes that the episode also "succeeds largely because of the sympathetic and pitiable trials of Vincent Price and the coldly villainous machinations of Basil Rathbone" (137). As such, it is the most thoughtful and complex of the episodes presented in the film.

One of the most intriguing aspects of *Tales of Terror* is its offering of three very different characters for Price to play. The actor takes full advantage of the opportunity to cross his former leading man image with his current horror star persona in "Morella," and then to play an amorous fop in "The Black Cat," a subtle acknowledgment of his growing status as a camp icon. Price's turn as the dying patient in "The Case of M. Valdemar" features the actor as a character much older and less vigorous than himself, a cinematic foreshadowing of the infirmities that would be visited upon him in real life. Ultimately these characters represent the actor's reel persona even as they become amalgamations of his real personality.

Furthermore, each Price character symbolizes significant challenges to traditional gender construction. In "Morella," Locke's obsessions with incest and necrophilia undermine his presumptive role as the paternal figure, compromising that role by allowing the sort of "unregulated permeability" of ethical and sexual norms that "constitutes a site of pollution and endangerment" (Butler 2493). A more obvious erosion of gender performance is associated with Price's interpretation of Fortunato in "The Black Cat," whose camp mannerisms suggest homosexuality and thus "disrupt the regulatory fiction of heterosexual coherence" (Butler 2497). Finally, the aged and infirm Valdemar can no longer function sexually and is reduced to the benevolent tyranny of directing his wife's existence after his death, vainly attempting to maintain "the illusion of an abiding gendered self" (Butler 2501) long past the point where gender norms are relevant. With each episode, the Price character decays as a representative of normal sex roles; the literal decay of M. Valdemar physically manifests the progressive dissolution that supplies *Tales of Terror* with an additional layer of psychological dread only intermittently present in the Poe sources.

8

NEVERMORE
The Raven and *The Comedy of Terrors* (1963)

Having produced and directed four Poe-inspired features in just over two years, Roger Corman began to feel he was in a rut. The thematic similarities among *House of Usher, Pit and the Pendulum, Premature Burial*, and *Tales of Terror* were beginning to wear thin through constant repetition; perhaps more significantly, box office receipts for *Tales of Terror* declined slightly in comparison to the gross for *Pit and the Pendulum*, suggesting that audiences were tiring of the formula as well. Denis Meikle claims that "preview audiences in the US had singled out 'The Black Cat' episode for special mention," which guaranteed "that the next film in line would be a comedy from start to finish" (89–90). Once again working with screenwriter Richard Matheson, Corman tackled the daunting task of transforming Poe's most famous poem — a dark meditation on the eternal misery of loss — into a rollicking light comedy that "exploit[s] the grotesquely humorous potential of horror-movie imagery" (Prawer 249). Furthermore, *The Raven* gently lampoons the famous poem, infusing elements of family dysfunction and gender politics that transform the narrative from a somewhat overheated lament for the death of a beautiful woman into a satire of both the Gothic tradition and the patriarchy of sixteenth century Europe.

Eleven months to the day after *The Raven* opened on January 25, 1963, fans of AIP's approach to comic horror received a Christmas treat in the form of *The Comedy of Terrors*. Once again the stars of *The Raven* (Vincent Price, Peter Lorre, and Boris Karloff) were brought together to provide shrieks of laughter as well as screams of fear, this time with additional support from Basil Rathbone, himself no stranger to horror and mystery films (in part thanks to his many performances as Sherlock Holmes). Richard Matheson again contributed the screenplay, but Jacques Tourneur took over the director's reins from Corman. While not at all connected to the works of Poe, *The Comedy of Terrors* begs comparison to *The Raven* because both films share the same comic sensibility and benefit from the by now well-established iconography of the AIP Poe series, particularly Price's presence. Simply put, neither film would be funny had 1963 audiences not been keenly aware of the Poe series and its Gothic tone; for that matter, contemporary audiences are unlikely to fully appreciate either movie unless they are familiar with the Price pictures that are being kidded. Therefore, *The Raven* and *The Comedy of Terrors* must be considered together.

The Raven tells the tale of three sorcerers and their competition for magical domi-

THE TERROR BEGAN AT MIDNIGHT!

American International presents EDGAR ALLAN POE'S THE RAVEN

FILMED IN PANAVISION AND PATHECOLOR

STARRING VINCENT PRICE · PETER LORRE · BORIS KARLOFF

CO-STARRING HAZEL COURT · OLIVE STURGESS · JACK NICHOLSON · Produced and Directed by ROGER CORMAN · Screenplay by RICHARD MATHESON · Executive Producers JAMES H. NICHOLSON · SAMUEL Z. ARKOFF · Music by LES BAXTER

Erasmus Craven (Vincent Price) slumbers while his daughter Estelle (Olive Sturgess) frets in this lobby card for *The Raven* (1963).

nation. Vincent Price stars as Dr. Erasmus Craven, a mild-mannered and retiring wizard mourning his dead wife, Lenore. It is Craven upon whom a talking raven calls for assistance. The night bird is actually a fellow magician, Dr. Adolphus Bedlo (Peter Lorre, reteaming with his "Black Cat" co-star), who has been transformed as a result of losing a magical duel with the infamous Dr. Scarabus (Boris Karloff). Bedlo is as cantankerous as Craven is kind; when Craven asks the "bird of ill omen" if he will ever again see his lost Lenore, Bedlo responds acidly, "How the hell should I know? What am I, a fortune teller?"

After he is restored to semi-human form, Bedlo discovers that Craven's father was once the "Grand Master" of a magician's brotherhood now controlled by Scarabus. The protocols of the brotherhood dictate that Craven should have become Grand Master upon his father's death, but Craven abandoned his birthright. When Bedlo sees a portrait of Lenore, he claims she lives with Scarabus; accompanied by Craven's daughter, Estelle (Olive Sturgess), and Bedlo's son, Rexford (an unusually dashing Jack Nicholson), the wizards set off to investigate. The party learns that Scarabus wants the secret of Craven's "hand magic," the ability to cast spells with mere gestures, and he has recruited Bedlo in a plot to lure Craven near. Furthermore, Lenore (Hazel Court) has faked her death and become Scarabus' mistress, taunting her husband and boasting of his replacement's greater prestige and power. Craven and Scarabus eventually engage in a battle of magical pyrotechnics; Craven finally triumphs over the older wizard, whom he leaves in the ruins of the castle with only the shrewish Lenore for company.

Much of the humor in *The Raven* is sophomoric and broad, with little of the black comedy Corman and Matheson brought to "The Black Cat" (and which Matheson and Tourneur would return to in *The Comedy of Terrors*). Price mopes around muttering about "the lost Lenore," occasionally bumping into his massive telescope, and Lex Baxter's unsubtle score cues each pratfall with overdone musical stings. The only consistently funny element in the film is Lorre's over-the-top mugging, his facial and body distortions foreshadowing "all the manic energy of rubber-limbed Jim Carrey," as Paul Castiliga observes (191). Even better are Lorre's ad-libs, bits of improvisation that allegedly confounded his more formal co-stars, especially Karloff (Meikle 92). While touring the long-neglected Craven laboratory, Bedlo muses, "Hard place to keep clean, huh?" Later he remarks that Scarabus would never have beaten him in their magical contest "if I was only sober, which I admit doesn't happen often." During a second duel with Scarabus, the older wizard's superior skills cause Bedlo's magic wand to wilt in his hand. "You dirty old man," Bedlo sneers, disgusted by the implication of phallic impotence.

Regardless of the hit-and-miss nature of the comedy, however, it is clear that the three legendary horror stars on display are enjoying themselves in their first cinematic team-up. More significantly, Price, Lorre, and Karloff lend the proceedings their substantial cinematic charisma, investing the gravity of their mysterious personas in the service of thematic, if not always comic, complexity. Although unabashedly crafted as a trifle by all parties concerned, *The Raven* nevertheless suggests deeper concerns than easy laughs; the film further develops certain Poesque concepts, in some cases illustrating ideas even more provocatively than the so-called "straight" Poe adaptations.

Initially quite faithful to Poe's original poem, the film opens with shots of Price's castle and the crashing waves along the nearby seashore (Corman's celebrated frugality would make use of this footage many times during his tenure at AIP), over which Price recites the opening stanzas of the poem. Corman's camera establishes the setting and suggests a somber mood for the film — a mood soon to be shattered by Lorre's comic improvisations. When the raven flaps into Price's study, he "[perches] upon a bust of Pallas just above [Price's] chamber door," precisely as does the avian intruder in the poem (Poe 944).

From this point on, however, any similarity to the events of the poem becomes strictly coincidental. The raven's famous one word comment, "Nevermore," is used only once in the film — at the conclusion, when Price utters the famous line "Quoth the Raven, 'Nevermore'" directly to the audience. In this context, the line is utilized for comic, rather than dramatic, effect. In the same vein, the film eschews Poe's central idea — the grim realization that there will be no end to the speaker's suffering, nor a reunion with Lenore even in Heaven (945). Within the context of the film this is a specifically antithetical conclusion, for Price's Craven is ultimately "cured" of his obsession with Lenore after discovering she yet lives, albeit consumed by avarice.

Also added to the film are suggestions of family dysfunction, a matter wholly absent from Poe's poem but prevalent in "The Fall of the House of Usher" and explored at great length in the previous Corman-Matheson-Price collaborations. It is significant that Lenore is identified as Craven's second wife; therefore, she is not the biological mother of his daughter, Estelle. The incorporation of a "wicked stepmother" perhaps seems slightly insensitive to modern audiences, as stepparents and "blended" families are more common today than in the early 1960s. Yet Lenore's stepmother status is evidence that *The Raven* is at least as much a comic variation on the traditional fairy tale as it is an adaptation of Poe. The fact that Lenore is not really Estelle's mother foreshadows her villainous nature and suggests a contest between the two women for Craven's attention and affection—a contest Lenore seems to be winning. In this sense, Lenore recalls Barbara Creed's description of "the monstrous-feminine in terms of the maternal figure" as a threat to "the patriarchal ideology" (47).

This depiction of Lenore is very much at odds with Poe's conception of the character as an idealization of feminine perfection; because the cinematic Lenore is so diametrically opposed to her literary model, Corman and Matheson apparently intend for her to suggest the camp aspects of Poe's too-perfect object of affection. The idealization of Lenore, as alluded to by Craven's initially excessive reverence for his second wife, serves as a sharp contrast to Lenore's true nature. As a result of what within the film's comedic context can only be interpreted as a burlesque of the notion of the feminine ideal, Lenore becomes (like Madeline Usher, Elizabeth Medina, and Morella Locke before her) a monstrous female who foreshadows the assertive contemporary woman associated with the sexual revolution of the 1960s.

The interplay between Dr. Bedlo and his offspring is also clearly dysfunctional. Rexford announces he has been sent by his mother to keep an eye on his father, an announcement that provokes considerable umbrage on the magician's part. Bedlo makes frequent disparaging remarks about his absent wife (note that the mothers of the magicians' children are not present in this film) and complains that Rexford "is just like [his] mother." Bedlo constantly reiterates his frustration and apparent hatred for his son, who remains doggedly loyal to him regardless of the ill treatment Rexford suffers. "I thought Jack and Peter managed to turn their scenes into some amusing little pieces," Corman recalls of the interaction between Nicholson and Lorre:

> This idea wasn't scripted, but it was a Method-type subtext worked out on the set.... Jack wants nothing in the world more than the love and approval of his father, and Peter wants nothing more than to get rid of his idiot son. So Jack is constantly playing up to Peter, and Peter is constantly pushing him away [85–86].

Much of the conflict between Rexford and Bedlo is illustrated through Rexford's annoying habit of straightening his father's cloak. According to Jack Nicholson, "The business with Peter's cloak was just actors' devices. I grabbed his cloak ... just to keep him alive to the fact I was trying to get him out of there. Of course, the good actor that he [was], he just reacted to it spontaneously, slapped me and acted out" (qtd. in Corman 86). The ongoing feud within the Bedlo family contrasts ironically with the relationship between Craven and his daughter, which is portrayed as more traditional and loving, if somewhat complicated by Craven's lingering obsession with his second wife.

Another Poesque theme explored in *The Raven* is the notion of the beloved but ambiguous (and apparently dead) woman. Like Madeline Usher and Elizabeth Medina before her, Lenore Craven is worshipped by the Price protagonist and proves to be the agent of his undoing; and, as with Madeline and Elizabeth, reports of Lenore's death are premature. Yet Lenore is a much more wicked character than Madeline — ostensibly a victim of her brother Roderick's fancies and the hereditary insanity that afflicts the Usher line — or even Elizabeth, who is metaphorically possessed by the inherent evil of the Medina household and may be literally under the influence of ghosts. In this instance, Lenore is quite sane and unapologetically evil.

Lenore is among the most overtly sexual of the female characters in the Poe series as well. "With refined good looks and haughty, self-centered nature," as Steven Thornton observes (241), Craven's wife first appears wearing the sort of low-cut gown associated with voluptuous females in the "Hammer Horror" films of the period — a subtle nod to actress Hazel Court's previous work in *The Curse of Frankenstein* (1957), the seminal Hammer Gothic thriller. Lenore utilizes her feminine wiles and charms in order to secure the attention and support of influential wizards. Although it is not explicitly stated that Lenore

Boris Karloff, Peter Lorre, and Vincent Price matched wits in two humorous 1963 AIP productions: here in *The Raven* (1963) and later in *The Comedy of Terrors*.

used her physical attributes to bewitch Craven, it is logical to assume they played no little role in making the magician fall in love with her. Lenore is not winning devotion for her chastity or her character; she cheerfully trades in her older husband on an even more elderly, albeit more powerful, wizard. Scarabus thus represents the patriarchal father-husband figure congruent to the early sixteenth century setting of *The Raven*; he is certainly the Grand Master of the *brotherhood* of wizards and magicians — an organization whose known members are uniformly male, which implies the total absence of women in the group.

Lenore must use her own feminine magic to counterbalance the social and sexual barriers that prevent her from being fully represented in the worlds of realism and fantasy dominated by males. As a result, Lenore cunningly performs her gendered role as *femme fatale* to acquire a degree of power and influence associated with men and thus becoming, in a sense, regendered as male. Her aggression and frank sexuality imbue her with substantial power of her own, which tellingly is never fully acknowledged by Craven or Scarabus. Lenore's aggression starkly contrasts with Craven's milder nature, suggesting the wife has incorporated the masculine traits of the husband and replaced him as the dominant partner, maneuvering him into a position of feminine submission. However, the sadomasochistic ramifications of this role reversal are belied by Craven's essential decency and sense of self, which will be reasserted and ultimately reconfirmed.

Carol J. Clover has theorized that the popularity of modern horror films stems in part from their association with "an s/m bang" (223), but sadomasochism informs older thrillers such as *The Raven* as well. There is little doubt that Lenore is as amused — and aroused — by sadism, as is Elizabeth Medina in *Pit and the Pendulum*. Lenore enthusiastically embraces the gender role reversal implied by her sexual dominance, appropriating masculine aggressiveness while simultaneously compelling the men in her life to assume attitudes of feminine passivity. She takes obvious delight in seeing her husband bound and helpless, smiling cruelly as she tells the shocked wizard that she is "very much alive." She also torments Bedlo, to whom she laughingly remarks, "I liked you better that way," in regard to his bird form.

The most blatant expression of Lenore's sadistic nature occurs when Scarabus announces his plan to place Estelle in stocks as a means of forcing Craven to give up his magical secrets. Displaying an excessive excitement at the prospect, Lenore breathlessly asks, "Are we going to have some torture?" She laughs as Scarabus remarks to Craven, "Perhaps the sight of your daughter's flesh being seared will clarify your thinking." The sadism indicated by these lines represents the sexual excitement Lenore associates with cruelty.

Dr. Scarabus seems as bewitched by Lenore as is Craven. In fact, Scarabus is as repulsed by his beautiful mistress as he is attracted to her — a common theme in both Poe's literature and the Price adaptations. When a smirking Lenore boasts about their triumph over her husband, Scarabus remarks, "I'm always fascinated by your lack of scruple" in a tone that mixes dread with admiration. Later he calls her his "precious viper." In a mocking tone, Lenore reminds her companion of the true nature of their relationship: "You knew what you were getting. Did I ever pretend I came here because of your charm?

I came here because of your wealth and power, and in return I gave you (*slight pause*) my company. And if you insist on anything more, I shall leave you as I did Erasmus!"

This speech illustrates Lenore's completely predatory nature and implies she is actually the dominant party in the relationship. For all his resources, magical and otherwise, the elderly Scarabus cannot resist the lure of a beautiful young woman. Because Lenore threatens to leave him should he "insist on anything more" than her "company," it can be inferred that there is no chance she will truly fall in love with Scarabus. Perhaps love is not the only thing Scarabus cannot have; Lenore's speech implies there is no sexual element to their relationship, in the absence of which the only possible benefit to Scarabus must be the prestige of being accompanied by such an attractive woman. Yet even this boon symbolizes an empty victory for the old sorcerer, for in his lonely castle the couple is devoid of company; therefore, it is rare that he can show off his lovely prize.

Given Scarabus' advanced age, it is likely he is too old to engage in regular or conventional sexual union; significantly, there is no evidence that his sorcery includes any tricks for restoring the vigor of youth. After being defeated by the much younger Craven, Scarabus sadly observes, "I'm afraid I just don't have it anymore"—the vague pronoun "it" symbolizing not merely lost magical skills but declining physical prowess, too. The line is delivered among the collapsed walls of the castle; the ruined house represents the ruin of Dr. Scarabus, his abilities as both man and magician irretrievably compromised by time and age. Ironically he still has Lenore by his side, but under the circumstances she has lost the allure of sexual and romantic promise. It is a fitting fate for the true villain of *The Raven*—Lenore herself.

As always in the Poe films, it is the character portrayed by Price that provides *The Raven* with a solid dramatic and thematic foundation upon which the action is balanced. Price atypically plays Craven as weak-willed and indecisive. Unlike the usual Price protagonist, Craven has no master plan or scheme in play; he is truly content to remain in seclusion in his castle, and his retiring attitude contrasts strongly to Bedlo's invective and energy. It is significant that Price plays a character named "Craven," with that word's association with cowardice and weakness. By contrast, Lorre's character's name, "Bedlo," implies playfulness and the humor Lorre brings to the film, while Karloff's name, "Scarabus," contains hard consonant sounds and the root word "scarab"—an Egyptian beetle—that suggest power, age, magic, and evil.

However, Erasmus Craven is without a doubt the hero of the film—an unusual aspect for Price to incorporate into one of his Poe characters. He never develops into a "man of action;" he remains quiet and self-effacing, even during the climactic duel with Scarabus. As a result, an implication of weakness and femininity informs the character, suggesting that he does not conform to gender assumptions. However, the character is ultimately depicted as the embodiment of masculine traits of wisdom, competence, and self-assuredness that confirms Erasmus as a "real man" of intellect even if he is not stereotypically defined as a masculine "man of action." In a subtle yet significant bit of business, Price bestows his character with a slight but confident smile throughout the showdown with Karloff. The implication is that Craven never seriously doubts the outcome of the duel; he knows his skill far surpasses that of Scarabus, and he feels no need to show off or unduly promote himself. Pride, honor, decency, and an uncompromising sense of self are all elements of Craven's personality expressed in Price's actions and expressions during the eight-minute magical battle.

Of all the characters in *The Raven*, only Craven truly grows and acquires wisdom from his experiences. Scarabus is defeated, and Lenore's power over Craven is entirely dissipated; they learn nothing in defeat, for they remain bitter about the failure of their evil plans. Bedlo remains a trickster character, his loyalty and motivations always suspect even when he becomes Craven's lackey at the film's conclusion. There is no evidence that Estelle or Rexford has matured, although as innocent youths they still have the potential to grow as individuals. Craven, on the other hand, has learned the error of his ways; it was a mistake to withdraw from the world at large and his attendant responsibilities within the brotherhood. As he remarks to his friends following the duel:

> Instead of facing life, I turned my back on it. I know now why my father resisted Scarabus: because he knew that one cannot fight evil by hiding from it. Men like Scarabus thrive on the apathy of others; he thrived on mine, and that offends me. By avoiding contact with the brotherhood, I've given him freedom to commit his atrocities unopposed.

Craven's speech suggests more than personal growth on his part. As a statement of personal responsibility, it echoes the famous observation attributed to Edmund Burke that "all that is necessary for evil to succeed is that good men do nothing." Like Burke's quote, Craven's speech applies to government and society as validly as it does to the individual. For the first time in the Poe series, a sociopolitical concept is explicitly expressed and emphasized by Corman and Matheson. Why this concept is so germane to a light project like *The Raven* is unclear — it could very well be a metaphor referring to the Cold War or an allusion to the struggle against fascism in World War II, a conflict in which Matheson fought — but its presence in the film contributes significantly to the moral authority of Erasmus Craven, the most purely heroic of Price's Poe protagonists.

The Raven met with both critical and popular favor, so AIP greenlit an original Matheson script, initially called *Graveside Story*, which began its rollout as *The Comedy of Terrors* on Christmas Day. Although the project sprang entirely from the imagination of screenwriter Matheson, the humor is clearly grounded in the iconography and ideas inherent in the Poe adaptations. Indeed, Matheson's black comedy reflects a familiarity with Poe's own wry sense of irony and wit that accurately predicts what Poe *would have* penned had the concept ever occurred to him. The final film is almost a sequel to *The Raven*, albeit with a slightly more sophisticated sense of the absurd.

The Comedy of Terrors casts Vincent Price as Waldo Trumbull, a corrupt and drunken undertaker whose lack of business acumen requires him to endlessly recycle his one coffin for each of his infrequent clients. Assisted by former bank robber Felix Gillie (Peter Lorre), Trumbull can't seem to make a decent living out of the funeral parlor he has acquired from senile old Amos Hinchley (Boris Karloff), whose lovely daughter Amaryllis (Joyce Jameson) Trumbull has married in an ill-conceived plot in take over the family business. Things are so bad for the undertaker that he desperately avoids his landlord, John F. Black

Opposite: The one-sheet for *The Comedy of Terrors* (1964).

(Basil Rathbone), who is understandably chagrined that Trumbull hasn't paid any rent on the business in a year.

Desperate to avoid eviction, Trumbull decides to smother elderly Mr. Pipps (Buddy Mason) in the middle of the night, then conveniently appear the next day when the beautiful young widow (Beverly Hills) is in need of a funeral director. After much bumbling, Trumbull and Gillie succeed in murdering the old man; unfortunately, the Widow Pipps leaves town without paying Trumbull's fee. "Is there no morality left in this world?" Trumbull wonders aloud in one of the film's best lines, which Price delivers with perfect mock chagrin. Trumbull then opts to kill his landlord, but Mr. Black turns out to be a cataleptic with an unusual habit of awakening just before or after the point of burial. Eventually everybody but old Hinchley seems to succumb in the film's comic climax, but only Trumbull himself actually expires — the senile Hinchley innocently doses his son-in-law with the very same poison Trumbull has threatened to give Hinchley at intervals throughout the movie.

There is less slapstick in *The Comedy of Terrors* than in *The Raven*, although plenty of knockabout high jinks remain to please lovers of low comedy. Indeed, the film opens with the sort of somber funeral scene than has been a standard of the horror genre since at least James Whale's *Frankenstein* (1931), merely one instance wherein director Tourneur — best known for his moody horror films for Val Lewton, such as *Cat People* (1942) — imbues the proceedings with a solid mood of Gothic dread. Tourneur wisely confounds audience expectations by showing Trumbull and Gillie retrieve their lone coffin in a high-speed manner created by undercranking the camera. This comic technique dates back to the days of silent cinema; the allusions to "old-fashioned" entertainment continue through the guest appearance of Joe E. Brown, a popular comedian of the early sound era, in his last feature film role as a frightened gravedigger. Additionally, there are a number of well-timed moments of physical comedy, including Gilley's hilarious attempt to avoid the Shakespeare-spouting, sword-wielding Mr. Black.

Nevertheless, the film's best element remains its dialogue, particularly the acidic lines Price delivers. Trumbull abuses everyone in sight, constantly belittling his hapless assistant and his long-suffering wife, who is particularly tormented by Trumbull's threats to poison her father with "medicine." Trumbull is particularly nasty when drinking: during one binge he says to Amaryllis, "If you could or would for one brief moment shut that vast resounding chasm of a mouth, I should be grateful!" Frustrated with her husband's insults, Amaryllis wonders aloud why she ever married him. The undertaker's reply is one of Price's classic diatribes: "That is a question I often inquire of myself, Madam, for which there is no satisfactory answer save one, perhaps — nobody else would have you!"

Although the Trumbull character is an exaggerated grotesque, it is significant that his greatest volley of invective is directed towards his wife. Amaryllis is a helpless victim, symbolic of the limited opportunities for autonomy available to women in 19th century America. As a single woman she has been completely dependent on her father, who can no longer protect or provide for her. Compelled to marry Trumbull as much by necessity as by his flattery, Amaryllis has no choice but to endure his cruelty. Her only defense is her own ability to hurl insults; "What know you of art and beauty, tosspot?" she hisses at her husband — a particularly ironic line given Price's well-regarded expertise in those very subjects in real life (and hence another example of how Price's real life is constantly referenced in his reel life).

Trumbull regards his wife as an inconvenient nuisance. During a celebratory scene following payment for Black's (premature) funeral, Amaryllis attempts to smooth matters over with Trumbull. "Aren't you coming to bed ... husband?" she asks suggestively, only to be curtly dismissed by the undertaker, who clearly prefers the company of the bottle to that of his wife. Elsewhere, Trumbull sums up his low opinion of females in general: "Women! You'd as soon put your trust in them as put a pistol to your head!" Yet Trumbull's misogyny is apparently directed at Amaryllis alone; while stealthily exploring the Pipps house in search of his next victim, Trumbull takes a moment to ogle the buxom Mrs. Pipps slumbering in her bedroom.

Price gets the choicest lines, but the rest of the cast make the most of their characters. Karloff completely mines the comic possibilities of his doddering character, delivering Hinchley's non-sequiturs about ancient burial customs with unrestrained glee. Rathbone seems to enjoy sending up his notoriety as a Shakespearian actor, bombastically reciting lines from *Macbeth* and later solemnly intoning, "What place is this?" every time Black revives. Lorre's delivery is as remarkable as ever, as when he explains about his bank robbing past, "I've never *confessed*— they just *proved* it!" As the put-upon Gillie, Lorre timidly carries a torch for Amaryllis (in a pointed reversal from the romantic triangle in "The Black Cat" episode of *Tales of Terror*, Jameson receives sympathy and affection from Lorre, not Price), humbly beseeching her to honor him with her singing — which happens to be every bit as terrible as Trumbull claims it to be. As the distaff foil to the horror boys' club, Jameson holds her own, never allowing her more famous co-stars to upstage her completely, as her willingness to sing so badly demonstrates.

Unfortunately, *The Comedy of Terrors* did not do well upon first release; Denis Meikle suggests the film failed because it was released soon after President Kennedy's assassination, a time "when no one felt much like laughing about death" (118). AIP tried to squeeze a few more dollars out of the project by re-releasing it in 1965 under its original title, but to no avail. Moreover, the film would mark Matheson's last theatrical collaboration with Price (although *The Last Man on Earth* would be released later in 1964, Matheson worked on the screenplay of this first version of his novel *I Am Legend* before *The Comedy of Terrors* went into production). Yet time has been reasonably kind to the film, earning *The Comedy of Terrors* a small but enthusiastic following and according it a place of honor alongside *The Raven* as two of Vincent Price's best efforts to blend horror with humor.

EVIL THINGS IN ROBES OF SORROW
The Haunted Palace (1963)

It is possible to divide the AIP series of Poe adaptations into two distinct periods: the initial period, 1960–1965, during which Roger Corman directed Vincent Price in six feature films at least partially derived from Poe's fiction, and the later period, 1968–1970, during which Michael Reeves and Gordon Hessler (selected to take over after Reeves' sudden death) directed Price in three films not literally connected to Poe but considerably influenced by the author's themes and iconography. Therefore, there are nine films in what can be termed the "canon" of the series because of their shared traits. Yet outside this canon are other productions that must be acknowledged in any discussion of the series. They do not fit comfortably because either Price or one of his key directors do not participate in their creation; in the case of *The Haunted Palace* and *Twice-Told Tales* (both 1963), the source material is not Poe. *Twice-Told Tales* isn't even an AIP production, although it is clearly inspired by the AIP franchise and is now owned by the same company (MGM/United Artists) that controls the AIP catalogue; therefore, all the films in question are now "siblings" within the same corporate entity.

Having completed four Poe adaptations by the spring of 1963, Corman wanted to try something new. Although marketed as yet another Poe adaptation and featuring quotations from the author's poem of that title, the plot of *The Haunted Palace* is derived from a short novel by H. P. Lovecraft (1890–1937). The film is a collaboration between Corman and Price, and it is based on material by Poe's most significant literary descendant; once the lines from Poe's poem are taken into account, *The Haunted Palace* transforms into a Poe adaptation almost in spite of itself.

Lovecraft wrote *The Case of Charles Dexter Ward* in 1927, but the novel remained unpublished until four years after the author's death. According to Lucy Chase Williams, it was AIP co-founder James H. Nicholson who insisted on changing the film's title out of commercial consideration (185). The Poe name was surely more familiar to the public than that of Lovecraft, although the number of casual fans who recognized "The Haunted Palace" as a Poe title was probably very small. Nevertheless, *The Haunted Palace* at least *sounds* more like the name of a horror film than the forensic-sounding *The Case of Charles Dexter Ward*. Interestingly, Alain Silver and James Ursini note that at some point during production the picture was called *The Haunted Village*, possibly in an attempt to compromise between the Poe and Lovecraft titles (*Roger* 206).

The Haunted Palace is reasonably faithful to the Lovecraft novel. The film pertains to Charles Dexter Ward (Price), a kindly nineteenth-century businessman who journeys to the mysterious New England village of Arkham to claim his ancestral home. The massive house in question — the "palace" of the title — was brought over from Europe stone by stone by Joseph Curwen, Ward's great-great-grandfather. Unfortunately for Ward and his beautiful young wife, Ann (Debra Paget, a holdover from *Tales of Terror*), Curwen was a sorcerer burned at the stake 110 years earlier, and his restless spirit begins to assume control over his descendant. Ward fights a losing battle for his soul; he seems to have reasserted himself at the film's end, but the baleful look of triumph on his face — and the sinister way Price delivers his final lines — indicates that Curwen is the final victor after all.

Included as an example of Roderick's verse in "The Fall of the House of Usher," the short poem "The Haunted Palace" uses the imagery of a royal palace to craft an extended metaphor representing the horror and tragedy of madness. Poe describes "a fair and stately palace" erected in "the monarch Thought's dominion" that is ultimately "assailed" by "evil things, in robes of sorrow" (959–960). Eventually the beauty and peace of the palace — a human brain — is destroyed by insanity. At the poem's conclusion, "A hideous throng rush out forever/And laugh — but smile no more" from the brain — a reference to the deranged babbling and laughter emanating from the hopelessly crazed protagonist (960). Poe's poem is a brilliant depiction of the way mental illness can destroy a sound mind.

While it is supernatural evil, not psychological dysfunction, that is the source of conflict in *The Haunted Palace*, the poem and the film share the notion of innocence destroyed by outside malignancy. Of all the protagonists portrayed by Price in the series, Charles Dexter Ward may well be the most tragic, for he vainly tries to resist his ancestor's dreadful influence until the very end. As Gary Morris points out about Corman's Poe cycle, "The appeal of corruption ... is always dangerously present for the innocent characters, and sometimes they succumb to it entirely like Charles Dexter Ward" (123–124).

Charles Beaumont wrote the screenplay for *The Haunted Palace* shortly before adapting *The Masque of the Red Death*, and his interest in Lovecraft is clearly indicated by his efforts to incorporate as much of Lovecraft's material as possible. Beaumont retains most of the important characters' names, and his script retains a portrait of Joseph Curwen that so strikingly resembles Charles Dexter Ward and exerts so strange an influence on the great-great-grandson. Beaumont's script features the hellish underground lair Curwen designs in the novel, and between Corman's atmospheric direction and Daniel Haller's typically elaborate set design, the basement of horrors suggests "some wide gulf of ultimate abomination" (Lovecraft 101).

In fact, certain additions to the script indicate Beaumont's desire to popularize Lovecraft (still very much a minor cult figure in the early Sixties) among general audiences. For example, Beaumont's script is set in Lovecraft's fictional New England town of Arkham; while Lovecraft certainly set many of his stories in Arkham, *The Case of Charles Dexter Ward* takes place in the author's very real hometown of Providence, Rhode Island. Similarly, Beaumont goes to great lengths to incorporate references to Lovecraft's famous "Cthulhu Mythos," but the original novel mentions only one of Lovecraft's pantheon, Yog-Sototh.

Perhaps the most effective scene in *The Haunted Palace* depicts Ward and his wife being accosted by mutated descendants of Joseph Curwen's ghastly attempts to mate human women with monstrous entities. The shots of deformed Arkhamites silently shuffling toward the Wards inspire horror and pity in equal measure, recalling the pathos intermingled with revulsion so prevalent in Tod Browning's *Freaks* (1932). As genuinely unsettling and well executed as the scene is, it has no antecedent in *The Case of Charles Dexter Ward*; Beaumont borrowed the idea from other Lovecraft stories, particularly "The Dunwich Horror" (1929).

Other changes in Beaumont's script reflect an effort to make the virtually unfilmable Lovecraft more cinematic. Lovecraft's Ward bears little physical resemblance to the character portrayed by Vincent Price; the author describes Ward as "tall, slim, and blond, with studious eyes and a slight stoop" who demonstrates "harmless awkwardness rather than attractiveness" and is initially a mere eccentric (10). Price's Ward, by contrast, is powerfully built, with good posture, dark hair, and full whiskers; he is a perfectly normal, even slightly boring person until Curwen's possession begins.

The psychic struggle between Ward and Curwen takes place largely offstage in the novel, so Beaumont necessarily places this idea squarely in the foreground. This fore-grounding of the battle of wills also serves as a dramatic reference to Poe's fiction and Corman's films; as in "The Fall of the House of Usher," "The Facts in the Case of M. Valdemar," and especially "Ligeia," and particularly in Corman's adaptations of these stories, the contest of wills symbolizes a struggle against loss of identity and self-determination. Like the stories and earlier films, *The Haunted Palace* suggests that a tragic end is inevitable in these conflicts, for the protagonists or victims are always killed or intellectually destroyed, their bodies now possessed by other entities. In a sense, this loss of identity resembles the mental deterioration associated with madness, which in turn is the theme of the poem from which the film takes its name.

One of Beaumont's additions to the plot is a familiar trope in horror stories: the conflict between the urban and the rural. As Carol Clover notes, "Going from city to country in horror film is in any case very much like going from village to deep, dark forest in traditional fairy tales" (124). Whereas Lovecraft's protagonist is initially accepted by his neighbors before his strange experiments alienate them, Beaumont's version of Ward and his wife experience outright hostility from the moment they set foot in Arkham. To a degree, this is so much a convention of the horror genre that it has descended into a cliché: the ignorant and superstitious villagers frightened and uneasy around strangers who inevitably display the trappings of sophisticated urbanity, including education and material wealth. Ward's professional success and his desire to claim his large house alludes to the underlying conflict between the rich and the poor; *The Haunted Palace* thus exemplifies Carol Clover's assertion that "one of the obvious things at stake in the city/country split of horror films ... is social class" (126). That Arkham has been tainted by the legacy of Joseph Curwen's forbidden knowledge further underscores rural distrust of excessive "education," and the Arkhamites fear that the return of his bloodline foreshadows further suffering on their part. The billowing layers of fog that enshroud the village subtly under-scores this theme, representing a cloud of ignorance and fear that paralyzes the townspeople while simultaneously contributing to the "dark and brooding atmosphere" Corman conveys throughout the series (Smith 150).

More significantly, Beaumont provides Lovecraft's young antiquarian bachelor with a wife. Ann's addition provides an element of sexual danger to the plot, for Joseph Curwen becomes quite lascivious when he gains control of Ward's body. "Surely a husband has certain rights," Curwen/Ward remarks to Ann; later he attempts to rape her, claiming he wants "merely to exercise [his] husbandly prerogatives." These lines indicate an awareness of the horror inherent in Ann's existence; as a wife in nineteenth century America, she is little more than property to her husband. The situation is not problematical when Ward is in control of himself— Ann's affection for her husband is clearly depicted, as is his reciprocation of her love and respect when he is in his right mind. However, Ann feels obligated to stay with her apparently deranged husband, both out of a sense of love and in acquiescence to the societal norms that make it her duty to remain.

Curwen/Ward's aggression towards Ann initially recalls Karen Hollinger's assertion that "the traditional maleness of the horror monster can be explained as ... an expression of the connection between the image of the monster and the filmic representation of castration anxieties" (297). Although Curwen/Ward's unwelcome advances clearly illustrate his cruel and lustful nature, they also suggest the restless spirit's need to assert himself

This poster advertising *The Haunted Palace* (1963) evokes the sexual threat inherent in many horror films, particularly Roger Corman's series of Poe adaptations.

and thus prove he is tangible, physical, and as "real" as his descendant. His incorporeal nature indicates a lack of physical form and thus a lack of body parts — including a phallus. He attacks Ann as much to confirm his sexual vitality — itself a manifestation of physical existence — as to fulfill his inherently wicked nature. Furthermore, Curwen/Ward's assault on Ann serves to undermine her personal autonomy and influence on her husband's better nature. By asserting his control over Ann, Curwen's spirit ensures she will not interfere with his control over Ward.

Because Curwen is Ward's great-great-grandfather, his molestation of Ann symbolizes incest. Yet Curwen's interest in his great-great-granddaughter-in-law seems more sadistic than sexual, for the undead sorcerer spends much of his time trying to revitalize the corpse of his mistress, Hester Tillinghast (Cathie Marshall). During one of his attempts to revive Hester, Curwen refers to Ann as a "stupid woman" and then observes, "She doesn't know what it is to love." Joseph Curwen is thus capable of genuine romantic attachment; his desire for Hester and his obvious anguish over their separation incorporates the Poesque notion of obsessive love for a dead woman not found in Lovecraft's novel.

The Haunted Palace is a muddled affair in many particulars. A glaring continuity error occurs when friendly Dr. Willet (Frank Maxwell) tells the Wards that Curwen's atrocities took place "150 years ago," yet an opening title specifically states that 110 years have passed between Curwen's execution and the arrival of his descendant in Arkham. At the film's climax, Dr. Willet rushes into the burning house to save Charles, but when he does so there is no sign of Hester and two other warlocks, Simon Orne (Lon Chaney, Jr.) and Jabez Hutchinson (Milton Parsons) — who just a minute earlier were plainly in the chamber with Ward. These and other shortcomings have earned *The Haunted Palace* little affection among Price scholars. Denis Meikle criticizes the film's "aimless wanderings through labyrinthine corridors, the endless repetition of key scenes, the loss of narrative direction halfway through, and the botched ending" (113), while Phil Hardy deems it "rich but flawed" (155). On the other hand, Lucy Chase Williams quotes *The Hollywood Reporter* and *Films and Filming*, which judge the film "a class horror picture" and "a powerful and unified surrealist fantasy," respectively (186).

Certainly the film contains a strong performance by Price in the dual roles. The way the actor subtly modulates his voice when switching between Curwen and Ward is impressive, as is the malicious gleam in his eyes he adopts when the Curwen persona is dominant. As always, Price's delivery of menacing dialogue is highly effective; as the film ends and the unsuspecting physician comforts what is now Curwen, Price utters the line, "I don't know how I can ever repay you for what you've done, Dr. Willet, but I intend to try" with a degree of mock sincerity that is nothing less than chilling. In her review of *The Haunted Palace*, Judith Crist observes that Price's delivery of a line referencing Torquemada "is almost worth the price of admission alone — but not quite" (qtd. in Smith 150). This left-handed compliment implies awareness of a camp element in Price's performance, yet this assumption is not accurate in regard to anything except a few wittily spooky bits of dialogue. For all intents and purposes, Price's turn as Curwen/Ward is as "straight" as most of his non-comic roles in the Corman films.

Interestingly, the film "became the highest-grossing feature ever released in Australia" at the time because of that country's large number of Lovecraft fans (Parish and Whitney 118). Complemented by a stronger than usual supporting cast — horror veteran Chaney, often condemned for being physically and vocally inappropriate for genre material, is particularly menacing as Simon — *The Haunted Palace* is reasonably effective and deserving of its success. It remains noteworthy as the first cinematic adaptation of Lovecraft, and it is certainly the only film to date that combines elements of Lovecraft with Poe, conveying a reasonable impression of both writers' sense of theme and tone even when not referencing specific characters and plot details.

10

AN EVIL MOCKERY OF BEAUTY
Twice-Told Tales (1963)

Vincent Price's success in the AIP Gothics was duly noted by other film companies, and in 1962 the actor signed with an outfit called Admiral Pictures. An operation so impoverished it made American International seem like a major studio by comparison, Admiral rather blatantly swiped the AIP formula for a trio of thrillers with literary roots similar to those in the Poe films. Roger Corman temporarily bolted from AIP to produce and direct *Tower of London* (1962), an adaptation of *Richard III* so loose that "what survives [of Shakespeare's play] is so little that its occasional occurrence almost evokes surprise" (Pendleton 140). A very young Vincent Price had played a supporting role in Universal's 1939 production of *Tower of London*, so it was appropriate that the now middle-aged thespian toplined the new version, essaying the part of Richard originally played by Basil Rathbone. Corman soon returned to the AIP fold, so writer-producer Robert E. Kent took over the remaining Price projects: *Diary of a Madman* (1963), directed by Reginald Le Borg from a story by Guy de Maupassant, and *Twice Told Tales*, (1963), directed by Sidney Salkow and based on the tales of Nathaniel Hawthorne.

Clearly inspired by AIP's success with the Poe-based anthology *Tales of Terror*, *Twice Told Tales* presented a trio of Hawthorne's weird tales to a modern audience that probably knew the writer only for *The Scarlet Letter* (1850). A contemporary and an admirer of Poe, Hawthorne (1804–1864) emphasizes moral lessons in his horror fiction, often suffusing his stories with a wry humor not always found in Poe's most significant tales. For *Twice Told Tales*, producer Kent chose to adapt "Dr. Heidegger's Experiment" (oddly the only adaptation taken from the actual Hawthorne collection that inspired the film's title), "Rappaccini's Daughter," and a condensed version of Hawthorne's novel *The House of the Seven Gables*, which like *Tower of London* was a remake of a vehicle from Price's early career at Universal. The results, while intermittently interesting, are ultimately less effective than the AIP Poe films because Kent's script and Salkow's direction are far more pedestrian that the early efforts from the Matheson-Corman team.

"Dr. Heidegger's Experiment" is a tale of old age temporarily reversed by an elixir of youth. On his seventy-ninth birthday, Dr. Carl Heidegger (Sebastian Cabot) celebrates with his best friend, Alex Medbourne (Price). A raging thunderstorm damages the crypt of Sylvia (Mari Blanchard), Carl's long-dead fiancée. When the two old men investigate, they discover Sylvia's body to be remarkably well-preserved due to its exposure to a mysterious liquid dripping from the roof of the crypt. Realizing the liquid can turn back the ravages of time, Carl distills a potion that restores his friend and himself to their youthful appearances and experiments on Sylvia's body, bringing her back to life. As it turns out, Alex spitefully poisoned Sylvia on the eve of her wedding to Carl; soon the two old friends are fighting over the woman they both love, spilling the vial of youth serum. During the struggle Alex accidentally kills Carl, and then he watches in horror as the serum's effects wear off. Sylvia's fate is worse; she dies a second time, reduced to the crumbling skeleton she ought to be after thirty-eight years in a grave.

As an adaptation of Hawthorne's story, "Dr. Heidegger's Experiment" is reasonably faithful, although significant changes are necessary to propel the plot and establish the romantic triangle. Hawthorne's story involves four elderly acquaintances of Heidegger being temporarily restored by drinking from the Fountain of Youth of legend, but Heidegger himself chooses to remain old. Heidegger does mention the loss of his fiancée, Sylvia, fifty-five years earlier, but no attempt is made to revive the dead woman. Nobody literally dies in the story, but all four of Heidegger's subjects are "melancholy old creatures ... whose greatest misfortune it [is] that they [are] not long ago in their graves"—in other words, their ruined and wasted lives have reduced them to figurative death (1). Once

Sex and horror are equally redolent in this still from *Twice-Told Tales* (1963), Sidney Salkow's uneven adaptation of Hawthorne.

restored, the three old men resume their bickering over who will marry the Widow Wycherly, whom they all once loved. The lesson here is that old age and experience are not certain to provide wisdom and understanding.

Hawthorne's basic message about not learning from one's mistakes is abandoned entirely in Kent's script, replaced by a Poesque obsession with a beautiful dead woman. In the wake of Heidegger's and Sylvia's passing, Alex is left to mourn the loss of his best friend and the love of his life, essentially condemned to the sort of metaphorical living death Hawthorne mentions at the beginning of his tale — a fate that recalls that of many brooding Poe protagonists, especially in the Corman films. By contrast, Hawthorne's bitter old quartet decides to "make a pilgrimage to Florida, and quaff at morning, noon, and night from the Fountain of Youth" (9), having yet to learn anything from Heidegger's experiment. There is no doubt Price's Alex has learned from his experience, sorrowful though that knowledge might be.

The most intriguing element in Kent's adaptation of the story is a peculiar emphasis on aberrant romantic connections (also found in Poe's output). The illicit passion between Alex and Sylvia is complicated by conflicting emotions. Both parties are tormented by their betrayal of Carl, and Alex is torn between his enthusiastic and lifelong bachelorhood and his apparent second chance at true love. "Nothing ever stopped me from living exactly the kind of life that I wanted," Alex tells Carl to explain his determination never to marry — yet Alex has resorted to murder to prevent Sylvia from marrying another man. "You love to take all a woman has to offer, then refuse to marry her," Sylvia accuses, to which Alex snidely replies, "You gave yourself to me" — an allusion to Sylvia's complicity in the affair. Yet this time Alex intends to marry Sylvia, urging her to leave Carl and run away with him.

Even more noteworthy is the relationship between Carl and Alex. Although there is no textual evidence of a homosexual relationship between the two elderly friends, their connection is clearly deep and abiding, similar to that of a happily married old couple. Only the two of them have gathered to commemorate Carl's birthday, and Alex playfully complains that it is only his affection for his friend that makes him "come out" on such a storm-tossed night. In his delight following exposure to the elixir's benefits, Carl immediately insists that Alex join him in recapturing youth; only later does he attempt to revive Sylvia. After his best friend and his true love have perished, Alex berates the now dried-up spring: "You've taken Carl and Sylvia away from me," he moans, placing priority on his relationship to the doctor by mentioning his name first. Alex and Carl are bound together on an emotionally intimate level; they are in terms of gender performance life partners whose idyllic existence is sundered by the intrusion of a woman, suggesting frustration at the idea of a "real" woman compromising their relationship and recalling the many romantic triangles of the AIP films.

Written in 1844, Hawthorne's story "Rappaccini's Daughter" concerns Beatrice, the daughter of a brilliant but eccentric botanist in sixteenth-century Padua, Italy. Rappaccini has utilized his scientific prowess to develop new strains of poisonous plants "no longer of God's making, but the monstrous offspring of man's depraved fancy, glowing with only an evil mockery of beauty" (Hawthorne 48). Furthermore, the scientist has exposed his child to his poisonous concoctions, rendering her touch and even her breath deadly to any living thing that gets too close to her. Giovanni, a medical student, falls in love with Beatrice but cannot engage in physical contact with her. Professor Baglioni, Giovanni's teacher and Rappaccini's chief rival, offers an antidote for the girl's condition, but it kills her instead. The story ends with Baglioni castigating his rival, sarcastically asking Rappaccini, "'Is this the upshot of your experiment?'" (Hawthorne 59).

"Rappaccini's Daughter" is the most faithful of Kent's adaptations. Kent includes such details as the purple hue that colors the flesh of those creatures unfortunate enough to feel Beatrice's touch, and he mentions Giovanni's arrival in Padua from Naples. Indeed, the episode differs significantly from the story in only two particulars: the cinematic Giovanni (Brett Halsey, Price's co-star in 1959's *Return of the Fly*) displays none of the ambivalent attraction-repulsion with which the literary Giovanni regards Beatrice, and the film eschews Hawthorne's rivalry between Baglioni and Rappaccini that provides the story with its ironic ending. It is the omission of the Baglioni-Rappaccini feud that eliminates Hawthorne's most obvious moral, a warning against unethical and unsupervised scientific experimentation. However, the excision of the crucial subplot allows Kent to develop a more provocative theme: the incestuous connection between Rappaccini (Price) and Beatrice (Joyce Taylor). Merely hinted at by Hawthorne, whose Rappaccini asks his daughter if she "prefer[s] the condition of a weak woman, exposed to all evil and capable of none" (59), the idea that the scientist suffers from an unhealthy affection for Beatrice is demonstrated frequently in Kent's script. Price's Rappaccini remarks to his daughter, "You will never understand how fortunate you are that none of the world's sin can touch you," which echoes of Hawthorne's reference to "all evil." These references to "evil" and "sin" are vague, but the absence of Rappaccini's wife in both story and film suggests that Beatrice has replaced her mother in her father's life on many levels and subtly associates sexuality with evil. Rappaccini realizes intellectually that committing incest is wrong.

Emotionally, however, the overzealous scientist cannot share his daughter with another man, so he poisons her system to prevent both himself and other males from touching her. "But all our years together! It can't be ended because of that boy," the cinematic Rappaccini complains to his daughter in the most blatant admission of his unacceptable love for her. These expressions of incestuous feelings and attendant guilt are similar to those displayed in such AIP films as *House of Usher* and *Pit and the Pendulum*.

The film's incorporation of Beatrice's enforced chastity is especially significant, as it is established early on that Rappaccini's wife deserted him and their young daughter to be with her lover. Thus the botanist's obsession is not merely incestuous in nature but vengeful as well; Rappaccini transfers his love and need for revenge from his unnamed wife to his daughter. Eventually—and illogically given his previous opposition to their union—the movie version of Rappaccini resorts to his literary antecedent's plot to imbue Giovanni with the same poisons that infect Beatrice, allowing the younger man to "make her [his] wife." This decision sets in motion the episode's conclusion: Giovanni drinks the antidote prepared by Baglioni (played by Abraham Sofaer earlier in the film but absent at the conclusion), but it kills the young man (just as it slays Beatrice in the story). Beatrice destroys herself by consuming the remainder of the antidote, and the distraught Rappaccini also commits suicide, intentionally grabbing the blooms of his deadliest creation (the source of the poison that contaminates Beatrice). As in his take on "Dr. Heidegger's Experiment," Kent chooses to solve a bizarre romantic triangle by killing off all the interested parties.

The version of *The House of the Seven Gables* (1851) that concludes *Twice Told Tales* is the least faithful of the episodes, due in large part to the brief running time the movie's anthology format demands. Most of the book's characters are jettisoned, but the central character of Gerald Pyncheon (called "Jaffrey" in the novel and played here by Price) remains, as does Gerald's spinster sister, here renamed "Hannah" in place of "Hepzibah" (Jacqueline de Wit). The centuries-old conflict between the Pyncheons and the Maule family is retained, as is the novel's quest to uncover various legal documents that bestow great wealth, which becomes the focus of the story. More overt supernatural elements are appended, including walls that run red with blood and the appearance of a none-too-convincing skeletal hand, which strangles Gerald at the episode's climax. Hawthorne's abrupt happy ending is replaced with a similarly unremarkable conclusion: Gerald's long-suffering wife, Alice (Beverly Garland), winds up in the embrace of the last Maule, Jonathan (Richard Denning), and the haunted house of the seven gables collapses à la the house of Usher.

In its brevity, the final episode of *Twice Told Tales* lacks even the rudimentary character development that contributes to the earlier sections of the film. Price's Gerald Pyncheon is a static character, a stereotypical villain who torments his innocent young wife and murders his admittedly unpleasant sister to keep from sharing the wealth with her. There is no love lost between Gerald and Alice, and a tantalizing detail suggests that their loveless marriage is also sexless: Alice insists upon taking a separate room when she and her husband arrive at his ancestral home, and when Gerald realizes his wife is falling for Maule, he bitterly demands, "Are you ready to open doors for Jonathan that you've kept locked to me?"

The sexual conflict between the film's third romantic triangle is more obvious but less radical than in the previous episodes; other than the startling shots of walls, ceilings, and portraits weeping blood, this conflict provides the only relief from the tedium otherwise pervasive in this Hawthorne adaptation. The author's message, that "the act of the passing generation is the germ which may and must produce good or evil in a far-distant time" (2) survives, but only by the hardest. Although more faithful to its sources than many of AIP's productions are to Poe, *Twice Told Tales* is ultimately hamstrung by a fatal combination of uneven performances, dreadful special effects in the final episode (the house is patently a cheap model, the skeletal hand is laughably fake), and Sidney Salkow's listless direction. Nevertheless, the film demonstrates the influence of the Poe-Price-Corman franchise on other producers and provides a contrast in quality that further enhances the charm of the early entries in the AIP series.

11

A Heartbeat Away from Hell
The Last Man on Earth (1964)

Nineteen sixty-three was one of the busiest years in Vincent Price's career. He appeared in seven theatrical releases, mostly in the sort of horror roles that by now were his specialty. During this hectic period, Price took a break from the popular Poe cycle to appear in a trio of pictures shot quickly and cheaply in Italy. Two of these films, *Rage of the Buccaneers* and *Queen of the Nile*, were historical action films; the third production, *The Last Man on Earth*, has developed something of a cult following, presenting Price in an unusual departure from the Gothic chillers audiences expected and allowing him the rare opportunity to portray a sympathetic protagonist. The film's failure to generate much interest among either critics or audiences in 1964 further mired Price in the period shockers that were already becoming formulaic, yet in some ways it has become the most consistently influential project of Price's 60s output, for *The Last Man on Earth* anticipates the rise of a new cinematic subgenre: the apocalyptic zombie horror movie.

The Last Man on Earth is the first adaptation of *I Am Legend* (1954), the first published science fiction novel by Richard Matheson. *I Am Legend* is the story of Robert Neville, the lone survivor of a plague that has killed most of the world and turned the rest into vampires. Set in the then-futuristic year of 1976, the novel is a masterpiece of lean, terse prose, terrifying not merely because of the legions of undead creatures who nightly taunt Neville in vain attempts to get his blood, but also because of the powerful sense of boredom, loneliness, and futility that Matheson brings to Neville's endless routine of staking vampires by day and enduring their attacks on his home-cum-fortress by night. In describing a typical day, Matheson observes that Neville "went from house to house and used up all his stakes. He had forty-seven stakes," a grim indication of the soul-crushing pointlessness of Neville's bloody work (28).

Eventually Neville stumbles across Ruth, a young woman who apparently shares his immunity to the vampire plague. However, his surprise and joy are short-lived; Ruth explains that she is one of a group of victims who maintain a semblance of humanity through drug therapy. Neville has unwittingly killed many of Ruth's cohorts (including her husband) while making his daily rounds of vampire staking. Inadvertently, Neville has become a monster, a creature that stalks the people of the new order and troubles their dreams: ironically, he is now the legend, "a new terror born in death, a new superstition entering the unassailable fortress of forever" (Matheson 170).

95

DO YOU DARE IMAGINE WHAT IT WOULD BE LIKE TO BE ...THE LAST MAN ON EARTH...OR THE LAST WOMAN?

Alive among the lifeless... alone among the crawling creatures of evil that make the night hideous with their inhuman craving!

VINCENT PRICE

STARRING AS

The Last Man on Earth

CO-STARRING FRANCA BETTOIA · EMMA DANIELI · GIACOMO ROSSI-STUART

Directed by SIDNEY SALKOW · Produced by ROBERT L. LIPPERT

Screenplay by LOGAN SWANSON & WILLIAM F. LEICESTER · From the novel "I AM LEGEND" by RICHARD MATHESON · AN AMERICAN INTERNATIONAL PICTURE

MP1621

Although George A. Romero and his collaborators have admitted that the Matheson novel was one of the main inspirations for their groundbreaking debut, *Night of the Living Dead* (1968), there is some question as to whether Romero and company had actually seen *The Last Man on Earth* before making their own account of a world being overrun by a plague of the undead. However, watching the 1964 version of the novel today, it is impossible not to think of Romero's film as Vincent Price locks himself up in a lonely house while an army of the living dead relentlessly attempt to gain entry. The vampires of *The Last Man on Earth* are slow-moving, stumbling creatures, seemingly incapable of reason and utterly dominated by their need to consume. Only the vampirized Ben Cortman (Giacomo Rossi-Stuart) seems capable of coherent speech, and his monotonous cry of "come out, Morgan!" (as Neville has been renamed) is utterly robotic and devoid of any hint of human emotion. Consciously or not, *Night of the Living Dead* borrows its most disturbing imagery from this far more obscure shocker lensed five years earlier and half a world away. The subsequent sequels, tributes, parodies, and outright rip-offs of Romero's film, then, are the indirect progeny of *The Last Man on Earth*.

The cinematic possibilities of Matheson's novel were obvious almost from the moment *I Am Legend* first appeared in print. England's legendary Hammer Productions bought an option on the novel in 1957, but ultimately the project was shelved because of objections raised by both the British censors and the Motion Picture Association of America (Meikle 104). Ten years passed between the book's publication and the release of the film version, which producer Robert L. Lippert shot in Europe to take advantage of cheaper production costs and economic incentives courtesy of the Italian government. Lippert hired Price to star and recruited American director Sydney Salkow, whose primary responsibility was to reshape the material shot by Ubaldo Regona in Rome. The results pleased nobody, at least at first.

For starters, Matheson himself disowned the film. The original screenplay Matheson crafted in the late 50s had changed hands, ultimately winding up in Lippert's possession; in turn, Lippert hired William F. Leicester to handle revisions. Unhappy with these changes, Matheson insisted on using the pseudonym "Logan Swanson" in the credits to protest the adulteration of his work (the author would revive the Swanson name later in his career when his 1982 novel *Earthbound* was published in unauthorized form). Even though later adaptations of the book—*The Omega Man* (1971), *I Am Legend* (2007)—would take far more liberties with the source material, Matheson's disappointment with the first film version remained acute for years.

Producer Lippert was associated with 20th Century–Fox through his management of one of the studio's subsidiary units, but Fox would not distribute the film in the United States. AIP bought domestic distribution rights, while Fox released the film in some foreign markets. The film was not released in Great Britain until 1966, and even then it did not receive the attention normally accorded a Vincent Price horror movie (Meikle 107). It is not surprising that an international box office disappointment with a convoluted

Opposite: **This poster for *The Last Man on Earth* (1964) is one of the most memorable— and suggestive—of AIP's promotional items.**

production history would fall through cracks in the legal system; as a result, *The Last Man on Earth* entered public domain in the 1980s.

Since anybody could distribute the film in any medium, it is no surprise that it has become readily available on TV and video. Ironically, the lack of interest that allowed the movie to slip into public domain is one reason why it has such a devoted following today. While many fans still castigate the low production values and Price's performance, it is nevertheless being watched and discussed more now than at any point since its initial release in 1964. For all of its flaws, *The Last Man on Earth* is frequently effective and inter-mittently quite powerful.

As noted above, *The Last Man on Earth* is the most faithful of the three cinematic adaptations of *I Am Legend* to date, particularly during the first hour. Price provides nar-ration, and the moody black-and-white cinematography gives the production a docu-mentary feel not duplicated in any of the actor's other genre efforts. In fact, this is one movie that actually benefits from the plethora of poorly duplicated public domain editions floating around — the muddy transfers and scratchy prints common in PD videos imbue the experience of watching a bad copy of the movie with a sense of realism that neither *The Omega Man* nor *I Am Legend* can match. Furthermore, the grimy, washed-out look of the Salkow-Regona film perfectly captures the atmosphere of futility and despair that mantles Matheson's book. There is something utterly chilling about watching Vincent Price wander the deserted Roman streets (substituting relatively well for the book's setting, Los Angeles) with only rotting corpses for company.

Price's turn as Robert Morgan has been a source of contention for years. At the time of the film's release, the *Hollywood Citizen* noted that Price "delivers his most restrained performance in some time" (qtd. in Williams 192). On the other hand, Denis Meikle condemns the star's "limp-wristed approach to the role" and "evident lack of interest" in the performance (106–107). Some fans of Matheson's book have complained that the fiftysomething Price is far too old and too debonair to play Neville/Morgan, who in the book is described as "a tall man, thirty-six, of English-German stock, his features undis-tinguished except for the long, determined mouth and the bright blue of his eyes" (Math-eson 14).

In spite of the fact that Price is significantly older than the book's protagonist is sup-posed to be, the actor is still effective in the role. For one thing, Neville is depicted as a working class joe, an Everyman; by contrast, Morgan is a research scientist, a person of greater education and sophistication than Neville, and thus the kind of character one might expect Vincent Price to play. For another, in a series of flashbacks the film depicts Morgan as a skeptic, a doubter who refuses to believe there is something in the old vampire legends that could be true — in spite of all the evidence that surrounds him, as pointed out by his friend and eventual adversary, Ben Cortman. At one point, a dismissive Morgan rhetorically inquires, "You'd prefer us to believe in vampires?" The fact that Morgan is a disbeliever finally forced to accept an impossible truth gives the character an extra layer of remorse and regret, which is precisely the sort of emotional trauma Price is so skilled at portraying.

Perhaps the most important element Price brings to the role is a sense of existential dread. Robert Morgan is a middle-aged, middle class professional—bright but perhaps otherwise unremarkable—who loses his entire world to unimaginable tragedy. Yet Morgan doesn't merely survive in the strange new world—he insists on recreating as concrete an illusion of normalcy as possible. The books he reads and the music he listens to don't serve merely to pass the time; they allow Morgan to demonstrate that he still exists, that the values and standards of his dead world remain relevant so long as he maintains them.

Price is quite believable as a man dedicated to an illusion, and he convincingly conveys the idea that Morgan is someone whose determination to survive is implacable. Nowhere is this determination more clear than in the film's ending, which represents the greatest change in both tone and action from Matheson's book. In the novel, Neville is captured by agents of the new order; although he suffers a possibly mortal gunshot wound and is thus likely to die anyway, Neville is to be executed to bring a sense of relief and catharsis to the other survivors. However, Ruth supplies Neville with poison, with which he kills himself and cheats his captors of their revenge. By contrast, the film climaxes with Morgan fleeing through the streets, finally locking himself in a building and fighting as long as possible. Eventually Morgan is pursued to a church, where he is shot and then staked, but not before he shouts "Freaks!" at his killers, insulting them when there is no other way to fight them. "They were afraid of me," the dying Morgan muses, apparently still not quite able to accept the new definition of "normal" his attackers represent.

One of the ways in which *The Last Man on Earth* is most effective is the way it captures the ennui and futility of Morgan's routine. From his very first line—"Another day to live through; better get started"—it is clear that Morgan requires some kind of routine to function at all in the postapocalyptic world. Salkow and Ragona spend considerable time following Morgan as he makes his rounds, which involve everything from disposing of vampire corpses (usually victims of their own kind) in an eternally smoldering burial pit to rummaging through the deserted supermarket in search of still-pungent garlic ("I can't live a heartbeat away from hell and forget it," he says in regard to the herb's legendary ability to ward off the undead). Morgan is even methodical enough to take notes on the houses he's visited and the number of vampires he's staked; after tallying up the day's work, Morgan offhandedly remarks to himself, "eleven kills." Yet when the entire world has been turned into vampires, of what use is it to have slain fewer than a dozen of the undead? The answer, of course, is none whatsoever; it is the routine itself, the notion of routine as "normal life," that makes it possible for Morgan to avoid going completely insane.

Another aspect of *The Last Man on Earth* that is almost unique among Price's horror films is that here the actor plays a completely sympathetic character. In the novel, Neville's dying acknowledgment that he is now the monster heightens the tragedy by adding ambivalence to the character. This ambivalence is never explicit in the movie, and to the end audiences are expected to root for Morgan and feel unmitigated sorrow when he finally succumbs to the inevitable. Scene after scene has depicted Morgan in a sympathetic light, including flashbacks to his daughter's birthday party and a moving segment in which Morgan watches home movies of his family, first laughing, then crying as despair overtakes him.

As Robert Morgan, the protagonist of *The Last Man on Earth* (1964), Vincent Price effectively captures the sense of existential dread suggested by Richard Matheson's source novel, *I Am Legend* (1953).

The tragedies that Morgan endures further endear him to viewers. Attempting to protect his dying daughter Kathy (Christi Courtland) from the government-mandated immolation of plague victims, Morgan forbids his wife, Virginia (Emma Danieli), from calling for a doctor. Terrified for her child, Virginia disobeys Morgan, and as a result soldiers claim the little girl's body. Morgan desperately follows the soldiers to the burial pit, where he accosts one in the act of tossing Kathy to the flames. The soldier replies, "Mister, a lot of daughters are in there — including my own!"

Poor Kathy is consigned to the pit — a very literal symbol of Hell — but Morgan is determined the same fate will not befall Virginia. He swears over her body he will not let her be burned, so he drives off to a lonely field and buries her there. That night, Morgan receives a visitor — it is Virginia, risen from the grave and begging her husband to let her in the house. This sequence, conscientiously adapted from the book, is perhaps the highlight of terror and tragedy in the film. Given the fates of his wife and daughter (to say nothing of the rest of the world), it is impossible not to feel kindly toward Robert Morgan.

In any case, there is still a degree of ambiguity to the character, albeit perhaps unintentional. When Morgan visits the pit to dispose of bodies, he dons a gas mask and drags the corpses out of his station wagon and tosses them into the flames. With his face obscured, Morgan is very scary; the mask effectively renders him monstrous. Furthermore, the gas mask makes Morgan unrecognizable, providing him with the same anonymity and lack of identity that obliterates any trace of individuality among the shrouded corpses. The walking dead are pretty much anonymous, but at least their leader, Ben Cortman, retains his identity — as long as Morgan lives to recognize it.

Perhaps the greatest ambiguity in the depiction of Morgan's character occurs during an early sequence that depicts him finding and staking vampires. This montage is clearly meant to show the extent of the horrific project upon which Morgan has embarked, but it also faintly suggests his personal lust for violence and destruction. The first image in the sequence Morgan finds is female, and he is showing breaking into her room and staking her in her bed. The sequence clearly suggests both home invasion and rape and is perhaps the most concrete evidence that Morgan is as monstrous as the vampires themselves.

Morgan's interaction with Ruth (Franca Bettoia) is mostly friendly, even though his first appearance when they meet in broad daylight frightens her. However, Morgan does insist on testing her blood to prove she is a normal human being — which, ultimately, she is not, at least by his definition. It is then that he discovers how terrible he is to Ruth's people, for she says that to them Robert is a monster, "a legend in the city ... leaving bloodless corpses." In spite of this revelation, Robert uses a serum derived from his blood to permanently cure Ruth — an idea borrowed in both the 1971 and 2007 versions of the story.

Accusations that the film is campy are not justified for the most part, but there are a couple of moments in which it appears the filmmakers, if not Price himself, are treating the material tongue-in-cheek. During Morgan's daylight adventures, he passes an abandoned automobile dealership. "There was a time I shopped for a car; now I'm looking for a hearse," Morgan says, the wistfulness of the delivery failing to disguise the absurdity of the line. Later, Morgan finds a dog, finally getting close enough to the sick animal to take him in — and discover he is infected with the vampire plague. The next scene opens with Morgan preparing to bury the dog, which is shrouded in a blanket and impaled with a wooden stake. The shot is supposed to be sad, but the stake is so enormous in proportion to the dog's small body that the effect is unintentionally hilarious.

In spite of these moments of accidental humor, *The Last Man on Earth* remains an interesting and memorable hybrid of science fiction and horror. For all the technical improvements represented by the larger budgets of *The Omega Man* and *I Am Legend*, neither of those films is as faithful to Richard Matheson's novel as the 1964 production based on the author's script. Bastardized though it may be, the screenplay retains enough of the novel's power and imagination to earn it a better reputation than the author himself would grant it. As Michael Weldon asks in *The Psychotronic Encyclopedia of Film*, "When have writers ever liked the way their work ends up on the screen" (416)? More importantly, the film is the first major cinematic depiction of a world overrun with the living dead and clearly foreshadows the cannibalistic ghouls popularized by George A. Romero and his imitators. Finally, the movie provides its star with a rare opportunity to play against type and portray a basically heroic protagonist. For all of its shortcomings, *The Last Man on Earth* remains the first and best adaptation of Richard Matheson's first and best fantasy novel.

12

THE BEAUTIES OF TERROR
The Masque of the Red Death (1964)

By the fall of 1963, the rising costs of film production had convinced the executives at American International Pictures to find cheaper venues to make movies. Having struck a co-production deal with the English company Anglo-Amalgamated, AIP sent Roger Corman and Vincent Price abroad for *The Masque of the Red Death*, the first of two British-made Poe adaptations. Released in the summer of 1964, *The Masque of the Red Death* (along with its 1965 successor, *Tomb of Ligeia*) marked a re-invigoration of the Poe cycle on all levels — particularly in regard to Corman and Price's enthusiasm for the series. The introduction of new screenwriters allows new perspectives on familiar themes from the series, including a different characterization for Price and some radical revisions in the area of gender politics.

Originally published in 1842, "The Masque of the Red Death" remains one of Poe's most famous and influential tales. In medieval Italy, the decadent Prince Prospero offers his castle as protection for his friends and other nobles from the Red Death, a plague that has "long devastated the country" and is identified by "the redness and the horror of blood" (Poe 269). Seven elaborate chambers are prepared, each festooned in different colors, in which the prince hosts an extravagant masked ball. The masquerade is interrupted by the mysterious appearance of a reveler costumed as the Red Death itself; angered and frightened by the repulsively realistic outfit, Prospero decides to kill the intruder. However, it is Prospero who drops dead upon approaching the stranger, the embodiment of the Red Death; the guests collapse as well, dying "each in the despairing posture of his fall" (273).

Corman's film is particularly faithful to the story, partially because it lends itself to adaptation more easily than many other Poe tales. Nevertheless, Corman felt the story was just too brief to sustain the longer, more elaborate film he had in mind. Therefore, the producer-director decided to supplement Charles Beaumont's "clever, literate, but not a little ponderous" screenplay with material from another Poe tale, "Hop-Frog" (1849), added at Corman's request by a second screenwriter, R. Wright Campbell (Meikle 122).

As in Poe's story, the film is set in medieval Italy, which is being ravaged by a horrifying plague known as the Red Death. Poe's protagonist (Price) is accurately portrayed as a proud and wicked nobleman who provides shelter and security for his aristocratic guests within the walls of his castle. Yet for the purposes of a full-length motion picture,

103

the Prospero of literature is too static a character; Beaumont's script, amended by Wright, Corman, and Price himself, develops the prince fully. On film, Prospero is a particularly cruel and hedonistic ruler whose villainy is compounded by the fact he is a committed Satanist.

Except for the ghostly but mute embodiment of the Red Death, Prospero is the only relevant character in the short story. Corman and company add additional characters, including two women of great importance to the prince: his ambitious mistress, Juliana (Hazel Court in her third Poe film for Corman), who zealously pursues her own initiation into the black arts; and Francesca (Jane Asher, a seventeen-year-old newcomer now best remembered for her then-boyfriend, Paul McCartney), an innocent peasant girl whom Prospero decides to corrupt. Francesca initially joins the prince in an attempt to save the lives of her lover, Gino (David Weston), and her father, Ludovico (Nigel Green), who have been imprisoned by Prospero. As the storyline develops, evidence mounts that Francesca is not entirely immune to the attractions of evil that Prospero offers.

Francesca is at first reluctant to spend time in the prince's company. Much older and almost irrationally proud of his evil nature, Prospero is a feudal lord who wields absolute power of life and death over his subjects long before the Red Death appears. The girl is horrified by Prospero's cruelty to his friends as well as her neighbors, whose village he orders burned even as winter approaches. Knowing full well how capricious is her host's temperament, Francesca fears he will decide to kill her or her loved ones simply for amusement. Almost as frightening is Juliana, who senses the younger woman may supplant her in the affections of Prospero and seems willing to do anything to prevent such a scenario from unfolding.

The nature of Francesca's innocence is complex. On the most literal level, she is innocent of any crime, being victimized by Prospero simply for trying to defend her lover and father. Francesca is also innocent in terms of knowledge; during one of her many philosophical debates with the worldly prince, she responds to one of his points by weakly admitting, "I cannot answer. I have no learning." While Gino is certainly her boyfriend, there is no suggestion that Francesca is sexually active with him; therefore, she is also innocent in the sense that she is a virgin. The threat to Francesca's virginity is constant throughout the film's running time; when she is first spotted by Alfredo (Patrick Magee), Prospero's most lustful associate, he asks, "Can such eyes have ever known sin?" With a slight smile that hints at unspeakable degradations, Prospero replies, "They will, Alfredo. They will!"

One of the most intriguing elements in the film is the way in which Francesca gradually develops as a person. Her innocence slowly fades as she spends time in the company of the more experienced Prospero. Her ignorance is replaced by knowledge, just as the fine gowns seemingly warehoused within the castle replace her grimy peasant dress. Francesca slowly gains the confidence to finally display the conviction to defend her Christian faith even as Prospero tries to persuade her otherwise. "Can you look around this world and believe in the goodness of a God who rules it?" he asks. "Famine, pestilence, war, disease, and death — they rule this world. If a God of love and life ever did exist, he is long since dead. Someone — something — rules in his place." Yet Francesca never falters, and it is her piety that keeps her safe from harm. As Prospero spends more time with her, he begins to suspect that she represents what little good might still exist in a world scourged by the Red Death.

Francesca's faith is tested, of course, and she is tempted by Prospero's worldview. On the most fundamental level, the girl is ignorant but not stupid: she realizes the material benefits that would come her way if she became the prince's consort. Francesca understands that Juliana enjoys fine clothes, jewelry, and food, as well as Prospero's protection in a time and place where life (particularly female life) is cheap and dangers of all kinds are constant. A powerful, learned man such as Prospero is attractive to a degree, physically and psychologically (it is no accident that Gino, played by the deliberately [?] wooden Weston, is portrayed as ignorant, impoverished, and dull). More than anything else, however, Francesca is tempted by the sheer lack of limitations that a life with Prospero promises. When Prospero tells Francesca, "I will initiate you into understanding," he suggests an understanding that includes more than awareness of sin and debauchery. The life of the mind — a life of art, poetry, and philosophy — would be denied to a mere peasant girl in medieval Italy. At his side, Francesca would experience all the beauty and mystery and possibility in the world beyond her simple village — that is, if the prince himself understood the world's potential.

Consumed by the darkness of his soul, Prospero has embraced the false promise of Satan. Seeing only the greed, hatred and violence in the world, the prince simply cannot believe that anything better lies beyond the walls of his castle — or of material existence itself. Wealth, power, and education offer Prospero no pleasure; although he exploits his station in life throughout the film, he gains no satisfaction from it. In spite of these conditions, Prospero is nevertheless a tragic hero, for he still has the potential to be a great man.

Regardless of his protests to the contrary, the Satanist subconsciously reveres goodness, or at least the *potential* for goodness. This is why Prospero spares a peasant child from the slaughter meted out to her fellow villagers and ultimately why he protects and nurtures Francesca. In the few innocent people he meets, Prospero sees the good he no longer believes resides within his own self. Prospero transfers experience to Francesca, yet ironically she resurrects a hint of his long-extinguished innocence. This transference between the principal characters is symbolized by the chaste kiss that Francesca places on the older man's cheek before she flees the crimson-robed figure of the Red Death (who agrees to spare her at Prospero's request). For Prospero, "the kiss seems to offer an eleventh hour antidote to the corrosive cynicism he has energetically preached throughout" (Rigby 105). Although the gesture is ostensibly made to express the girl's appreciation for her life, it also epitomizes her acknowledgment of the remnants of good within Prospero's soul and the promise of what their unconsummated relationship might have been.

Prospero and Francesca's complex relationship of innocence and experience is not the only irony that abounds in *The Masque of the Red Death*. Fittingly, both Prospero and Juliana are rendered naïve by the very worldliness they so proudly display. Prospero believes that he understands the true nature of existence and that the Red Death is his master, Satan. When the Red Death (John Westbrook) insists he is not Satan, Prospero ignorantly insists that "there is no other God — Satan killed him." To this the Red Death responds, "Each man creates his own God for himself— his own heaven, his own hell." Increasingly frantic at his growing awareness of how poorly he has understood the nature of existence, Prospero insists upon removing the Red Death's mask (note the pun on "masque"), only to find the demonic figure's face is his own. Prospero attempts to flee, but the Red Death pursues, asking the prince, "Why should you be afraid to die? Your soul has been dead a long time." As he expires in a torrent of blood, Prospero finally understands that his worldview and misplaced faith in evil represent the folly of his Satanic beliefs; this epiphany identifies him as a tragic hero.

Prospero's fate is foreshadowed by Juliana's doom. Having begged her lover to initiate her fully into the practice of Satanism, Juliana decides to pursue the matter on her own. She offers herself as the bride of Satan, branding her own breast with an inverted cross in a scene suffused with an atmosphere of sexual horror. Corman depicts Juliana's initiation in a delirious dream sequence, during which various shamanistic figures torment her. When she awakens, Juliana triumphantly announces that she "has tasted the beauties of terror." She believes her place as the devil's bride provides security and comfort. Yet her triumph is short-lived; Prospero tells his consort there is one more step in her initiation,

Hints of sadomasochistic horror abound in Roger Corman's Poe adaptations, as suggested when Juliana (Hazel Court) brands herself as a bride of Satan in *The Masque of the Red Death* (1964).

at which point she is attacked and killed by his falcon. Later the prince says to his guests, "I beg you, do not mourn for Juliana. She has just married a friend of mine." Price delivers this line with his usual sardonic glee, suggesting Prospero's wicked sense of irony in regard to his mistress' demise yet forecasting his own moment of ironic epiphany to come.

Juliana is an interesting character, ostensibly a villainess yet also a victim of Prospero's hegemony and of the repressive society in which the film takes place. That she so enthusiastically follows the dark beliefs of the prince does not change the fact that her opportunities as a woman in medieval Europe would be limited at best. Beyond the walls of Prospero's castle, Juliana would enjoy few rights except as the wife or mistress of another male aristocrat. Her acceptance of Satanism is a tacit admission of the constrictions the world places on her because of her gender, not just a signal that her morality and intellect have been compromised by Prospero's nihilistic philosophy. Intriguingly, it is Juliana's assertion of independence — the quest to complete her study of Satanism — that dooms her. Apparently even within the construct of Satanic philosophy, women cannot be allowed independent initiative and must remain under the control of a transgressive but nevertheless patriarchal system.

Juliana's conflict with Francesca has less to do with her affection for Prospero than it does with her anxiety over losing her status. Juliana fears being replaced by Francesca, in whom, perhaps, she sees a reflection of herself. Corman never firmly establishes Juliana's history, but considering that she and Francesca are both beautiful redheads, it is possible Juliana was herself an innocent young woman corrupted by Prospero. As Steven Thornton puts it, "One suspects [Juliana] is observing a vision of herself from the not-too-distant past" when she gazes upon Francesca (230). Thus the appearance of Francesca results in another variation of the romantic triangles that are emblematic of Corman's Poe adaptations. In this context, the Price character is the apex of a relationship with two women; for once he does not contend with a male rival, for it is the women who are in conflict for Prospero's attention and good will. The triangle is another representation of the motif of innocence contrasted with experience, and once again innocence is the key to survival while experience is the path to destruction.

Like Corman's previous Poe projects, *The Masque of the Red Death* contains numerous references to unusual sexual practices and obsessions. Although for once the Poe story does not contain any recognizable suggestion of romantic/sexual transgression, by the time the film was produced such notions had become central tenets of the series' iconography; therefore, sexual deviation must be present even if it must be imported to the plot. Touches of sadism and masochism are hinted at throughout the film. Juliana's branding is a form of self-mutilation and a symbol of ownership often referenced in sadomasochistic behavior. Prospero constantly ridicules and insults his friends, deriving some kind of perverse fulfillment through their humiliation. In one of the film's most disturbing sequences, the prince insists that his guests emulate "the lives and loves of the animals," a bizarre humiliation redolent with suggestions of bestiality.

In a sequence that makes manifest the devaluation of women only suggested by the presence of Juliana and Francesca, Prospero considers the pleas of Scarlatti (Paul Whitsun–Jones), a guest who has arrived too late to enjoy the prince's protection. When Prospero refuses him admittance, Scarlatti begs for sanctuary from the plague and offers his wife (Jean Lodge) as a bribe. "I've already had that doubtful pleasure," Prospero sneers at the prospect of having sex with the married woman. This scene is noteworthy for the way Scarlatti's wife mutely stands next to her husband and meekly acquiesces to the idea of being traded like property — although it must be admitted that Prospero is their only hope to avoid the Red Death, so her co-operation can be construed as a logical means of self-preservation. In another example of his cruel sense of humor, Prospero finally agrees to spare the Scarlattis from the ravages the Red Death; he orders his archers to fire upon Scarlatti, and then tosses a dagger to Scarlatti's wife so that she may kill herself — a note-worthy and cruelly ironic gesture that acknowledges the woman's right to autonomy only if she wields it for the purpose of self-destruction.

The film establishes that Alfredo is at least Prospero's equal in decadence; at one point, Prospero remarks, "I'm sure you wonder about every female in my household." Later the lascivious Alfredo displays particular interest in Esmeralda (Verina Greenlaw), the diminutive companion of the dwarf, here renamed Hop Toad (Skip Martin). Alfredo's unhealthy attention to Esmeralda implies he is sexually excited by her dwarfism. Because Corman cast a child (whose voice was later dubbed by an adult actress) in the role of Esmeralda, Alfredo's attraction to her also strongly suggests pedophilia. This idea is further underscored because young Greenlaw wears adult makeup — heavy rouge, eyeliner, and lipstick — in an unsuccessful attempt to make her appear older. Apparently Corman and his associates could not locate an appropriate female dwarf in all of Great Britain, thus requiring the use of a child actress. As a result, modern audiences familiar with the sex-ualized images of young girls in films like Martin Scorsese's *Taxi Driver* (1976) and Louis Malle's *Pretty Baby* (1978) and aware of tragedies like the 1996 JonBenét Ramsey murder are acutely distressed by Alfredo's unwholesome taste for eroticized "children."

Alfredo's fate is grim, albeit richly deserved. Enraged by Alfredo's abuse of Esmeralda, the grotesque dwarf Hop Toad plots a hideous revenge, chaining the ape-costumed Alfredo to a chandelier and setting him afire. The onlookers are too horrified to prevent the dwarf and his companion from escaping the castle; instead they are transfixed by the "fetid, blackened, hideous, and indistinguishable mass" (Poe 509) that remains of Alfredo. Pros-pero himself seems greatly amused by Hop Toad's "entertaining jest"; the prince announces a reward for the dwarf before ordering his guards to "clear [Alfredo's smoking remains] out of the way. How can my guests be expected to dance around *that*?" Although borrowed from a different story, the scenes with Hop Toad fit seamlessly into the overall narrative and provide another example of an innocent female (Esmeralda) who survives the destruc-tion of an experienced male (Alfredo). The reiteration of this theme is particularly sig-nificant because it represents a revision of the usual male-female relationship in the Poe series.

The Masque of the Red Death met with the best overall reception of any entry in the Poe cycle since *House of Usher*. According to James Robert Parish and Steven Whitney, the picture made more than $1.4 million in North American rentals alone (118), and a critic in *Sight and Sound* observed,

Corman's first British film ... is strikingly handsome, with vast, impressive sets, fluid camerawork, and majestically tasteful [color]. Moreover, none of this the work of Corman's usual collaborators, but of British technicians ... who have succeeded in making a refreshingly un–British (or at any rate non–Hammer) British horror movie [qtd. in Rigby 103].

While Corman did indeed work with a predominantly British cast and crew, one crucial "usual collaborator" did accompany the filmmaker to England, providing an aesthetic connection to the Hollywood-lensed films: Daniel Haller, the imaginative art director who had done such a brilliant job dressing up the low-budget sets on the previous Poe adaptations. Now working with leftover elements from such earlier British productions as *Becket*, Haller devised a far more opulent castle for Prince Prospero than the piles occupied by Roderick Usher, Nicholas Medina, or Erasmus Craven. Similarly, Laura Nightingale's elaborate costumes far surpass those featured in earlier AIP films in elegance, design, and verisimilitude. The most impressive technical achievement is the cinematography of Nicholas Roeg, future director of *Performance* (1970), *Don't Look Now* (1973), and *The Man Who Fell to Earth* (1976), all of which contain elements of horror and the fantastic, whose compositions subtly reference medieval woodcuts depicting the Black Plague. Roeg's efforts "won him a Best Cinematography award at a major European film festival" (Corman 87). No less an authority than Stephen King acclaims *The Masque of the Red Death* as "interesting and rather beautiful" (190).

Corman had planned to shoot *Red Death* immediately after *Usher*, but a threatened lawsuit by rival producer Alex Gordon, who had planned to star Price in a version of the story as early as 1958, postponed the project. Furthermore, Corman feared that his interpretation of the demonic Red Death would be too derivative of Bergman's conception of Death in *The Seventh Seal*, a film Corman greatly admired. Corman's film is certainly informed by the Bergman classic, with the figure of the Red Death appearing in surprising places and reading tarot cards instead of playing chess (Bergman's Death's favorite pastime). Regardless of its sources of inspiration, *The Masque of the Red Death* is rich in symbolism and style. Alain Silver and James Ursini observe,

Jane Asher as the innocent Francesca in *The Masque of the Red Death* (1964).

> Death's role in Corman's film is much more elaborate [than in *The Seventh Seal*]. His two-fold role is that of destroyer and liberator. To ... Prospero and his aristocratic guests ... he

is their own reflection, their own hell — an inferno they have created through self-indulgence, callousness, and arrogance.... Concurrently, Death is a liberating force for the innocent victims of Prospero's depredations.... [*More* 52].

The film would not hold together without a strong cast anchored by Vincent Price. The actor varies his line readings, delivering some lines with a dripping irony and sarcasm and others with a chilling edge accented by his wickedly gleaming eyes. Given Price's tendency to overplay such characters, it is a tribute to his dedication to the project and Corman's careful direction that Prince Prospero never becomes a camp stereotype. As Mark Clark observes, "Price oozes oily charm and radiates icy indifference to human suffering" yet conveys "an undercurrent of pathos," resulting in a performance that shows the actor "at his most colorful, energetic, and entertaining" (96–97).

The Masque of the Red Death maintains its high critical standing even after the passage of more than forty years (and a 1989 remake, produced by Corman and featuring Adrian Paul as Prospero). Technically impressive and graced with several excellent performances, the film demonstrates a thematic richness even greater than its predecessors in the Corman/Price/Poe series. By avoiding cheap scares and infusing the source material with philosophical musings on gender roles, sexual obsession, and the possibility of enduring good in a world beset with chaotic evil, Corman's production honors Poe's tale and brilliantly succeeds in suggesting that "Darkness and Decay and the Red Death [hold] illimitable dominion over all" (Poe 273).

13

NOR LIE IN DEATH FOREVER
The Tomb of Ligeia (1965)

In his landmark 1973 survey *A Heritage of Horror*, David Pirie pronounces *The Tomb of Ligeia* (1965) "perhaps the more important of Corman's two English Poe films," praises Robert Towne's "highly literate script," and declares Vincent Price's performance to rank among his greatest (190). According to Lucy Chase Williams, the original notice in the *London Times* deemed Roger Corman's latest Poe adaptation worthy of "without absurdity be[ing] spoken of in the same breath as Cocteau's *Orphee* (1950)" (198). On the other hand, Jonathan Rigby concludes that in spite of its strong script, production values, and principal performances, "the film is also rather [slowly] paced and for a long time doesn't seem to be going anywhere" (117). Of all the films in the Poe cycle, none is more critically divisive than the final entry, as Michael R. Pitts observes: "Many enthusiasts [feel] this [is] the best of the Price-Corman-Poe series, while others [find] it colorful but short on plot" (372–373). Whether critics praise or damn the final cinematic collaboration of Corman, Price, and Poe, *The Tomb of Ligeia* is visually rich and symbolically stunning — perhaps more so than any of its predecessors, particularly in its depiction of gender subversion.

Once again, Corman and his screenwriter were required to develop a feature-length narrative to graft onto a brief Poe tale. Originally published in 1838, "Ligeia" features another of Poe's typically unnamed narrators — suffering from a "memory so impaired it ought to disqualify him from narrating" (Kendrick 177) — caught up in yet another obsessive love affair laced with supernatural elements. In this case, the storyteller describes "the Lady Ligeia," his mysterious first wife who insists, in the words of seventeenth century English philosopher Joseph Glanvill, that man dies "only through the weakness of his feeble will" (654). In spite of her own potent will, Ligeia sickens and dies, and the narrator takes a second wife, the Lady Rowena Trevanion of Tremaine (note the author's use of alliteration here, borrowed from one of his favorite poetic techniques). Soon, however, Rowena falls ill and expires; her body rises from the deathbed, her features transformed into those of Ligeia, whose will seems more powerful than death after all.

"Ligeia" is in many particulars reminiscent of Poe's "Morella," which while written *earlier* did not appear in print until two years *later*. Both stories involve women versed in arcane and mystical knowledge returning from the grave; in both cases, their spirits seem to possess the bodies of other women. Yet "Ligeia" is better developed, involving comparatively fewer stretches of credibility (such as "Morella" narrator Locke's unlikely refusal to name his daughter until she is ten) and a greater focus on a central theme — the idea that sufficient willpower will conquer death itself. Certainly *The Tomb of Ligeia* is a more polished film than the "Morella" episode of *Tales of Terror*, although *Tales* was produced earlier and introduces more specific notions of spiritual possession than either of Poe's stories — notions that seem to have been liberally borrowed for *Tomb*.

Thanks to the brevity of Poe's tale, Towne's screenplay manages to incorporate essentially all of its details, including a paraphrase of the Glanvill quote that introduces "Ligeia" and the interest in Egyptian mythology and culture demonstrated by the title character. For example, Poe refers to the Egyptian deity Ashtophet, the god of "marriages ill-omened" (654), and the reference is paraphrased by the film's protagonist, here christened Verden Fell (Vincent Price). Towne's script also depicts the Lady Rowena (Elizabeth Shepherd) expiring and reviving several times before her possession by Ligeia (also played by Shepherd), a bit of action taken directly from Poe's text. The recreation of such details in the film is a comparatively minor matter, yet Towne's fealty demonstrates his and Corman's desire to maintain as faithful an adaptation of Poe as possible. Such devotion to the source material is particularly significant given the tremendous number of additions necessary to develop a feature length film, and it presages the attention to detail that distinguishes Towne's most notable script, the Academy Award-winning screenplay for Roman Polanski's *Chinatown* (1974).

Towne's additions include the presence of a black cat — apparently to recall Poe's story of that name and the episode of *Tales of Terror* it inspired. The nameless cat seems to be Ligeia's familiar and may be possessed by her restless spirit. It rarely misses an opportunity to startle Verden's new love interest; the animal screeches at the very moment Rowena mutters the dead woman's name, which startles Rowena's horse so badly it throws her to the ground. During the film, the cat scratches Rowena's face when she attempts to kiss Verden, nearly causes her to plunge to her death in the bell tower, and attacks her locked door with supernatural fury.

Throughout the film, Towne and Corman offer bits of feline symbolism. Early on, Verden argues with the local parson (Ronald Adam), who tries to deny Ligeia's burial in the abbey's consecrated ground. The black cat suddenly leaps upon Ligeia's coffin, stunning the funeral party into silence; Fell sardonically inquires if the cat made off with their tongues. Rowena demonstrates her "catty" nature on several occasions; like a cat, she playfully swats Fell's dark glasses, yanking them off his face and causing him to collapse in pain due to his "morbid sensitivity" to sunlight. Later Verden attempts to choke Rowena, apparently while he is consumed in some psychotic reverie. After regaining his composure, he remarks, "I can't very well send you off shivering like a frightened kitten." Elsewhere, Verden orders Kenrick (Oliver Johnston) to kill the cat, but saucers of milk to sustain the beast keep turning up. The destruction of the animal seems almost impossible, suggesting it has nine lives.

Perhaps most significantly, Towne's script acknowledges the many associations between felines and females in Western culture. The cultural assumption that women and cats are mysterious, complicated, and independent is clearly present in Towne's screenplay, for both Rowena and Ligeia demonstrate similarly catlike personalities. It is no accident that the feline in *The Tomb of Ligeia* is a black cat; Towne and Corman are clearly banking on the superstition that black cats are bad luck and are associated with witches to build audience tension. The presence of a black cat also serves as a suggestion that Ligeia is herself a witch, and certainly it seems possible that her incredible will power is augmented by supernatural means — in effect, witchcraft.

In time, it is revealed that Ligeia had mastered the art of hypnosis and mesmerized Verden before her death. Although hypnotism itself is now generally associated with science, at the time of the film's setting it was perceived as some kind of magical manifestation. The use of mesmerism also alludes to the third episode *of Tales of Terror*, "The Case of M. Valdemar," which also involves hypnotism and a conflict of psychic wills. In any event, this "scientific" explanation of Ligeia's ability to posthumously control her husband is undermined by the apparently legitimate supernatural phenomena that take place during the film.

From the very first, eyes and vision play important thematic roles in the film. This is a natural thematic development from the original story; at one point, the narrator reveals that it is Ligeia's eyes that so fascinate him:

> The expression of the eyes of Ligeia! How for long hours have I pondered upon it! ... What was it ... which lay far within the pupils of my beloved? What was it? I was possessed with a passion to discover. Those eyes! Those large, those shining, those divine orbs! They became to me twin stars of Leda, and I to them devoutest of astrologers [Poe 656].

The cinematic protagonist demonstrates an interest in eyes every bit as intense as his literary antecedent's. When Verden shows one of his waxen copies of an Egyptian bust to his childhood friend, Christopher (John Westbrook), he suddenly exclaims, "The eyes! They confound me!" Of course, Fell isn't just talking about the statuary — he is referring to Ligeia as well.

The significance of visual symbolism is recognizable in several ways. On one level, the beauty of Ligeia's eyes in the story alludes to Poe's usual depiction of beautiful and highly idealized females. However, Ligeia's eyes also suggest the antithesis of Poesque idealization because they have frozen Verden in an emotional stasis of her own creation. The freezing power of Ligeia's gaze recalls the Greek legend of Medusa, who could petrify men by turning them to stone. As Barbara Creed notes, Sigmund Freud theorizes Medusa as a symbol of female genitalia, which in turn represents "the monstrous-feminine as constructed within and by a patriarchal and phallocentric ideology [associated with] the problem of sexual difference and castration" (36). In effect, Verden is simultaneously petrified by Ligeia, suggesting a state of constant sexual arousal within her thrall, and castrated by his inability to fully engage on an emotional (and at times physical) level with Rowena.

By endowing Ligeia with such an overwhelming hypnotic gaze, Corman and Towne imbue her with a powerful symbol of sexual aggression and a pointed parody of the masculine gendered gaze. This symbol is particularly potent within a visual medium such as film; indeed, the production largely depends on the filmmakers' presumption that the audience will unconsciously recognize the conflict and danger represented by the character's act of looking. In this context, *The Tomb of Ligeia* also exemplifies Laura Mulvey's definition of the cinematic gaze as inherently male, recognizing that "the woman as icon, displayed for the gaze and enjoyment of men, the active controllers of the look, always threatens to evoke the [castration] anxiety it originally signified" (2188).

The striking nature of Ligeia's eyes suggests an iconoclasm beyond beauty and sexual allure. In the funeral scene, Ligeia's eyes pop open when the cat jumps onto her coffin. Fell explains the incident away as "a nervous contraction — nothing more," but the staring eyes nevertheless foreshadow Ligeia's undead state. The intense blackness of the cat's appearance is relieved only by its baleful green eyes.

Most significantly, "Verden Fell's eyes — the windows to his soul — remain hidden behind his dark glasses whenever he stands in sunlight (a visual symbol for purity and goodness)" (Lampley 221). Even when he is indoors and removes his glasses, Fell's eyes remain squinted, implying physical limitations to his sight equivalent to his inability to fully comprehend what Ligeia's baleful influence is doing to him. Finally, Fell is literally blinded by the cat during their final confrontation within the blazing abbey; helplessly stumbling about the burning room (significantly, the secret bedchamber he shares with Ligeia's corpse), he embodies Mulvey's theory of a male castrated as a result of gazing (2180).

Roger Corman praises Robert Towne's ability to "understand the psychology of characterization" and "conceive a world entirely inhabited by tormented characters" (qtd. in Silver and Ursini, *Roger* 226). The script for *The Tomb of Ligeia* conveys a strong indication of how characters are tortured for their inability to fully comprehend what they are witnessing. To put it another way,

> What characters see — or fail to see — is of considerable importance. When Lord Trevanion [Derek Francis] arrives to check on his daughter, he is more concerned with the rare fox he's captured. Trevanion fails to acknowledge his child's injuries, and he assumes Fell is a doctor simply because the bespectacled stranger is bandaging Rowena's foot. Later, Verden fails to recognize Rowena on two occasions, for his perceptions are muddied by Ligeia's evil influence [Lampley 220].

It is very interesting that the story unfolds in nineteenth century England — 1821 is given as the year of Ligeia's death. The social, sexual, and political opportunities for women would therefore be very limited, and both Ligeia and Rowena can be seen as rebels against the patriarchal system in which they exist. In fact, the emphasis on will power in the film underscores the primary form of rebellion both women practice: they are both stubborn beings who demonstrate highly unusual strength of will, at least for women of the period. Ligeia's will is directed towards preserving her existence on a literal level; her demand for life inspires her ominous epitaph, "nor lie in death forever."

Rowena's will is focused on a slightly more figurative preservation of existence — her independence in a world run by men. Her own father asks rhetorically, "Willful little bitch, ain't she? Hell to be married to." This line is especially telling in regard to the repressive conditions in which the Lady of Tremaine finds herself. Other comments about Rowena's willfulness are littered throughout the film; at one point, Verden tells her, "Willful? You don't even know the meaning of the word," a subtle admission that he believes Ligeia's will is stronger than Rowena's.

It is significant that Ligeia embraces the religion of ancient Egypt, which includes powerful female deities such as Isis and a materialistic view of the afterlife that implies a false death for the first Mrs. Fell. Furthermore, her interest in Egyptian mythology represents her preference for a non–Christian orthodoxy, an orderly society at least nominally free of the institutionalized sexism and philosophical dogma of that period in English history between the Regency and the Victorian era. Rowena's preference for Verden's company implies, in part, a preference for his decidedly non-traditional modes of behavior. By the same token, Rowena's jilting of Christopher symbolizes her rejection of a "proper" husband and her subsequently submissive role in marriage.

The tendency to rebel against "normal" society is influenced partially by the unconventional sexualities exhibited by Verden Fell and his two wives. Verden's obsession with Ligeia implies that his subjugation to her will is at least partially sexual in nature. Certainly Ligeia's dominant tendencies are apparent in her deathbed statement to Verden: "I will always be your wife—your only wife." When it is revealed that Verden keeps Ligeia's peculiarly well-preserved corpse (another conceit on loan from the "Morella" segment of *Tales of Terror*) in a secret bedchamber, it is obvious that Fell has practiced necrophilia with the remains of his first wife. Especially disturbing is the fact that when Rowena discovers Ligeia's remains, the corpse's arms are specifically positioned as if to embrace another person—which is, of course, precisely what has been happening.

Rowena's romantic and sexual impulses are at first glance unremarkable, but a careful reading of her scenes and dialogue reveals the subtle emotional and physical yearnings that propel her into Verden Fell's arms and thus the center of the story. Already constrained by the rules of society, Rowena seems unwilling to settle for the conventional sexual life that marriage to Christopher promises. It is Fell's dark appearance and mysterious behavior that convey his unconventional personality and promise an unconventional sexuality as well, an anticipation of Linda Williams' claim that "the monster's power is one of sexual difference from the normal male" and evidence "of a frightening potency precisely where the normal male would perceive a lack" (20).

During one of their early conversations, Rowena tells Verden, "You make me want to offer *you* something" when he asks if he can offer her refreshments. This remark indicates Rowena's bold sexual nature and reveals how far she has already fallen for her dark beau. The reply also suggests the sexual frankness that formal period social customs repressed, particularly among females. As Steven Thornton claims, Rowena's willfulness and adult sexuality "make her an uncharacteristically respectable (and admirable) genre film heroine" of horror cinema's Silver Age (238).

Yet whatever carnal delights Fell seems likely to share are almost entirely frustrated by his obsession with Ligeia. Verden and Rowena marry and depart on an extended honeymoon, during which their marriage is presumably consummated. Significantly, Verden seems happier and even ceases wearing his shaded glasses, which represent blocked vision and diminished sexual autonomy. After their return to the abbey, however, Verden refuses to spend nights with his wife, cloistering her in a separate bedroom. He even resumes the practice of wearing his dark glasses. Verden has regressed, resubmitting to Ligeia's erotic dominance and the "castration anxieties, the underlying threat of nonphallic female sex-

Vincent Price as Verden Fell and Elizabeth Shepherd as Lady Rowena Trevanion in *The Tomb of Ligeia* (1965), Roger Corman's visually rich and symbolically stunning farewell to the Poe series.

uality, and the power in sexual difference" (Hollinger 300) that his first wife represents. When it is discovered that there is no death certificate and thus no legal proof that Ligeia is dead, Rowena complains about her lot to Christopher: "I eat alone, I sleep alone, and that's how it should be. After all, I'm not his wife, am I?" The nature of her frustration is thus physical as well as emotional.

In his last performance for Roger Corman, Vincent Price is more restrained and subtle than in any of the earlier Poe adaptations. Costumed in all black, complete with curly black hair and black-lensed glasses, Price's Verden Fell is striking and mysterious, a precursor to the modern "Goth" fashion. In fact, this dark-clad character functions as a visual bookend to the series of Poe adaptations, since Fell "looks like a photographic negative of white-haired Roderick Usher," according to Bruce Lanier Wright (125). Price shaved his trademark moustache to play Fell, another allusion to his portrayal of Roderick Usher (and a subtle nod to the actor's well-regarded turn as the protagonist in 1946's *Dragonwyck*, his most relevant experience as a Gothic hero prior to the Poe series). The actor uses his velvety voice beautifully, offering a seductive purr that, coupled with his eccentric appearance, makes him seem believably fascinating to a "normal" young woman like Rowena.

Price has been praised — and often condemned — for his barnstorming performances in his horror films, acting turns that are often considered over-the-top. Here, however, his refusal to overplay his part keeps lines such as "She will not die because she is not dead — to me" realistic and straight. Even when he must suggest Fell's crumbling mental state through a frantic monologue, Price manages to deliver potentially risible dialogue such as "If only I could lay open my own brain as easily as I did that vegetable! What rot would be freed from its gray leaves!" with a sort of excited gravity that (almost) prevents the lines from inducing laughter.

Yet for all of Price's skill and sensitivity, his efforts would be blunted if he were cast opposite a weak co-star. In the dual roles of Rowena and Ligeia, Elizabeth Shepherd provides the horror star with his most worthy acting foil, successfully creating two distinct characters in what becomes the finest performance from a female actress in the entire Poe series — a stunning achievement given the previous work of Hazel Court and Barbara Steele. Shepherd's performance as a being divided between two personas, both of which are sexually aggressive, exemplifies Rhonda J. Berenstein's theory that

> monsters do not fit neatly with a model of human sexuality. Instead, they propose a paradigm of sexuality in which eros and danger, sensuality and destruction, human and inhuman, male and female blur, overlap, and coalesce. In this schema, sexuality and identity remain murky matters, stepped in border crossings and marked by fuzzy boundaries [27].

Like Price, Shepherd possesses a physical appearance that is more striking than conventionally attractive, a trait that suggests elements of alienation and oddity within their respective characters. Also like her co-star, Shepherd is gifted with especially strong vocal abilities; her deep voice suggests Rowena's latent sexuality but remains soft and kindly. However, the actress adopts a slightly harder-edged voice when Ligeia's personality overwhelms Rowena, suggesting the evil and domineering nature of the first Mrs. Fell. Jonathan Rigby identifies Shepherd's ability to "[create] a petrifying effect in a scene, where, under hypnosis, she suddenly switches from reliving her childhood to speaking in the braying, masterful tones of Ligeia" (116).

What in Poe's hands is essentially a three-character story becomes a multi-character film, of whom six are especially relevant. In addition to Poe's three characters, the film introduces Christopher Gough, a childhood acquaintance of the protagonist (an idea swiped from *House of Usher*) who serves as the Trevanion family lawyer and is Rowena's intended husband; Lord Trevanion, Rowena's comically boorish father; and Kenrick, Fell's faithful old servant (yet another idea derived from *House of Usher*). The presence of these new characters opens up the storyline and allows Towne and Corman to craft more dramatic tension and develop additional thematic concerns.

Throughout the Poe cycle, the nominal heroes of the individual films are uniformly dull and largely ineffectual, evidencing the essential truth of Roy Huss' assertion that "the horror film genre seems to reserve no place for the dashing young savior-hero" (qtd. in Berenstein 5). Beginning with Philip Winthrop in *House of Usher* and continuing with Francis Bernard (*Pit and the Pendulum*), Dr. James ("The Case of M. Valdemar" segment of *Tales of Terror*), Rexford Bedlo (*The Raven*), and Gino (*The Masque of the Red Death*), each of the "romantic leads" in the series is an unexceptional character who comes across as forgettable and sometimes incompetent, even in situations wherein the "hero" finally defeats the threat at hand. As a result, there is an implication of ineffectual sexuality among these allegedly romantic leads that serves to underscore the charisma and allure of Price's protagonists. To a certain degree, these characters appear weak because they are portrayed by actors of dubious merit; indeed, of all the romantic leads in the Poe adaptations, only one is played by an actor of note: Jack Nicholson as Rexford, who in any case is *supposed* to be somewhat dim-witted, a circumstance that justifies Nicholson's deliberately wooden performance.

As Christopher, John Wexford turns in arguably the strongest performance in this sort of role, even though he spends most of his time impotently grimacing at Price and Shepherd. Yet Westbrook is a much stronger actor than most of his predecessors, and he uses pained expressions and tense posture to convey the barely masked rage and disappointment within the attorney's heart. The character is a man of reason and logic, a lawyer who by training and inclination must deal with the realities of the material world. Therefore, Christopher is uncomfortable with emotions, romantic or otherwise, and wholly incapable of dealing with supernatural phenomena. Westbrook's expressions, gestures, and body language expertly convey this notion; later, the actor subtly suggests the lawyer's rising sense of triumph when Gough arrives at the abbey to check on Rowena late in the film. Here Gough seems excited, almost happy, at the prospect of unraveling the Fell marriage and perhaps winning back the hand — if not the heart — of his erstwhile companion. Yet even at this moment of apparent victory, Christopher can only comfort Rowena with sober logic, not romantic declarations: "I can't promise all will be well, but it will be done with soon."

Gough's practical turn of mind is nevertheless very useful during the film. It is Gough who discovers that there is no death certificate for Ligeia and consequently establishes, as he tells Verden, "Legally Ligeia is still alive — still your wife!" Gough also reveals that the abbey and much of the estate is still registered in Ligeia's name, so Verden's plan to sell the abbey and take Rowena away is hobbled. The attorney is also inquisitive enough to wonder exactly who is in Ligeia's grave, so he hires workmen to help him disinter her coffin. When he exposes Ligeia's body to a flame, it melts; Gough therefore establishes that a waxen effigy, apparently crafted by Fell, lies in Ligeia's grave.

Unfortunately for Christopher Gough, he can never match Verden Fell in Lady Rowena's affections, much less surpass him. Because he is such a rationalist, Gough can never really participate in the Romantic world of obsessive emotion and intense imagination that Fell represents to Rowena. Even more importantly, Gough could never accept the embodiment — the visualization — of sexualized power exchange that informs the relationship between Rowena and Verden (and Ligeia as well, to complete yet another of Corman's romantic triangles). This world of Poesque mystery and imagination is irresistible to Rowena, for it represents freedom from the hyper-rational and practical life symbolized by Christopher and Lord Trevanion. Rowena has already confounded the expectations of her fiancée and her father in that she is not the typical quiet and proper wife-to-be; her discomfort with the real world and her role in it does not end simply because Fell dies in the abbey conflagration. The ambiguous expression on Rowena's face at the film's close does not merely suggest her continued possession by Ligeia's spirit; it also implies that she cannot — or will not — return to the conventional life against which she was already rebelling when she first met Verden. In a sense, Christopher has not really saved Rowena at all, proving that "horror's heroes often fail miserably in their efforts to save the day" (Berenstein 91).

The presence of the aging Lord Trevanion and elderly servant Kenrick adds another layer of psychosocial symbolism to *The Tomb of Ligeia*. These representatives of established patriarchal order exist both to protect their charges from excessive sexuality and to subtly encourage an exploration of unconventional desires. At first glance, Trevanion appears to be something of a lout, a wealthy and titled man who is not really the refined gentleman generally associated with the British aristocracy. Living only for his foxhunts and other material diversions, Rowena's father seems as unaware and unappreciative of a more metaphysical conception of the world as is Christopher, whom Trevanion clearly considers an appropriate and socially acceptable potential son-in-law. Yet there is in Trevanion's boisterous, comical attitude a suggestion of the same distaste for social convention that his daughter displays. Lord Trevanion seems uneasy, or at least impatient, with the expectations and protocols of his station. On some level, Rowena has inherited her independent and contrary nature from her father, a notion further underscored each time he inquires or makes a comment about her: even when he seems to complain about his contrary offspring, there is a hint of admiration, pride, and even amusement in Trevanion's voice. The old man understands that his daughter's willfulness portends sexual aggression, yet he is not particularly bothered by this challenge to society's expectations. In the child's iconoclastic demeanor, the parent sees himself.

As Fell's faithful retainer for decades (perhaps for Verden's entire life), Kenrick initially seems like a mere servant loyally trying to protect his master. However, a lifelong servant such as Fell's aging butler definitely symbolizes the hegemony of the venerable aristocracy — who else, after all, could expect to employ the same staff — perhaps even generations of the same family of retainers — but the British aristocracy? Thus Kenrick functions as a gatekeeper, vainly attempting to separate and maintain the expected lifestyle of the aristocracy while dealing with the radical disorder of Verden Fell's obsessive romanticism and fascination with the "wrong" sort of woman — Ligeia. At the film's climax, the old servant finally admits that he has tried to help Fell, but Ligeia's post-hypnotic command was too strong to resist. "Only she can release him, and she's dead," Kenrick sadly concludes. Like Lord Trevanion, Kenrick is an old man who symbolizes a carefully defined and traditional interpretation of reality and propriety; also like Trevanion, Kenrick is charged with the paternalistic duty of protecting a willful, younger person who is captivated by the possibility of an unconventional existence. Yet by providing the protection he does, Kenrick subtly encourages Verden to pursue a lifestyle that culminates in sexual obsession and the mental decay Kenrick claims to dread.

The Tomb of Ligeia offers less in the way of pure shock and intense physical terror than the previous Poe-Price pictures, which is probably why such naysayers as Jonathan Rigby prefer earlier entries in the series. However, there is much to be said for the film, particularly its success as "a pure Gothic tale in the traditional style" (Lampley 218). Like its predecessors, the film undoubtedly deserves more respect than the dismissive conclusions of Tom Hutchinson and Roy Pickard, who conclude "in the final analysis most of the Corman films [are] little more than sappy little burlesques and spoofs" (105). Graced by a fine British supporting cast, gorgeous cinematography by Arthur Grant (a veteran of the Hammer Horror school), striking use of real locations (including Stonehenge and a real crumbling abbey in Norfolk), and a provocative suggestion of sexuality as social rebellion, *The Tomb of Ligeia* deserves its place as the final — and finest — of Roger Corman's memorable collaborations with Poe and Price.

14

THE TRAGEDY, "MAN"
The Conqueror Worm (1968) and the Reeves Legacy

With the departure of Roger Corman, AIP temporarily abandoned its Poe series. After the domestic release of *The Tomb of Ligeia* in early 1965, the studio proceeded with *The City Under the Sea*, a (misquoted) title derived from Poe's "The City in the Sea." While Vincent Price stars in and even reads a few lines from the poem, *The City Under the Sea* has essentially nothing to do with Edgar Allan Poe. In fact, the title was changed to *War-Gods of the Deep* for American consumption, an indication that even AIP wasn't disingenuous enough to connect just any old thing with Poe — at least, not yet. Three years would pass before another putative Poe picture would be offered to the public. In this case, the faux Poe title situation involving *The City Under the Sea/War-Gods of the Deep* was reversed, and the latest project was called *Witchfinder General* in England but given a Poe title in the United States — *The Conqueror Worm*.

From this point on, any similarity between the so-called Poe films and their alleged source material would be increasingly coincidental. In fact, *Witchfinder General* was conceived and produced as a stand-alone project, with no conscious connection to the Poe series; AIP changed the title for the sole purpose of attracting fans of the Corman-Price-Poe collaborations. Nevertheless, associations with the spirit of Poe, if not the letter of his work, make *The Conqueror Worm* a suitable renaming of Michael Reeves' final and best project, a powerful if unsettling mediation on the corrosive consequences of violence — even when allegedly committed in the name of justice — on both the individual and society — particularly women.

Critical reaction to AIP's desperate title change was understandably sharp. Dave Worrell and Lee Pfeiffer claim that AIP "shamelessly retitled [*Witchfinder General*] *The Conqueror Worm*, based on one of Poe's more obscure tales [sic]" (29). Philip Waddilove, the film's co-producer and a close personal friend of the director, deemed the title change "inappropriate" in his introduction to Benjamin Halligan's biography of Reeves (xiii). Even Vincent Price himself believed "*The Conqueror Worm* was the most ridiculous title for *Witchfinder General*" (qtd. in Senn 232). The overall impression conveyed by both observers of and participants in the production is that the title change is misleading, silly, and wholly contrary to the themes of both Reeves and Poe.

Yet the American title of *Witchfinder General* was not chosen at random. According to AIP co-founder Samuel Z. Arkoff, "We came across an Edgar Allan Poe verse which included a line that spoke of a 'conqueror worm.' We weren't exactly sure what it meant ... but it was pure Poe and seemed to fit..." (qtd. in Senn 231). Arkoff himself may not have understood the poem, but Poe clearly intends the work to be an extended metaphor for human life and (especially) death; the poet describes "a play of hopes and fears," associating life with a theatrical performance (960). Poe calls life a "drama" pursued by protagonists "Through a circle that ever returneth in/To the self-same spot," suggesting the inevitable cycle of existence, and concludes that as "The curtain, a funeral pall,/Comes down with the rush of a storm" and "the play is the tragedy 'Man,'/And its hero the Conqueror Worm" (961). In other words, human life is a futile pursuit of "hopes and fears" in which everybody dies while new generations rise to perpetuate the grim cycle.

Although "The Conqueror Worm" has nothing to do with witchcraft, it conveys an utterly dark and pessimistic worldview that dovetails nicely with the tone of *Witchfinder General*. One of the most provocative and thoughtful depictions of violence and death ever committed to film, it is the primary evidence supporting the cult status of Michael Reeves (1943–1969), a brilliant but troubled young director whose potential as one of the world's great filmmakers was cut short by his untimely death at the age of twenty-five. Reeves completed only three features (and finished the director's duties on *Castle of the Living Dead* [1964] when the original helmsman abruptly quit the production) before an (apparently) accidental overdose of barbiturates killed him; interestingly, each of Reeves' movies features a noted horror star: Christopher Lee in *Castle* (although Reeves apparently did not direct any of Lee's scenes), Barbara Steele in *The She Beast* (1966), Boris Karloff in *The Sorcerers* (1967), and Price in *The Conqueror Worm*. In spite of the meager number of titles on his resume — or perhaps because of it — Reeves has gained a small but ardent following over the decades, with some observers going so far as to call Reeves the James Dean of horror cinema. Perhaps a better analogy is the career of country-rock musician Gram Parsons (1946–1973), whose unique fusion of sonic styles continues to influence other artists in spite of the fact that he recorded only two solo albums.

Loosely based on *Witchfinder General*, Ronald Bassett's historical novel, *The Conqueror Worm* concerns Matthew Hopkins (Price), who profits by extracting confessions from supposed witches and extorts sexual favors from young women who fall into his power. Hopkins and his assistant, John Stearne (Robert Russell), torture Catholic priest John Lowes (Rupert Davies) until the clergyman's niece, Sara (Hilary Dwyer), offers herself to Hopkins. After Stearne rapes Sara, Hopkins abandons her and orders Lowes' execution. Sara's fiancé, Richard Marshall (Ian Ogilvy), swears vengeance on Hopkins, but Hopkins captures the couple and tortures Sara in a vain attempt to compel Richard's confession of witchcraft. Richard escapes and begins hacking Hopkins with an axe, but arriving soldiers shoot the witchfinder. Thwarted in his desire to repay Hopkins' evil in kind, Richard angrily cries, "You took him from me!" over and over again; her mind finally destroyed, Sara screams despairingly as the frame freezes on her tormented image and the end credits roll.

The nihilistic vision and atmosphere of utter helplessness that permeate *The Conqueror Worm* are, as Arkoff maintains, quite relevant to Poe's poetic conceit. "It is safe to say that no director in cinema history exhibited such a consistently depressing and angry

Vincent Price as one of his most despicable characters, Matthew Hopkins, in *Witchfinder General,* aka *The Conqueror Worm* (1968), which functions as a Poe adaptation in spite of the fact it was conceived without any conscious connection to the author or his works.

view of the world and humanity as Reeves," claims Danny Peary, further linking the film to the poem (56). The dark tone of the film is established from the pre-credit sequence, over which Price reads the first verse of Poe's poem (in the American version). Peaceful shots of the English landscape are punctuated by hammering sounds, which are ultimately revealed to emanate from a hangman building a gallows. A terrified old woman is dragged to the place of execution. The accused witch's screams are cut off with chilling finality when the stool is kicked out from under her feet; a zoom shot to the figure of Hopkins on horseback ends in a freeze frame, and as Paul Ferris' music swells, murky and disturbing images play out behind the opening credits. As the film progresses, we recognize these illustrations as photographs altered to suggest period woodcuts of the film's principal victims and victimizers. At the film's conclusion, Price narrates the final verse of the poem (again, only in the American version) while a final image of horror — Sara's screaming face — provides a terrible mute testimony to the truth contained in the poem's last lines, which imply that life contains "...much of Madness, and more of Sin" (961).

Throughout the film, a litany of violent and gruesome images is displayed, images far more horrifying in their realism than the fantastic shocks of the previous Poe entries. Reeves himself insisted that such intense realism was absolutely necessary to convey his intentions; as he explained to John Trevelyan, the British censor (and incidentally a distant relation to Reeves), the film's "overall message ... is as anti-violence as it can be. Violence breeds violence ... violence itself is insanity" (qtd. in Murray 210). To a considerable degree, it is the unromantic and brutal attitude towards violence that has won the film so much admiration, but from the moment of first issue, the film has also suffered the umbrage of shocked critics. Playwright Alan Bennett condemned the film in no uncertain terms, first preparing a recipe list of the films brutalities before launching into his rancorous review:

> It is the most persistently sadistic and morally rotten film I have seen. It was [sic] a degrading experience, by which I mean it made me feel dirty.... The world of film is not an autochthonous world: sadism which corrupts and repels in life continues to do so when placed on celluloid. It is not compounded by style nor excused by camera-work [qtd. in Halligan 196–197].

Ken Russell, whose own controversial witch hunting film *The Devils* (1971) seems greatly influenced by Reeves' earlier work, once told Benjamin Halligan that Reeves' final production was "one of the worst films I have seen and certainly the most nauseous" (162). In his survey of British horror, Andy Boot argues that the subtext of the film is "that man is an animal, never happier than when he is perpetrating acts of wanton violence for nothing more than his own gratification" (183). Even Stephen King, himself often an admirer of graphic movie violence, judges *The Conqueror Worm* "surely one of the most revolting horror pictures to be released by a major studio in the Sixties" (194). Yet these comments fail to consider the purpose of the violence within the context of the story.

There is no question that the violence and brutality of *The Conqueror Worm* is grimly effective even after four decades. As rough as the picture may have been in 1968, it is crucial to remember that AIP co-financed the film with Tigon British, a production company founded by infamous British "sexploitation" kingpin Tony Tenser. While Tenser himself was very supportive of what he knew was a provocative and intelligent thriller, his association with Reeves' film undoubtedly colored many contemporary reviews. Thus *The Conqueror Worm* must be removed from its sleazy low-budget background to appreciate it without the terrible weight of British cultural norms of 1968 — perhaps the year of the worst social and cultural upheaval of the 1960s (Halligan 195).

Although set in 1645, *The Conqueror Worm* alludes to the anxiety associated with the revolutionary spirit so pervasive in 1968. Following the opening credits, Patrick Wymark (who also plays Oliver Cromwell in a cameo appearance) provides a brief prologue to set up the action. "The structure of law and order has collapsed," Wymark explains, and "local magistrates indulge in individual whims. Justice and injustice are dispensed in more or less equal quantities, and without opposition." Thus the stage is set for Reeves' treatise on the nature of law and justice and the shortcomings of those charged with maintaining the standards of both, whether in the seventeenth or the twentieth century. Much of the film's ability to horrify stems from the fact that Matthew Hopkins is not only an actual historic personage, but also a sadistic killer operating with "the full blessing of what law there is." In its depiction of cultural upheaval sparked by Puritan repression sanctioned by government, *The Conqueror Worm* functions as an allegory, much as Arthur Miller's *The Crucible* (1952) uses a literal witch hunt as a metaphor for the ideological witch hunts of the McCarthy era.

Several scenes include conversations between Hopkins and various local authorities, and Hopkins, a former lawyer, frequently alludes to the legal aspects of his witch hunting. He continually reminds Stearne to follow the "prescribed methods" for extracting confessions, often following his instructions with some reference to the necessity for due process. When Hopkins and Stearne first meet the villagers who have summoned them, Hopkins initially expresses the possibility that the accusations against Lowes are unfounded. "By the way, do you know what they call me now? Witchfinder General," Price later remarks to his assistant with no little pride. "There are those who think I should be appointed such for all of England — appointed by Parliament," he continues. These and other lines, delivered straight-faced by Price, indicate that Hopkins believes his holy crusade is necessary and acceptable because it is legally sanctioned.

Yet at no point does Reeves forget the corruption that mars Hopkins' soul and ultimately reveals his sanctimonious pronouncements as hypocritical ramblings. As soon as he meets Sara, Hopkins is willing to exchange his so-called legal responsibilities — in this case, torturing her uncle — for the carnal delights she promises. The lawyer deliberately interjects legal terminology into his negotiations with Sara: "And you will make every attempt to present the facts to me?" he asks, later telling her, "I've come to question you," when he arrives for their first rendezvous. After deciding that John Lowes must die, Hopkins claims the battered priest's incoherent mumblings are a confession and instructs Stearne to make sure the witnesses concur, demonstrating the witchfinder's willingness to resort to false confessions when it suits his purposes. Prior to their final confrontation with Richard and Sara, Hopkins points out to Stearne that they can get rid of their enemies by condemning them as witches. "We have the power to do it legally," Hopkins remarks.

Throughout the film, Hopkins bolsters his connection to secular law by referring to the religious motivations that inspire witch hunting. "Go on, Stearne, you're doing God's work," Hopkins says during the torture of Sara at the film's climax. Elsewhere, Hopkins accepts payment and tells the magistrate the money is "to be spent in the service of our Lord." Hopkins frequently exhorts Stearne to discover if "the mark of Satan" is upon their victims. From these comments and actions, it is clear that Matthew Hopkins is truly "a disturbed Puritan — part true believer, part opportunist" (French and French 230). The apparent sincerity he possessed when he began hunting witches has been diluted by greed, sadism, and a growing sense of entitlement and superiority.

Avarice and pride certainly motivate the witch hunter, propelling him to grander and more elaborate schemes to win confessions from his victims. Yet an important component in Hopkins' psychological makeup is his thinly concealed disgust and hatred for the people around him. He constantly insults Sterne, never missing a chance to remind him that "you ride with me because you help me in my work." Price adds a touch of overzealousness to the expressions of piety Hopkins makes to the local authorities upon the completion of a job, clearly transmitting Hopkins' insincerity without allowing his delivery to descend into camp. Furthermore,

> Price conveys the scorn that someone of Hopkins' breeding and intelligence would have for a world which allows him ... to commit what he knows to be monstrous, sadistic acts. Hopkins is a god in an England full of greedy, hypocritical, superstitious people who he feels are inferior to him. He ... debases them by raping their women, taking their money, and executing the few among them brave enough to protest... [Peary 57].

Especially telling is a quick shot of Hopkins at the conclusion of his initial conversation with Sara. As he turns away, Hopkins shoots Sara a stern look of disapproval; even though he is essentially blackmailing her into having sex with him, he is still disgusted by what he perceives as her immorality. It is a subtle gesture subtly made, but this facial expression justifies Mark Clark's comment that the role of Hopkins represents "Price at the pinnacle of his career" (97).

Another example of Hopkins' distaste for the people around him — and by extension, all of humanity — is the fact he is never portrayed actually torturing anybody. John Stearne does all the actual interrogation, slapping suspects and pricking them with a long spike in search of the Devil's mark. When the physical exertion is too much for one man, locals are recruited to assist Stearne while Hopkins grimly observes. The witch hunter barks orders to Stearne and other underlings, but he keeps his hands to himself. Tellingly, the dark clothes Hopkins favors contrast with the white gloves he wears throughout the movie. The white gloves symbolize a bizarre kind of purity in Hopkins' nature; furthermore, they imply the "kid gloves" worn by wealthy playboys of later generations, symbols of the escape from physical labor — the dirty work, in other words. Interestingly, Hopkins penchant for the color of purity extends to his mount; Hopkins' choice of a white horse symbolically associates him with Death, who according to the Book of the Revelation rides "a pale horse."

When Hopkins and Stearne are reunited after being chased by Roundhead troops, Stearne blames Hopkins for his arrest and injury at the hands of soldiers. Hopkins dismisses the complaints, pointing out, "I even saved your share of the pay [for the latest executions] even though I did all the work." Of course, Hopkins never actually touched any of the victims — once again the bloodletting has been assigned to other hands. In fact, the only physical act of torture Hopkins attempts is the branding of Sara at the film's climax, and even that action is interrupted before it begins when Richard breaks free. Hopkins is more than willing to shoot anybody who threatens him — and he does so more than once — but these expressions of physical violence are necessary for self-defense, not the pursuit of Satan's consorts. Price's restraint and subtlety make these aspects of the character significant and allow Hopkins to appear "as a superb presence of inexorable vindictiveness around which the other characters move with fascinated repulsion" (Pirie 154). Rick Worland accurately assesses Price's turn as Hopkins "one of [his] best performances" (30).

In the earlier Poe-inspired films, there are relatively clear distinctions between the villain and the hero. *The Conqueror Worm* is so memorable because it blurs the line between villainy and heroism, calling into question the boundaries that separate the more general, less emotionally charged terms of protagonist and antagonist. In the case of Richard Marshall, the nominal hero, there is a gradual transformation from stalwart to psychopath. When we first meet Richard, he is smirking to himself while riding in a Roundhead cavalry patrol and is teased by his friend Swallow (Nicky Henson) about "ungodly" thoughts of Sara. This exchange suggests the innocence and inexperience of Richard, who is a simple farmer and neophyte soldier. Soon, however, Richard kills his first man: he saves his captain's life by firing on a lurking sniper behind the officer. "He was trying to kill you, sir," Richard remarks almost to himself, dumbfounded at the event.

Richard's innocence is compounded by a strong sense of idealism. He sees the world in simple, stark terms — black and white, good and evil. His love for Sara is sincere, and it is perfectly reasonable for Richard to be angry when he discovers the terrible violations visited upon his fiancée and her kindly uncle. However, Richard's idealism — a positive trait in almost any other film — is the source for his own descent into violence and madness. Because he cannot abide the murder of John Lowes and the abuse of Sara, he becomes obsessed with vengeance. Richard temporarily deserts his command to investigate the trouble at home, and he makes it clear to Swallow that he intends to desert again if necessary — even if his actions lead to a court martial — in order to hunt down Hopkins and Stearne. "It's madness!" Swallow declares. "It's justice — my justice," Richard grimly replies. Richard's ideals of home and hearth have been compromised, and it is the transgression against his conception of the world around him that propels his quest for vengeance, causing him to abandon his honor and everything else he claims to value. He claims to seek justice for Sara, but it is revenge for his shattered worldview that Richard truly pursues.

In one of the film's most resonant scenes, Richard and Sara kneel at the desecrated altar in her murdered uncle's church. Richard declares that Sara and he are married, although significantly there is neither a priest (symbol of religious authority) nor witnesses (aspects of legal authority) to sanction the nuptials. Furthermore, Richard swears an oath before God that he will punish the criminals who have visited disorder on his life. The contrast between a vow of life (marriage) and a vow of death (revenge) foreshadows Richard's growing obsession.

At the film's climax, Richard refuses to confess before Hopkins and Stearne, even though to do so would spare Sara further torture. Richard cries out in frustration and promises to kill Hopkins, but the shards of his compromised idealism — perhaps a mirror of Hopkins' own decayed principles — prevent him from uttering the words that would relieve his wife. When Richard attacks Hopkins, he intends to prolong the witchfinder's suffering. Swallow bursts in and fires the bullet that slays Hopkins — sparing him additional torture. Richard's repeated cry of "You took him from me!" not only conveys the anguish he feels at being cheated out of Hopkins' final destruction but also hints that he realizes how his murderous quest has reduced him to Hopkins' level.

Richard's devotion to his personal *weltanschauung* (worldview) provides an interesting insight into masculine conceptions of order and justice. Although Richard's behavior and devotion to duty prior to Hopkins' depredations imply acknowledgment of and consent to support pre-existing social conventions, Richard quickly abandons this adherence to the established system in order to force the world around him to conform to his personal notions of right and wrong. In this sense, Richard embraces violence and aggression to achieve his goals, which with their emphasis on action and disregard of consequences implies an inherently masculine approach to problem solving. When the rules of society no longer undergird his personal convictions and assumptions, Richard does not hesitate to compel a unique and individual sense of order in a "manly" fashion. As a result, Richard becomes a mirror image of Hopkins, placing his own self-centered agenda above the prescriptions of the laws and customs that both men have pledged to support. In short, Marshall and Hopkins battle one another partially to express their domination and control of the situation — with little regard for the consequences to others.

Perhaps the greatest tragedies visited upon any character in *The Conqueror Worm* are those suffered by Sara. Initially she is portrayed as an innocent country girl, yet it is highly significant that she is not a virgin by the time she crosses Hopkins' path. Sara willingly offers herself to Richard — with the tacit approval of her uncle, who wishes Richard to carry her far away from the brewing trouble — but not before briefly chiding him for an overly amorous advance: "The army has taught you rough manners," she complains. Soon, however, she is consummating her love affair with Richard; as an unmarried woman engaging in sexual congress, she has transgressed against the values of her society.

Sara is quite aware of her sexual powers. When she rushes to her uncle's aid, Hopkins confronts her. The terrified girl initially admits she is the priest's niece, but when Hopkins observes, "You, too, may be corrupted by Satan," she changes her story, now claiming to be a foundling. "And you have remained innocent all these years?" Hopkins asks deliberately, fully cognizant of the double meaning of the word "innocent" in this context. Sara replies, "If you would release [my uncle] now, you might be convinced tonight that all this is needless." In other words, it is Sara, not Hopkins, who makes the first suggestion that there is a carnal solution to the matter at hand. Throughout the scene Sara seems flirtatious, cutting her eyes and smiling knowingly at Hopkins. The witch hunter takes the bait, and it is a highly distressed Sara who quickly turns away from him.

Hopkins thinks he has bargained for Sara's maidenhead, not just her body itself. He understands after they sleep together that she was not a virgin (and not "innocent") before he came to her in the night. Therefore, the idea is already planted in his Puritanical mind that she is "unclean" — a whore. When he discovers she has had sex (albeit unwillingly) with Stearne, he is too disgusted to touch her again. Reeves shows a villager telling Hopkins that he has witnessed Stearne and Sara together; there is no dialogue in the shot, meaning it is unknown whether or not the villager, who is depicted observing the attack with a salacious look on his face, has made it clear that Hopkins' assistant raped the girl. Would Sara's lack of consent have made a difference in Hopkins' attitude? Probably not, as Hopkins has already decided she is unworthy of fundamental human dignity and respect.

Sara realizes the terrible mistake she has made in sleeping with Hopkins. Her honor is destroyed, as is her fidelity to Richard; her sacrifice delays her uncle's death but cannot prevent it. Stearne has been spying on Hopkins, which is how he knows his employer has been sleeping with the girl. In his brutal logic, Stearne has as much right to the girl's body as does his employer — whether the girl likes it or not. Thus, Sara also gets raped for her good intentions to save her uncle, further compounding her misery and shame.

Beyond the sexual abuse she suffers and the death of her only known relative, Sara is subjected to pricking and other tortures near the film's conclusion. She must suffer physical agonies because her husband refuses to confess. Then she must witness Richard's brutal attack on Hopkins, which inspires conflicting feelings of appreciation and loathing in her heart. When Swallow shoots Hopkins and Richard becomes enraged, Sara is confronted with the final destruction of her sense of perspective and propriety. She is an unchaste woman, practically a harlot in the repressive standards of her time; her husband has abandoned his love for her in his quest for vengeance, and he has at last lost his mind. When one of the troopers mutters, "May God have mercy on us all," it is the last straw: Sarah herself cracks under the strain of her ordeal, her screams of madness a cruel epiphany recognizing the lack of godliness — of any sense of order, supernatural or man-made — in the rural England that is her world — and, perhaps, the world beyond.

Just as Richard and Hopkins have rejected established society's rules in order to further their own ends, Sara has attempted to manipulate matters for her own benefit. She has violated the social contract to develop her own *weltanschauung*, even though her intentions are ostensibly benevolent. Yet in seventeenth century rural England, no woman can expect to challenge the male-constructed hegemony, no matter how honorable the purpose. An independent feminine worldview threatens just and unjust males alike, and any attempt to foster such a transgressive order must be violently suppressed, as suggested by Barbara Creed's theory of the monstrous-feminine. Indeed, the witchfinder/witch opposition is a highly potent expression of the concurrent gender conflict within the larger society. Although Hopkins metes out punishment to those women who stand accused of witchcraft, Richard's loss of focus regarding his wife's violation and the established society's lack of concern for her plight indicate a tacit support of misogynistic brutality to suppress female hegemony.

The abuses heaped upon Sara are unquestionably horrible, but with the exception of John Lowes, all of the victims depicted are women. There is, then, a remarkable streak of misogyny running rampant in *The Conqueror Worm*, a further acknowledgment of the intense gender struggle symbolized by the witchfinder/witch conflict. Every woman in the film is portrayed as property, as something to be "taken" or "kept" but never fully or consistently appreciated. When one elderly suspect claims she can't be executed because she's going to have a baby, Stearne cracks, "Who'd want to make *you* pregnant?" His joke draws appreciative laughter from the gathering crowd — yet another mob of villagers who, as they do throughout the film, are drawn to the spectacle of witch killing out of a mixture of fear, excitement, and boredom — but who never express dread or disgust at the executions. This lack of disturbance among the townspeople indicates a general agreement that witches must be destroyed — as must any other woman who challenges the status quo.

Further evidence of seventeenth century English misogyny occurs later in the film during the execution of accused witch Elizabeth Clark (Maggie Kimberly). Hopkins decides to experiment with burning witches, and Elizabeth is the first victim of this brutal method of execution. The unfortunate woman is tied to a ladder and lowered into the flames with excruciating deliberateness, her body slowly immolated while her head flares up like a bonfire. Elizabeth's screams pierce the soundtrack until they finally trail off. Once again Reeves intercuts shots of villagers watching the execution with stoic expressions of acceptance (except for Elizabeth's husband, played by composer Paul Ferris, who will later be mortally wounded in a failed attempt to assassinate Hopkins), even approval; most disturbing of the villagers' faces is that of a little blonde boy, grinning with excitement. Later he and other children are depicted roasting potatoes in the smoldering remnants of the fire, a shot that conveys the ignorance of "innocent" children eating food cooked in human remains and foreshadows their unquestioning acceptance of their culture's anti-female attitude. Women, it seems, are only valuable when they are performing utilitarian functions — including, in this grim sequence, literally providing themselves as fuel for the fire that cooks children's dinners.

In a move insisted upon by AIP executives, Reeves was forced to shoot additional footage of topless actresses playing the tavern whores. This decision, clearly made to increase the exploitability of the film, betrays a 1960s-era sexism only marginally less virulent than that found in 1645. For all of his lascivious behavior, Hopkins seems to genuinely despise women. "Strange, isn't it, how much iniquity the Lord vested in the female," he muses at one point. When he introduces the idea of burning witches by announcing, "I intend to initiate a new method of execution ... it's a fitting end for the foul ungodliness in womankind." Sara, of course, is ultimately a pawn traded back and forth between Hopkins and Richard in their own bizarre contest of ego and will. In the end, Sara, the "witches," and the wenches are reduced to the same level: they are all commodities to be traded, not people to be respected.

One factor that cannot be ignored is the power of cinematography in *The Conqueror Worm*. Reeves found an extremely capable cinematographer in John Coquillon, whose vistas of the English countryside imply an epic dimension to the film that its budget would never have allowed otherwise. The "overpowering use of landscape" is one of the film's most stimulating elements, according to David Pirie (155). Tracking shots of Richard Marshall riding across the countryside and two sequences in which Hopkins and Stearne are pursued by either Richard or other Roundhead troops imbue the picture with a sensibility associated with the Western genre. This was in fact a deliberate effect Reeves pursued in his desire to create what amounts to an English Western (Murray 131). In his juxtaposition of "natural beauty with human depravity," Reeves "contrives to make the natural scenery and its rootedness a strong positive force against the shifting nomadic evil of the characters; in this respect the film is almost mystical and pantheistic" (Pirie 153). Given that the earth is frequently gendered feminine, the scenes of Richard, Hopkins, and other men fighting, killing, and otherwise performing masculine aggression against a background of natural beauty suggest that it is the phallocentric patriarchy that is "unnatural" and destined, eventually, to be consumed by the feminine.

In the wake of its strong critical and popular reception, *The Conqueror Worm* inspired a number of direct and indirect copies. Because the film was particularly popular in West Germany, it inspired a "grotesquely sadistic sex movie" released as *Mark of the Devil* in the United States (Hardy 206). As Michael Weldon puts it in *The Psychotronic Encyclopedia of Film*, "This is the one with the famous 'stomach distress' bags given to viewers ... in a brilliant American ad campaign stressing the gore ..." (Weldon 460). Far bloodier and less intelligent than Michael Reeves' film and suffused with an even greater streak of misogyny, *Mark of the Devil* featured Herbert Lom, a contemporary of Vincent Price, as the witch hunter, Udo Kier blatantly aping Ian Ogilvy in his performance as the hero, and Reggie Nalder as an assistant witch hunter even more repulsive than Robert Russell's John Stearne. The German production even borrowed an English director, Michael Armstrong, who was an associate of Michael Reeves and had — like Reeves — made films for Tigon. In turn, Armstrong's take on witch hunting spawned a sequel, *Mark of the Devil II* (1972).

While *Mark of the Devil* and its follow-up exploited the basest elements of *The Conqueror Worm* and eschewed most of its artistry, Reeves' film did influence a number of respectable efforts, including the aforementioned Ken Russell production of *The Devils*. The Hammer film *Twins of Evil* (1972) stars Peter Cushing as a very Matthew Hopkins-esque Puritan, only this time focused on burning suspected vampires. Because these films depict the torture and murder of women who at least nominally threaten the patriarchal social construct, they also ultimately confirm their anxiety regarding a firmly identifiable feminine worldview. Robin Hardy's *The Wicker Man* (1973) touches on notions of religious fanaticism that can be traced back to *The Conqueror Worm*. Perhaps the most interesting films presaged by *The Conqueror Worm* are two of Sam Peckinpah's most notable — and violent — productions: *The Wild Bunch* (1969) and *Straw Dogs* (1971), which features the brutal rape of the protagonist's wife in rural England, as does Reeves' film (Halligan 191) and thus expresses a similar anxiety about a gynocentric social order. Interestingly, Peckinpah hired John Coquillon to photograph *Straw Dogs* on the basis of his work on *The Conqueror Worm*; the two would collaborate on additional films thereafter.

The success of his third feature did not guarantee Michael Reeves further glories; he spent the last few months of his life vainly trying to set up new productions, none of which ever jelled. More ominously, Reeves battled severe emotional problems including depression and insomnia, a battle that ended with his fatal drug overdose on February 11, 1969. Yet Reeves' death did not prevent AIP from trying to build on his legacy; several projects he had discussed wound up being produced, often featuring Vincent Price and other veterans of *The Conqueror Worm* on both sides of the camera. Two of these productions are relevant here: *The Oblong Box* (1969) and *Cry of the Banshee* (1970).

Although the title comes from a Poe tale, *The Oblong Box* takes nothing from the original story, which concerns a mysterious, coffin-like container being transported on a ship by a most peculiar passenger. In fact, a more logical name for this film would be *Premature Burial* — the notion of being buried alive is in fact borrowed from that Poe classic — but Roger Corman had adapted the story once before, so AIP did not wish to recycle the title. There is a scene in the film wherein anguished madman Sir Edward Markham (Alastair Williamson) recounts the terror of being buried alive: "Waking up in that horrible oblong box; no air to breathe; trapped, and no escape. The earth raining down on the lid, every shovelful burying you more deeply." These lines recall the horrific highlight of Poe's "The Premature Burial":

> It may be asserted, without hesitation, that *no* event is so terribly well adapted to inspire
> the supremeness of bodily and of mental distress, as is burial before death. The unen-
> durable oppression of the lungs — the stifling fumes of the damp earth — the blackness of
> the absolute Night — the silence like a sea that overwhelms — the unseen but palpable pres-
> ence of the Conqueror Worm — these things, ... carry into the heart ... a degree of
> appalling and intolerable horror from which the most daring imagination must recoil
> [262–263].

Beyond this distant allusion to the source tale and the shared themes of guilt and live
burial, there is nothing to connect the film to any Poe story at all.

A confused hodgepodge of various genre clichés, *The Oblong Box* "is a somewhat
contrived combination of Burke and Hare with echoes of Jack the Ripper and *The Phantom
of the Opera*. The most interesting aspect is that ...like a guilty conscience, the evils of
British colonialism come home to haunt and destroy its perpetrators" (Hardy 210). Vincent
Price stars as Julian Markham, a wealthy Briton who owns a plantation in Africa. His
brother, Sir Edward, has been tortured and cursed by a native tribe for killing one of their
children; suffering from occasional lapses of sanity as well as a hideously scarred face, Sir

Edward must be kept locked in
his attic room. With the assistance of his confederate, Trench
(Peter Arne), Sir Edward arranges
for an African witch doctor
(Harry Baird) to slip him a potion
in order to feign death. Sir
Edward is accidentally buried
alive; body snatchers subsequently bring his coffin to the
surgery of Dr. Neuhartt (Christopher Lee, "outfitted in an
appalling silver Beatle wig,"
according to Lucy Chase
Williams, [217]), who becomes
the madman's unwilling accom-
plice in a campaign of murderous
revenge.

Michael Reeves had been
slated to direct *The Oblong Box* as
a follow-up to *The Conqueror
Worm*, but his rapidly eroding
health, coupled with the many
weaknesses inherent in Lawrence
Huntingdon's jumbled original
script — which Benjamin Halligan terms "profoundly un-

Elizabeth (Hilary Dwyer) comforts Julian (Price) in *The
Oblong Box* (1969).

Reevesian" (211)—ultimately led to the director's replacement by Gordon Hessler (b. 1930), whom AIP groomed as its principal horror specialist. Former film critic Christopher Wicking was brought in to streamline the script. According to the screenwriter, he "made the theme of imperial exploitation of the natives the subtext, the cause of the curse" (qtd. in Meikle 155). It is through this then-innovative theme that the movie accomplishes what little sense of originality it possesses; moreover, the guilt of the Markham brothers faintly recalls the overwhelming guilt of actual Poe protagonists, both in the author's fiction and in the earlier AIP adaptations.

Sir Edward's punishment at the hands of the natives fills his brother with dread and shame. Several times during the course of the film, Julian remarks upon his regrets. During one of his many long walks with new bride Elizabeth (Hilary Dwyer), Julian announces his intention to "abandon" his plantation, even though to do so will essentially impoverish him. Elsewhere, Julian observes that "we" (his family in particular and Europe in general) have "plundered the land" in Africa and must deal with "sin and retribution"—a peculiarly Poesque line that underscores Wicking's take on the proceedings. It is finally revealed that Julian, not Edward, was the Markham who killed the native child; therefore, it is Julian who should have paid for the crime.

Certainly Julian's guilty conscience troubles him in regard to his role in his brother's tragedy, yet he never seems willing to pay an appropriate retribution. Eventually, Edward and Julian confront each other on the family estate; Julian shoots his sibling, who bites him before expiring. The film ends with Elizabeth going to Edward's former attic abode, only to be informed by her deteriorating husband that it is his turn to be locked up. "This is *my* room," he announces sadly. Thus do the Markham brothers both pay for their avarice and inhumanity; in doing so, they represent the liability shared collectively by Western civilization for the exploitation of the Third World.

Beyond the notions of guilt and premature burial, *The Oblong Box* offers no significant connection to Poe. It offers the least intriguing depiction of female characters in the entire series as well: the only women of consequence in the film are Elizabeth, who is depicted as a rather one-dimensional stereotype of the frightened heroine; a few servants; and a prostitute (Uta Levka), whom Edward murders. The most important servant, Neuhartt's maid, Sally (Sally Geeson), is depicted as a sexually aggressive character; she even beds Edward, whose face is covered by a crimson hood, out of a combination of pity, curiosity, and greed (she thinks the aristocrat will take her as a mistress). In its casual assumption that women exist in horror films simply to function as clichés, *The Oblong Box* marginalizes women, exploiting them without any of the thematic weight Michael Reeves brought to *The Conqueror Worm*; in the end, Reeves' film may depict more women suffering more abuse, but there is no hint of approval, much less blasé acceptance, of the female condition as is found in Hessler's project.

Whether or not Reeves could have improved the troubled production is a question that cannot be answered at this late date. In fact, given Reeves' very public distaste for Vincent Price and his failing health, it is likely Reeves' participation would have made the film worse or made no difference at all. Yet the presence of actors Price, Dwyer, and Rupert Davies (as an artist neighbor of the Markhams), coupled with the vibrant photography of John Coquillon, all veterans of *The Conqueror Worm*, makes it impossible not to wonder "what if."

Furthermore, the missed opportunities that abound in *The Oblong Box* are singularly confounding. Why make a film featuring Vincent Price and Christopher Lee, together for the first time on screen, and then give them only one scene together? Why not cast Lee as Sir Edward? Perhaps Hessler's most effective cinematic trick is to incorporate Edward's point of view in many shots; this, coupled with the fact that Edward's horrible face is kept hidden until the climax, builds a modicum of suspense. However, when his face is finally revealed, the makeup job is more laughable than frightening; Denis Meikle describes Edward's appearance as "a big hooter" upon which sprout "evil-looking acne heads" (157). Without exception, the performances are lethargic or uninspired or both; even his own daughter thinks Vincent Price "reverted to camp" in the film, particularly in comparison to *The Conqueror Worm* (Price 270).

As ineffective as *The Oblong Box* may be, it is considerably better than *Cry of the Banshee*. Although blatantly promoted as a Poe adaptation, there is absolutely nothing in the Poe canon appropriated for the film — not even the title. A verse from "The Bells" affixed to an opening title is the one reference at all to the American author — and even it consists of "incongruous lines — nonsensical in context" (Rigby 164). What results is a confusing hodgepodge of elements swiped from earlier AIP efforts and an atmosphere of

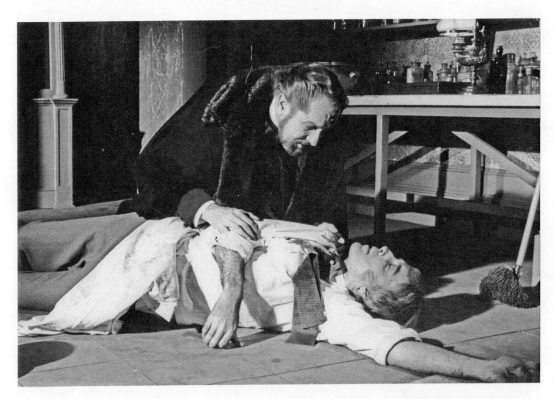

Among the many lost opportunities that abound in *The Oblong Box* (1969) is horror stars Vincent Price and Christopher Lee sharing only one scene in the entire film!

desperation — permeated by suggestions of almost contemptuous indifference for the long-running series, and by extension, its star — that make *Cry of the Banshee* a poor coda indeed for Price's Gothic screen personally. For in the wake of this film, the actor would never again appear in a period (pre-twentieth century) horror movie.

Veterans of *The Oblong Box*, director Gordon Hessler and scripter Christopher Wicking (in collaboration with Tim Kelly) reteamed for *Cry of the Banshee*. Hessler and Wicking occasionally demonstrated wit and style in their previous efforts, but the only imaginative element in *Cry of the Banshee* is the opening credit sequence designed by Monty Python regular and director Terry Gilliam. Set in the sixteenth century, the film concerns the Whitman clan, headed by magistrate Lord Edward Whitman (Price), who determines to wipe out the "witches" who practice "the Old Religion" in his rural English community. Whitman stops short of killing Oona (Elisabeth Bergner), the leader of the witches, but this decision turns out to be a mistake of uncharacteristic mercy: Oona calls upon Satan to "send [her] an avenger" to retaliate against Whitman and his family. The avenger turns out to be a *sidhe*, an evil spirit that possesses the Whitman groom, Roderick (Patrick Mower), turning him into what appears to be a bargain basement werewolf (the *sidhe*, incidentally, are Celtic faeries, not lycanthropes) who then stalks and slays the Whitmans one by one.

Hessler and Wicking unabashedly steal from earlier — and better — entries in the Poe series. Lord Edward presides over several elaborate balls attended by his wealthy friends; during these, he makes sport of impoverished villagers, teasing and abusing them (and killing them when it suits his mood). These scenes echo Price's activities as Prospero in *The Masque of the Red Death*, and the fact that his guests' merriment is frequently interrupted by the howl of the *sidhe* recalls Poe's short story, in which the tolling of Prospero's black clock causes "a brief disconcert of the whole gay company" attending the party (270). The fact than the possessed groomsman is named "Roderick" is an obvious allusion to *House of Usher*. Most significantly, the hunt for witches and the scenes of brutality associated with the treatment of suspects are obviously derived from *The Conqueror Worm* (although in this case the witches are genuine).

Unlike the Reeves film, however, the brutal scenes of torture and abuse in *Cry of the Banshee* do not underscore any significant intellectual or artistic point of view. The only purpose of these scenes, apparently, is to exploit the more controversial and provocative aspects of *The Conqueror Worm*. Without Reeves' grim artistry to justify the inclusion of such brutality, Hessler's movie becomes more sordid and repulsive than even AIP itself desired. The scenes in question emphasize the sexual abuse of women; many dresses are ripped, allowing flashes of bare breasts designed to whet the basest appetites of viewers. "According to the law," Lord Edward tells a suspect, "as a witch you are to be whipped through the streets until your back is bloody and then to look on the world through the stocks," a sentence carried out under the unblinking eye of Hessler's camera. The disturbing result of such artless sexual violence is that it seemingly "authorizes impulses toward violence in males and encourages impulses toward victimization in females," according to certain critical assumptions noted by Carol J. Clover (43).

The only potentially innovative notion in *Cry of the Banshee* pertains to the depiction of the Whitman clan as an example of social and sexual dysfunction. Lord Edward is even more intent on exploiting his power over the less fortunate than his cinematic model, Matthew Hopkins; Edward notes that "authority is the main point of government, and maintaining authority is the main purpose of law," but his authority over his own household seems to encourage debauchery among his children. Edward himself ridicules and torments a captured "heathen" girl, even going so far as to roughly kiss her before his amused party guests. The magistrate even looks at his emotionally fragile wife, Patricia (Essy Persson), in lascivious triumph, then turns back to assault his victim further. Lord Edward's concept of justice confirms the patriarchal hegemony and is used to viciously repress any indication of a feminine revision to the established order, whether it stems from the pagan celebrations of witches or the somewhat more conventional social norms that Patricia meekly represents.

Interestingly, *Cry of the Banshee* is one of the few horror films in which Price's character fathers children — and the only one in which a Price character has more than one child or a male offspring. Given the boorishness of their father, it is unsurprising that the Whitman children imitate his behavior, particularly favored son Sean (Stephan Chase), who spends most of his screen time forcing himself on serving wenches and even attempts to rape Patricia (his stepmother, as it turns out). Whitman's other son, Harry (Carl Rigg), returns from a college sojourn and initially seems somewhat distanced from his family's unpleasant behavior, yet he demonstrates affection for his sister, Maureen (Hilary Dwyer), that borders on the incestuous — affection that Maureen reciprocates in kind.

The single most thoughtful scene in the entire film features an argument among Edward, Harry, and Maureen that disintegrates into a shoving match between father and son. Suddenly the scuffle ends, and the three family members soon break out into laughter, amused at the realization that they are all truly alike. In its acknowledgment of the humor and the horror inherent in the Whitman family dynamic, the scene illustrates David J. Skal's observation that the decay of the family unit is one of the most pervasive thematic developments to emerge in the Vietnam era fantasy film. As Skal puts it, "The family is a sick joke, its house more likely to offer siege instead of shelter" (*Horror* 354) in the horror films of the 1970s (for example, Tobe Hooper's 1974 horror classic *The Texas Chain Saw Massacre*) and becomes the agent of destruction, not salvation, for traditional values and the "normal" social order.

Maureen is the nominal heroine of the project, ostensibly just another young woman menaced by a monster. However, Dwyer's performance hints at how closely Maureen takes after her father. Maureen is a stubborn, haughty young woman, her superiority over the villagers a perhaps unconscious assumption derived from her father. Like Edward and her brothers, Maureen displays a profoundly active sexuality; she is depicted as being the aggressor in her affair with Roderick. In their first scene together they recline in the woods, and in other scenes they are in bed together; in all of these scenes, Maureen cuddles with her lover in positions of repose indicative of postcoital bliss. While Maureen makes an effort to be more discreet about her sexual activities than her male relatives — a nod towards the sexist double standard of the period — she is nevertheless comparatively bold. While she seems genuinely fond of her "groom" — a most intriguing title for the possessed servant—she ultimately sides with her father: at the film's climax, Maureen saves Edward from Roderick's attack by shooting her lover in the face.

The entire Whitman family ultimately pays the price for their embrace of their father's misdeeds. They are all killed by the *sidhe*, although we don't see Edward himself die. Price's character is still alive at the end; having insisted on seeing Roderick a final time, the patriarch visits the cemetery and insists on opening his erstwhile servant's coffin, which is empty. Whitman flees to his carriage, only to find Harry and Maureen murdered in his absence by the still lively Roderick, who takes the reins and drives Whitman into the forest towards an unknown fate. The evil he has practiced and encouraged among his offspring has apparently consigned Edward Whitman to a fate worse than death.

In this, her third and final appearance alongside Vincent Price, Hilary Dwyer achieves a record of sorts: she becomes Price's most frequent leading lady (in horror movies, at any rate). Furthermore, the actress plays significantly different roles in each production, moving on from Price's victim in *The Conqueror Worm* to his wife in *The Oblong Box* before winding up as his daughter in *Cry of the Banshee*. This variety of relationships within Dwyer's

roles was not lost on the horror star; the actress recalled that Price joked, "If I get to play his mother, we'd get married" (qtd. in Halligan 210). Dwyer's presence logically reflects her membership in the Reevesian "stock company" and potent chemistry with Price, but it also establishes her onscreen persona as a reflection — and refutation — of the Price persona. Innocent where Price is corrupt in *The Conqueror Worm*, young where he is older in *The Oblong Box*, and daughter to his father in *Cry of the Banshee*, Dwyer comes to represent the conflicts inherent in constructs of male-female relationships whether adversarial, romantic, or filial in nature.

There is no question that Michael Reeves helmed one of the most effective and aesthetically rich of Vincent Price's horror movies. Whether or not *The Conqueror Worm* is rightfully classed among the Poe adaptations may be debatable, but whether or not the

A rare shot of the *sidhe*, one of the least convincing monsters in horror movie history, from *Cry of the Banshee* (1970). Sadly, a lame makeup job is far from the film's worst deficiencies.

film was appropriately retitled for American consumption is not. How high Reeves' reputation may have soared had he completed more films is impossible to determine, but it seems likely the tragic director would have amounted to more than a footnote in British film history. Yet Reeves' reputation is not disputed; his one fully realized feature continues to elicit commentary — positive and negative — years after its creation, and his influence on screen violence is clear. It is perhaps unfortunate that the horror films made by AIP shortly after the filmmaker's demise so crudely exploit the very elements that Reeves handled which such sensitivity, but diluted or not, they remain the clearest examples of Michael Reeves' cinematic legacy.

Triple Distilled Horror
Scream and Scream Again (1970)

While many of Vincent Price's horror films presented the actor in some variation on his *Dragonwyck* character — a Gothic aristocrat — in the eyes of some fans he remains more immediately associated with the "mad doctor" archetype. Price's knack for portraying medical madmen was established early in his career, going back at least as far as *Shock* (1946). Indeed, the number of films featuring Price as an insane or criminal physician, scientist, or scholar slightly exceeds the number of films featuring Price as a Poesque protagonist — and by a considerable degree if one includes his sympathetic turns in films like *The Fly* (1958) and his comic turns in movies like *Dr. Goldfoot and the Bikini Machine* (1966), to say nothing of his many TV roles (dramatic and comedic) in which he appeared as a "doctor" type. It is as a very daft scientist indeed that Price appears in *Scream and Scream Again* (1970), one of the most bizarre and misunderstood productions in the Merchant of Menace's career — or anybody's career, for that matter.

Based on a 1966 pulp novel called *The Disorientated Man* by "Peter Saxon" (a house pseudonym), *Scream and Scream Again* marks the first time Price was billed alongside England's leading horror stars of the period, Christopher Lee and Peter Cushing. Such a casting coup might seem like a horror fan's dream come true, but the three stars don't all appear together in a single scene (and Cushing's third-billed role is in fact a cameo, with neither Price nor Lee anywhere in sight) in what must be one of the great missed opportunities of fantasy cinema. Interestingly, the film also marks the first and only time Price appears in a production from Amicus (in collaboration with AIP), England's greatest purveyor of horror films after Hammer. Upon its release, *Scream and Scream Again* earned more money than any previous Amicus effort, although nobody at either Amicus or AIP seemed able to understand why (Nutman 71). The reasons, however, are pretty obvious in hindsight: regardless of their actual screen time, the movie still boasts three of scary cinema's leading names — hence the pun contained in the film's promotional copy, which promised "triple distilled horror" — and it remains a unique and fascinating (if often vexing) exercise in genre-blending 40 years after its creation.

Scream and Scream Again opens with a long shot of a jogger (Nigel Lambert) running along a busy London street to the accompaniment of an incongruously peppy jazz score (courtesy of David Whitaker). At intervals the screen freezes on the jogger (unnamed in the movie but called Ken Sparten in the novel) as credits appear. By the end of the credits, the jogger has collapsed. He wakes in a mysterious hospital bed, attended by a silent nurse (Uta Levka) who provides him with no clue as to the nature of his confinement. The jogger throws back his blanket to discover that one of his legs has been amputated at the knee.

The film cuts to an unnamed totalitarian state (but clearly identified as East Germany in the book), where an operative named Konratz (Marshall Jones) reports to his superior, Schweitz (Peter Sallis). Schweitz is displeased to learn that Konratz somehow knows about a super-secret surveillance project. Before Schweitz can have Konratz arrested, the operative kills his superior with some kind of nerve pinch (which, according to the novel, induces blood clots).

The film cuts again, this time to the scene of a vicious sex murder. Hard-boiled Detective Superintendent Bellaver (Alfred Marks) is disgusted by the violence of the act and traces the victim back to her employer, Dr. Browning (Vincent Price). Bellaver and his officers arrange a meeting with Browning, who is horrified to hear the grim details of the crime. During an autopsy, Professor Kingsmill (Kenneth Benda) and his young assistant, David Sorrel (Christopher Matthews), discover that the victim's injuries include two odd punctures on her arm.

From this point on, the film switches back and forth between the three disparate storylines. More and more of the jogger's body is removed, and Konratz rapidly advances through the hierarchy of his nation's quasi-military command structure by killing the officials above him, including Major Benedek (Peter Cushing), who wishes to remove Konratz because his propensity for torture "has been taken to an unnecessary and gruesome extreme" in a case involving a young girl trying to flee the country (Yutte Stensgaard). A brooding young man named Keith (Michael Gothard) turns out to be the sex maniac Bellaver seeks — and like a vampire, he drinks his victim's blood.

Eventually the various plot strands start to come together after Keith is finally cornered and handcuffed to a police car — only to tear his own hand off and flee across the countryside. Tracked to a barn on Dr. Browning's property, Keith commits suicide by throwing himself into a convenient vat of acid. Bellaver wants to question Browning further, but he is abruptly ordered to close the case after Konratz shows up in London and offers intelligence specialist Fremont (Christopher Lee) a captured British spy in exchange for every scrap of evidence relating to the "vampire murders." Dr. Sorrel has examined Keith's severed hand and discovered it is composed largely of an unknown synthetic substance. In spite of Bellaver's orders to forget the matter, Sorrel and policewoman Helen Bradford (Judi Bloom), who has survived an earlier encounter with Keith, attempt to investigate Browning's laboratory. Browning captures Sorrel and explains that Keith and others like him are cybernetic beings — incredibly strong "composites" made up of various body parts, including the jogger's, à la the Frankenstein Monster — that Browning has created. The mad scientist intends for his race of perfect beings to eventually assume control of the planet.

At first, Browning seems to want Sorrel to join him in his scheme to populate the world with artificial supermen, but when Browning announces his plan to put Helen's brain in a composite body, Sorrel tries to stop him. However, Browning himself is a composite — "You didn't think I was doing this alone?" he asks Sorrel as he overpowers the younger physician. Before the operation can continue, Browning is interrupted by the arrival of Konratz, who is also a composite. Konratz announces that the attention the vampire killer has brought to the public has compromised the project's security; he intends to destroy all evidence of the project in England, including Browning. The two composites fight, and Konratz winds up submerged in Browning's acid vat, which has been moved into the laboratory.

During the struggle, Sorrel and Helen manage to flee. Outside the house, they run into Fremont, who tersely orders them to wait in the car. Fremont makes his way to Browning's laboratory, where by force of will alone he compels the doctor to destroy himself in the acid. When Fremont returns to the vehicle, Sorrel asks, "Is it all over, sir?" Grimly Fremont replies, "It is only just beginning" as the film ends with yet another freeze frame.

As the above synopsis attests, *Scream and Scream Again* is a complicated and complex motion picture that borrows liberally from any number of generic models. In this sense, it remains one of a kind in the annals of cinema history: it is the only police procedural/Cold War espionage thriller/vampire shocker/serial killer mystery/science fiction film ever made. Furthermore, the involvement of various high-ranking government officials from all over Europe in a secret plot to take over the world identifies the film as a conspiracy thriller, one that looks back to *The Manchurian Candidate* (1962) while simultaneously prefiguring the paranoia of TV's *The X-Files* (1993–2002). Like Browning's composite creations, *Scream and Scream Again* is a patchwork of many different parts.

Vincent Price has frequently been accused of playing his horror roles tongue-in-cheek and of deliberately camping up his performances. While this charge is sometimes overstated, Price's turn as Dr. Browning is pretty over-the-top. When he is informed that one of his domestics has been raped and murdered, Browning responds, "Oh, that's terrible! Perfectly terrible!" in an exaggerated tone that suggests annoyance far more than sympathy. Later on, Browning acts like an overeager schoolboy when he offers to show Sorrel his work. "As a doctor, I think you're going to be fascinated with what I'm trying to do," Browning beams, adding ominously, "but once you fully understand, your life will have to wind down a very different road." Perhaps the most florid line follows Sorrel's observation that Browning is attempting to create a "super race." "Well, yes," Browning replies, "but not an *evil* super race." The emphasis Price places on the word "evil" underscores the essential silliness of the line.

These and other lines are certainly exaggerated, and many critics have opined that Price's deliberately camp approach to parts in such films as *Scream and Scream Again* masks his professional frustration and lack of respect for the low-budget horror fare in which he found himself typecast. It may well be true that Price felt he was capable of much better things and longed for better roles in higher profile movies, but there is one important point to keep in mind regarding his performance as Dr. Browning: the character is as mad as a hatter and *needs* to be played with a degree of exaggeration. When Sorrel remarks that Browning's attempts to create life are "the old mad scientist's dream," he speaks the truth. Only a madman would attempt such a thing, a fact that Price recognizes,

Poster art for *Scream and Scream Again* (1970), the only police procedural/Cold War espionage thriller/vampire shocker/serial killer mystery/science fiction film ever made.

consciously or not, and therefore he plays the part as he understands such a character ought to be portrayed.

In fact, Browning's eroded mental state is particularly interesting given that the deranged scientist is strangely naïve and idealistic. Browning truly believes he is working on a noble project, and he is shocked and demoralized when he realizes that other members of the conspiracy don't share his cockeyed dream of a better world. As Konratz attempts to destroy Browning's work, the scientist comments angrily, "You've turned every scientific advance into a weapon" before attacking his opponent. A few minutes later, Browning protests to Fremont that "we" aren't perfect and can be corrupted. Instead of sharing Browning's desire to track down and reform the corrupt composites, Fremont simply gets rid of the immediate problem — Browning himself.

As evidenced by his obsession to build synthetic people out of spare parts stolen from unwilling donors and his naïve expectation that those around him share his romantic vision, Browning is detached from reality. These are qualities taken directly from Saxon's novel. In the book, the doctor is named Malcolm Sanders and prattles on about how his process is "'a boon to mankind. Think of the race of super beings we shall be able to create. Not singly, but in vast numbers'" (Saxon 139). Elsewhere, Sanders insists that his artificial people must be perfect, hence the need to take the best elements from his victims and discard the rest.

Yet for all his insistence on perfection, Sanders continually takes shortcuts when it suits him. For example, the silent nurse, Jane, is black in the novel. However, Sanders admits to Dr. Pine (as Sorrel is called in the book) that he got "impatient" with a lack of suitable black body parts, so he has grafted Jane's head, arms and legs to a Caucasian trunk "so neatly to the milk-white torso that a quick glance [gives] the impression that Jane [is] wearing a white swimsuit" (Saxon 141). Unfortunately, the idea that Jane is a transracial composite is dropped from the film; such a startling image would be quite in keeping with the conspiratorial and paranoid mood. In any case, this odd detail in the novel underscores the point that while Sanders insists on utter perfection in his creations, he doesn't always take the time to uphold his own standard of excellence. This inconsistency is further evidence of Sanders' shaky mental state.

What finally becomes clear in both the novel and the film is that the composites are nowhere near as perfect as they claim to be. Thus in the film Keith is an amoral serial killer with vampiric tendencies, Konratz is a brutal assassin who gets sadistic joy from killing and torturing people, and Browning is a well-meaning but unrealistic lunatic. These aberrations among featured characters suggest innate shortcomings among others of the so-called "perfect race," which leads to an inevitable conclusion: the composites are just as imperfect as humans. This conclusion reveals a level of ironic horror to the conspiracy at the root of *Scream and Scream Again* — even if the composites did succeed in taking over the world, it is impossible for the dream of order and perfection Browning espouses to ever come true.

The female characters in *Scream and Scream Again* are pretty typical horror film tropes. They exist as victims of the murderous Keith and the sadistic Konratz, except for Browning's minion, Jane, and plucky policewoman Helen Bradford. Yet Jane demonstrates very little individuality or autonomy; she speaks only a few words of minor dialogue in the film (and is completely silent in the book). She is little more than a robot dispatched to do Browning's will, as when she breaks into police station to steal Keith's severed hand from the lab where Kingsmill and Sorrel have been studying it. Interestingly, Jane kills a female officer who surprises her in the middle of the theft, which proves that Jane is as homicidal as the other composites.

As for Helen, she at least survives the events of the film (in the book the vampire killer, who calls himself Kenneth, manages to kill her before his arrest). It is significant that she is recruited for the undercover mission to lure the vampire killer primarily because she is pretty. Helen is the girlfriend of another officer, Griffin (Julian Holloway), who is extremely reluctant to let his "old woman" be exposed to danger. In one scene, Griffin watches unhappily as Sgt. Joyce (Clifford Earl) places tracing equipment in Helen's clothes and even tries to stick a device down the front of her pants — and effort the young woman quickly rebuffs.

While listening in on Helen's encounter with Keith, Joyce and other cops snicker and make jokes, rebuffing Griffin's urging to interrupt the scene by telling him to let her have "fun." In effect, Helen's comrades allow Keith to nearly asphyxiate her because they want the cheap thrill of hearing her engage in sexual activity with a psychotic murderer. The implication is that women in *Scream and Scream Again* are already depersonalized long before Dr. Browning operates on them; their body parts, particularly their sex organs, are significant only for the perverse pleasures they provide to killers and cops alike.

It is true that Helen does accompany Dr. Sorrel to investigate Browning's workshop, but in typical horror film tradition she is almost immediately captured and becomes Browning's next potential project. Browning notes that he wishes to place the policewoman's brain in a female body he has recently completing, which raises an intriguing question: had the operation in fact been completed, what would have happened next? Would Browning be able to control the composite with Helen's brain? Would she have revolted against the scientist — perhaps even possess the physical strength to overwhelm him? Given the difficulty other mad scientists of the movies have had when it comes to controlling contrary female creations — see Peter Cushing's problems with Susan Denberg in *Frankenstein Created Woman* (1967) or how Natasha Henstridge deals with her makers in *Species* (1995) — it is quite possible Browning would have been in trouble even if Konratz hadn't shown up.

The narrative structure of *Scream and Scream Again* is fascinating to contemplate. A number of mainstream productions have similar interweaving plotlines, such as the Academy Award winning *Crash* (2005), but few other horror and science fiction projects attempt such ambitious storytelling. Here the credit belongs to writer Christopher Wicking, who substituted his script at the last minute when AIP executive Louis M. Heyward tossed out Amicus co-producer Milton Subotsky's unacceptable screenplay (Nutman 68). Wisely, Wicking went back to Saxon's source novel, changing most of the characters' names and jettisoning an explanation that alien invaders are at the center of the conspiracy — a change that Christopher Lee apparently never quite grasped, as years later he recalled that Price, Cushing and himself were supposed to be playing aliens (Meikle 163). Otherwise, however, Wicking's script is remarkably faithful to *The Disorientated Man*.

The complexity of the story Wicking and director Gordon Hessler attempt to tell would be daunting to any production team, and the makers of *Scream and Scream Again* don't completely succeed in wrapping up the proceedings. Viewers who haven't read the book — in other words, the vast majority of viewers — are surely confused when Konratz suddenly appears in England for his meeting with Fremont. For that matter, it is not entirely clear why Fremont shows up at Browning's house at the film's climax. Is he a composite as well? If not, is he still part of the conspiracy, or is he working against it? And how, exactly, does he have the power to make Browning destroy himself in the acid vat? In the novel, the alien scientist uses hypnotic suggestion to control both humans and composites (Saxon 143), but nowhere in the film is it made clear that Browning, Fremont, or anybody else has similar mental powers.

In his study of Amicus productions, Philip Nutman refers to disagreements about the film's budget and editing schedule between "Deke" Heyward and Milton Subotsky (70). Perhaps these disagreements contributed to the confusion and continuity errors in the final cut. When the police pursue Keith in a high-speed car chase, both the cops and the killer pass the same cars over and over again. Several characters, such as Helen and Sylvia (fourth-billed Judy Huxtable), one of Keith's victims, are never clearly referred to by name, and Konratz is often called "Konrad." Peter Cushing's Major Benedek refers to Schweitz as "Sallis" — the actor who plays the character — while in the movie's trailer, Marshall Jones is misidentified as Cushing in a stunning editorial faux pas.

The continuity errors and unexplained plot points in *Scream and Scream Again* have earned the film plenty of ire from critics and fans alike. Leonard Maltin dismisses the film as "tired" and "confusing" (1159); echoing the complaints of horror fans who decry the wasted opportunity to team up Price, Lee, and Cushing, Denis Meikle asserts that the movie would be more effective had the horror stars' parts been played by other actors (163). As the mixed-up credits in the trailer suggests, at the very least Peter Cushing should have played Konratz to Lee's Fremont (or vice

Dr. Browning (Vincent Price) makes a point in Gordon Hessler's *Scream and Scream Again* (1970).

versa), which would have brought the terror trio together at the climax. Even Deke Hey-ward admitted to bringing the horror stars together at the last minute solely "to take advantage of the names, for marquee value" and regardless of their limited screen time (qtd. in Nutman 68).

Yet in spite of the many shortcomings and squandered opportunities, there is some-thing inherently powerful about *Scream and Scream Again*. It has a very small but devoted cult following, including those who admire the Amen Corner, a successful British rock band who appear as themselves in club scenes and sing two songs, including one called "Scream and Scream Again." Allegedly the great German director Fritz Lang admired the picture, perhaps because it reminded him of his own conspiracy-laden films such as the Dr. Mabuse series. Proponents of the film point to the sheer audacity of the plot and acknowledge the film's dreamlike qualities. Especially in the depiction of the jogger's grad-ual and unexplained dismemberment, *Scream and Scream Again* is truly nightmarish, even hallucinatory.

Although not regarded as either a critical or fan favorite, director Hessler adds a number of bold flourishes to the picture, including some disturbing close-ups and effective use of hand-held cameras. These touches greatly contribute to the sense of waking night-mare that permeates the film. Perhaps the most accurate description of the film's power comes from a cotemporary reviewer for *The Los Angeles Times*, who claimed *Scream and Scream Again* is "infinitely more terrifying than any of the Gothic witchery of *Rosemary's Baby*" and concluded that Hessler's film "is a minor masterwork of style and suspense" (qtd. in Nutman 71).

A Strange Presence Even in Death

The Abominable Dr. Phibes (1971) and
Dr. Phibes Rises Again! (1972)

By 1970, it was obvious that AIP's Poe series was out of steam. In that year, the publicity department shamelessly promoted *Cry of the Banshee* as a Poe adaptation even though there wasn't a Poe work by that title, much less any tentative thematic association with the writer's output as suggested by *The Conqueror Worm*. Vincent Price was himself growing weary of his typecasting as a horror star and was particularly unhappy with the overall quality of his AIP material, which he frankly dismissed as "crap" in a letter to his agent (qtd. in Williams 44). It was obvious that the King of Horror (and his devoted audience) needed a change of pace. Fortunately that change came in the fall, as Price began production on what would become one of his landmark films, *The Abominable Dr. Phibes* (1971). This blend of horror and humor, so perfectly attuned to the actor's unique screen persona, has also earned a place among the best dark comedies in screen history.

The year is 1925, and prominent London doctors are being murdered in various ghastly ways. Dr. Dunwoody (Edward Burnham) is devoured by starving bats, and psychiatrist Dr. Hargreaves (Alex Scott), a self-proclaimed "head shrinker," finds his own skull fatally reduced when he dons an opulent, constricting frog mask. The body of Dr. Longstreet (Terry-Thomas) is discovered drained of blood. Inspector Trout (Peter Jeffrey) of Scotland Yard quickly realizes there is a pattern to the murders, but his superiors, Chief Inspector Crow (Derek Godfrey) and Superintendent Waverley (John Cater), are skeptical. After consulting with a rabbi (Hugh Griffith), Trout ascertains that the murders are based on the G'Tach — the Biblical curses visited upon the pharaohs for keeping the Israelites in bondage. With the assistance of Dr. Vesalius (Joseph Cotten), Trout determines that the surgical team that attended young Victoria Regina Phibes (Caroline Munro) in her last illness has been marked for death — but by whom? Victoria's husband, musician and theologian Anton Phibes, reportedly died in a car crash while trying to get back to his ailing wife, and there are no living relatives who might conceivably seek revenge on the doctors — of whom, incidentally, Dr. Vesalius was the leader.

Of course, Dr. Phibes isn't really dead — not entirely, at any rate. Although horribly mutilated in the crash — his face has been destroyed, he must eat and drink through a hole in the side of his neck, and he uses his "knowledge of music and acoustics to recreate [his] voice" electronically—Phibes is alive and well enough to spend years plotting his revenge. As portrayed by Vincent Price, Phibes is both brilliant and deranged, a mournful, lovesick widower who uses his familiarity with the Bible to give a suggestion of divine intervention at work in his pointedly Old Testament-style pursuit of justice. Assisted by the beautiful but mute Vulnavia (Virginia North), Phibes successfully dispatches his victims one-by-one, each murder more inventive than the last. Thus Dr. Hedgepath (David Hutcheson) is pelted to death with ice chips in his own car, a reference to the curse of hail, while Dr. Kitaj (Peter Gilmore) crashes his personal airplane when rats attack.

Trout and his assistant, Sgt. Schenley (Norman Jones), do manage to reach Dr. Whitcombe (Maurice Kaufmann) before Phibes does, but, in the film's most outrageous set piece, Whitcombe dies anyway, impaled on a brass unicorn's horn fired via catapult from across the street (an allusion to the curse of beasts). An attempt to protect Nurse Allen (Susan Travers) is similarly in vain; while she is sleeping and a policeman stands outside her door, Phibes cuts a hole through her bedroom ceiling and douses her with green liquid, then releases a swarm of locusts to strip the flesh from her skull. Only Dr. Vesalius remains of the surgical team's nine members (one surgeon, Dr. Thornton, is stung to death by bees — thus covered with boils, another Biblical curse — before the film opens). Yet there are two curses left — the death of the first-born and the plague of darkness. Which is it to be?

It turns out that Phibes has a particularly diabolical fate in mind for Vesalius. The mad musician kidnaps the surgeon's son, Lem (Sean Bury), and performs an operation of his own, planting a small key over the boy's heart. Having summoned Vesalius to his secret lair, Phibes explains that the physician has six minutes to operate and remove the key, which must unlock the operating table to which Lem is shackled. If Vesalius fails to free his son in time, acid will rain down and disfigure the boy. "He will have a face like mine!" proclaims Phibes, who removes his realistic (if somewhat immobile) makeup to reveal his horribly burned true visage, a revolting human skull.

Trout and the other policemen arrive, and Vesalius manages to free Lem in the nick of time (Vulnavia, however, stumbles into the acid stream and is apparently killed). Phibes plays his elaborate organ, which doubles as an elevator to the basement. Phibes sequesters himself in a hidden tomb under the floor, where another of his fantastic inventions replaces his blood with embalming fluid. Accompanied by Victoria's carefully preserved corpse, Phibes eludes the mystified authorities. Vesalius remarks that one curse (darkness) is still left. "Well, he'll be working on it—wherever he is," Trout replies, as the closing credits begin to roll to the tune of "Over the Rainbow." The film fades out to the sound of Price's mischievous chuckle.

At first glance, *The Abominable Dr. Phibes* sounds quite gruesome; apparently the original screenplay by James Whiton and William Goldstein placed more emphasis on screams than laughs. That Phibes and Vulnavia are at least partially as artificial as their private fantasy world is strongly suggested, and this suggestion survives in some of the film's promotional materials, which include references to Phibes being a literally self-made man. According to William N. Harrison,

The humor evident throughout much of the film is not evident in the original script....
Phibes (referred to as Pibe) performs the same ritual murders but with several changes....
Vesalius hypothesizes that a man as badly disfigured as Pibe must be in terrible, constant
pain, and must require regular injections of powerful painkillers.... The original concept of
Vulnavia ... is that she is a windup robot ... covered in real flesh. Pibe's other robots, the
Clockwork Wizards, are far more versatile than in the film, defending the Pibe mansion
against the police, using their instruments as weapons. Pibe himself is implied to be less
human and leaks oil when shot by police [8–9].

While the initial script was conceived as a more straightforward horror film, it nevertheless included some slight hints of the broad approach the final production would
take. According to Denis Meikle, Whiton and Goldstein depicted Phibes escaping from
the police via hot-air balloon at the film's climax (170); an echo of this idea survives in
the form of one of Trout's musings, when at one point he admits he wouldn't put it past
Phibes to use a balloon to assist in his invasion of Nurse Allen's hospital.

It seems that the original screenplay, then, unconsciously foreshadows the slasher
films of the 80s. Interestingly, the notion of a madman using a series of elaborate "theme
murders" would be revisited in David Fincher's *Se7en* (1995), wherein the conceit is played
completely straight. In Fincher's film, psychotic killer "John Doe" (Kevin Spacey) looks
to the Seven Deadly Sins to provide inspiration for his bizarre murder spree. It seems
likely that Fincher and his screenwriter, Andrew Kevin Walker, recognized the disturbing
possibilities inherent in a serious take on the *Phibes* storyline.

Whatever the original intentions of the screenwriters, once AIP hired Robert Fuest,
a former set designer and veteran TV director (*The Avengers*), to helm the picture, *The
Curse of Dr. Phibes* (as it was then called) became something else again. Fuest brought in
Brian Clemens and Albert Fennell, his collaborators from *The Avengers*, to provide uncredited script doctoring and producing assistance, respectively (Meikle 176). The director
quickly realized the comedic potential of the project, wisely choosing to make the film
both a tribute to and a parody of the kind of old-fashioned shocker that had become a
trademark for both Price and AIP. Furthermore, hitherto unexplored elements of Price's
multifaceted public image were incorporated into the characterization.

For example, following the murder of Dr. Longstreet, Phibes walks past a painting
on his victim's wall and then returns briefly for a second look. The disparaging glance
Phibes throws towards Longstreet's corpse before departing fully conveys his negative
opinion of Longstreet's taste. Later Phibes is depicted in a cook's apron, fussily throwing
out the less appetizing Brussels sprouts from which he is distilling the locust bait that he
will shortly use on Nurse Allen. These nods to Price's real life are what make *The Abominable Dr. Phibes* "an effective horror thriller and self-conscious play on Price's dual per-
sonae" as both horror star and aesthete (Worland 32).

The fact that Anton Phibes continues to pine for his dead wife and even keeps her
perfectly embalmed body around is a direct reference to the earlier Poe series, particularly
The Tomb of Ligeia. The apostrophes Phibes recites to his beloved strengthen this connection to the earlier films; they also recall such famous Poe poems as "The Raven" and
"To One in Paradise." For example:

My love, sweet queen and noble wife,
I alone remain to bring delivery of your pain.
Severed, my darling, too quickly from this life
Of fires drawn and of memories met,
I shall hold our two hearts again in single time.

Of course, Poe never added promises of vengeance to his poetry, although the quest for extreme revenge is incorporated into such stories as "The Cask of Amontillado" and is certainly a recurring theme in Price's Poe adaptations. Thus it is appropriate that Phibes demands personal satisfaction for the wrongs he perceives:

Nine killed you! Nine shall die
And be returned your loss.
Nine killed you! Nine shall die!
Nine times nine!
Nine eternities in doom!

Other references to Price as pop culture icon abound. While the actual number of mad or evil doctors and scientists Price had portrayed in earlier films is relatively small, by the early 70s his status as the Horror King automatically presumed his expertise in such roles even as it exaggerated their frequency in the public's mind. Even the name of Mrs. Phibes — Victoria Regina — serves (perhaps unconsciously) as an allusion to Vincent Price's first great acting triumph, opposite Helen Hayes on Broadway in the 1930s. It is ultimately impossible to imagine any actor besides Vincent Price in the title role, which may well explain why no studio has yet attempted to mount an actual remake of *The Abominable Dr. Phibes.*

Certainly Price's particular style of acting lends itself particularly well to the material. Because Phibes can only speak with mechanical assistance, Price actually delivers fewer lines here than in most of his other horror films, and when Phibes does speak, Price's legendary voice is electronically distorted. Though still recognizably Price's, the Phibes voice is harsh and cold, which makes the degree of expressiveness Price gets out of it all the more remarkable. The actor's penchant for exaggerated eye movements — dismissed in other films as "eye rolling" by some critics — is in fact necessary for the Phibes role since the character's face is supposed to be artificial. Price manages to convey the character's rage and insanity almost exclusively through his eyes; perhaps more significantly, Price also manages to display the character's genuine devotion and tenderness toward his dead wife in the same manner.

The degree of sympathy that Price brings to the role is a key ingredient in the film's enduring appeal. While Fuest's highly stylized direction and Brian Eatwell's opulent set design nicely underscore the darkly comic aspects of the film, there is throughout a subtle but constant tone of lonely wistfulness. For all its dry jokes and sly witticisms, *The Abominable Dr. Phibes* is a profoundly romantic picture. As the film's most famous tag line, "Love means never having to say you're ugly" (a goof on the tag line from 1970's *Love Story*), suggests, Phibes' feelings for his beloved Victoria would be right at home in any standard tear-jerker. Yet it is precisely the legitimacy of those feelings that imbues the film with an emotional verisimilitude not found in many other so-called "black comedies."

In spite of the terrible crimes he commits, it is very easy to identify with Anton Phibes. That he truly loves Victoria is indisputable; her unexpected death has upset his sense of the orderliness of the universe, driving him insane and doubling the tragedy of the situation. Phibes pours out his lamentations to a slide show of Victoria's pictures, and he is depicted caressing her clothing, jewelry, and other mementoes. Though she is dead Phibes preserves her body and finally buries himself with it, suggesting a hint of necrophilia that is less disturbing than heartbreaking—a significant difference between suggestions of necrophilia in *The Tomb of Ligeia* and other Poe adaptations. His love for Victoria is so complete that it becomes almost palpable, which in turn makes his quest for vengeance seem almost reasonable under the circumstances.

Of course, the fact that almost all of Phibes' victims are portrayed as twits or scoundrels makes sympathizing with the maddened musicologist almost unavoidable. We get a sense that the world is better off without the pompous Dr. Whitcomb or the sex-obsessed Dr. Longstreet. It is only when he threatens a child that Phibes becomes a true monster, and even then he gives Vesalius' son "the same chance that [his] wife had." Once it is clear that Lem will survive the ordeal, it is again easy to root for Phibes as he entombs himself with Victoria and literally gets away with murder. Anton Phibes may be an anti-hero, but he is a carefully delineated and substantial one.

Considerable credit for this element of emotional substance must be paid to screen-writers James Whiton and William Goldstein. Fortunately the sympathy and understanding the screenwriters demonstrated for their bizarre protagonist were not jettisoned during shooting. In turn, a sense of the authors' original intentions can be surmised from the film's novelization, titled simply *Dr. Phibes*. Although the majority of movie novelizations are adapted into prose form by writers who have nothing to do with the original films, in this case Phibes' co-creator Goldstein was selected for the job. As a result, the novelization complements and expands the viewer's appreciation of the film. Goldstein's book provides interesting information, such as Phibes' genealogical descent (his family originated in Austria) and the first names of Trout (Harry), Vesalius (Henri), and other characters. Goldstein also devotes considerable effort to develop the characters of the victims, humanizing them almost as much as he does Phibes. However, it is the not-so-good doctor for whom Goldstein insists we still feel the greatest sympathy:

> [Phibes] moved about [Victoria's] possessions stiffly. Their nearness only seemed to have submerged his grief rather than deadened it. His gloved hands touched the furniture and traced futile patterns from piece to piece. Against their varied colors, against the vivacity of his young dead wife, he seemed to grow even more forlorn.... One can only approximate the perception of this ravaged, forlorn man as he lost himself again in the reaches of this strange domain on Maldine Square [65].

Thus the saga of Dr. Anton Phibes is in a very real sense a story of romantic love. However, the story is also romantic in the sense of its emphasis on strong emotions and in its veneration of the past. Phibes is nostalgic as well as lovesick, as demonstrated by his careful recreation of the home he shared with Victoria and even the café and ballroom where once he drank and danced with his wife. The film itself shares a romantic preoccupation with the past, which explains why the original script's undefined but presumably

Dr. Anton Phibes (Vincent Price) dances with Vulnavia (Virginia North), his ambivalent assistant, in *The Abominable Dr. Phibes* (1971).

modern setting has been replaced with Jazz Age London. The use of such Tin Pan Alley standards as "Darktown Strutter's Ball," "One for My Baby (And One More for the Road)," and "Over the Rainbow" adds to this bittersweet emphasis on the past (even when the use of such songs is anachronistic, as with the last two examples cited above). It is interesting that *The Abominable Dr. Phibes* does not share the traditional Gothic setting of Price's Poe films, but it nevertheless is grounded in a similar approximation of a bygone era—significantly, in this case, one well within living memory of many of the filmmakers and audience members.

The notion that women in Vincent Price's horror films are both victims and objects of veneration is apparent in *The Abominable Dr. Phibes*. Nurse Allen is the only female whom Phibes clearly victimizes, and Victoria is the one woman whom Phibes obviously venerates. Indeed, the casting of rising "scream queen" Caroline Munro is one of the more inspired elements in the film, for the actress boasts an uncommon combination of exotic beauty and "girl next door" charm. Victoria has "a strange presence, even in death," according to Vesalius, and thanks to Munro's embodiment it is quite believable that Victoria Phibes could drive a man to murderous distraction.

Be that as it may, there is an intriguing notion that Victoria is in a sense a victim of Phibes as well. In the film as released, the exact nature of Victoria's final illness is not specified. As Trout skims Victoria's medical report, he notes the "diagnosis" is "immediate radical resection" and then asks Vesalius what happened to the young woman. "We were too late," Vesalius replies, but a quick cut to one of Phibes' elegiac recitations interrupts Vesalius before he can explain himself. By contrast, Goldman's novelization explicitly states that Victoria suffered from "metastic [sic] carcinoma of the uterus" that required "ten hours of dissection" that proved useless (*Abominable*, 69–70). In other words, Victoria had uterine cancer, and the surgical team staged a desperate operation—presumably a full hysterectomy—in a vain attempt to save her life. This diagnosis is present in the original screenplay, which also features Vesalius' comment that "in cases like this it is often difficult to persuade the husband" that the sterilization of the wife is necessary (Harrison 8).

The idea that Phibes in some way delayed or interfered with the treatment for Victoria's medical condition, particularly for selfish reasons, would seriously compromise the audience's sympathy for the mutilated avenger but would be appropriate to the screenwriters' original vision of their antihero as a traditional villain. It is therefore understandable why the dialogue in question was excised from the film, but nevertheless a suggestion of guilt on Phibes' part remains. If Anton Phibes realizes that either directly or indirectly he contributed to his wife's demise, it is likely that he is consumed with guilt as well as rage and regret. In fact, it is possible that Phibes has repressed his sense of guilt to the extent that it has exacerbated his mental decline; it is likely that he has subconsciously transferred his guilt to Vesalius and the doctors, in turning leading to his bizarre revenge plot. The notion that Phibes inadvertently initiated the film's chain of events is both tragic and ironic.

It is significant that Victoria's condition involves her sexual and reproductive system. The potential loss of her ability to bear children is presumably the reason Phibes (in the original script) might have resisted the surgical recommendation, but it is also possible that Phibes, a confirmed aesthete, would associate the "mutilation" of Victoria's womb as an assault on the very standards of beauty and artistry that have always been so important to him. Moreover, the emphasis on Victoria as a vessel for reproduction suggests that Phibes, like many men of his era, may have valued his wife more as a commodity than a full partner in his life. Significantly, there is no mention in the script, the release print, or the novelization of Victoria having a say in whether or not she undergoes the operation. In a sense, Victoria is what in modern parlance is called a "trophy wife," a beautiful and charismatic young ornament in a wealthy, cultured older man's life. Considering that Victoria is perfectly preserved in Phibes' coffin for two, she can be considered a trophy wife in the most literal sense as well.

The importance of Victoria as both a symbol and an inspiration is obvious, but she is dead and thus does not take an active role in the film's plot. By contrast, Vulnavia is an active participant in the proceedings; indeed, it is apparent that Phibes could never achieve his elaborate plot without assistance. Vulnavia remains the most mysterious character in the film, and by keeping her motivations and origins a secret, the filmmakers make her particularly fascinating. Nevertheless, the audience cannot help but wonder: exactly why does Vulnavia help the demented musician? What is the exact nature of her relationship to Phibes? For that matter, what is Vulnavia's exact nature *period*?

These questions are left unanswered in both the film and Goldstein's novelization, although the original screenplay provides a few additional clues. William N. Harrison notes that originally Vulnavia was conceived as a flesh-covered robot of Phibes' own design (9). This concept makes sense given that Phibes himself was originally conceived as more mechanical than human; for that matter, the idea that Phibes and Vulnavia are mechanically enhanced suggests that they are both cyborgs, an excitingly futuristic notion to find in an otherwise period setting. The fact that Vulnavia never speaks during the film further suggests her artificial origins; in effect, she comes across as a more elaborate version of Dr. Phibes' Clockwork Wizards, functional but mute and devoid of intelligence or free will. Yet if Vulnavia is not a real person, why does she scream in horror and pain when showered with acid? Certainly she seems to have died as the film ends — but if she is truly dead, then how can she reappear, unharmed and unscathed, in the sequel?

It is also interesting to note that the name "Vulnavia" is similar to and suggestive of the name "Victoria." Furthermore, Vulnavia even resembles Victoria somewhat, suggesting yet another connection between the two women in Anton Phibes' life. If Vulnavia is an artificial construct, did Phibes model her on his late wife? If she is some kind of cyborg, is her flesh derived from Victoria, perhaps through some hitherto unknown process invented by Phibes to clone his beloved? The idea that Vulnavia is Phibes' daughter, either literally or figuratively, occurs, although it seems unlikely, given the film's chronology, that she is also Victoria's child. Thus the notion presents itself that Phibes fathered Vulnavia, perhaps providing the sperm to an unknown donor or to the hypothetical process of his invention. In turn, this notion recalls the alchemists of medieval times, who supposedly provided their own seed in an attempt to create artificial familiars to serve their needs. Given Phibes' awareness of history and theology, it is easy to imagine him imagining himself as a 20th century alchemist and Vulnavia as the homunculus of his own design.

The homunculus theory of Vulnavia's origin in turn suggests a sexual connection between Phibes and his assistant. This suggestion is pretty well spelled out in the film's most famous poster (itself derived from a publicity still), which depicts Phibes (sans makeup) in a passionate embrace with Vulnavia that never takes place in the movie itself. With her seemingly infinite wardrobe and her companionship on the dance floor, Vulnavia certainly acts like Phibes' girlfriend in many scenes. When she gazes at Phibes, there is an expression of devotion in her eyes that could be construed as romantic attraction. Perhaps most intriguingly, the unusual name "Vulnavia" suggests the word "vulva." However, there is no overt evidence of a romantic or sexual relationship between Phibes and Vulnavia. His assistant may provide chaste companionship for the bereaved murderer, but at no point does Dr. Phibes actually seem to take Vulnavia to bed. Of course, the fact that Phibes and Vulnavia never actually have sex does not eliminate the *suggestion* of sexual chemistry between the couple.

Whether Vulnavia is a human being, a mechanical being, or some combination of the two, she is clearly subservient to and completely controlled by Phibes. She exists only

Vincent Price and Virginia North demonstrate that "love means never having to say you're ugly" in a publicity still from *The Abominable Dr. Phibes* (1971). Interestingly, this scene does not appear in the film, as Price's Dr. Phibes is completely devoted to his dead wife, not North's Vulnavia, his mysterious assistant.

to serve and amuse him, and she is willing to die or be destroyed (temporarily, at least) in order to achieve Phibes' goals. However capable she may be in whatever fields of endeavor, Vulnavia is ultimately valued as a possession, not a person. In this sense, her similarity to Victoria persists: however well he treats them, both women are trophies in the self-made world of Dr. Anton Phibes, testimonies to his self-absorbed, narcissistic world view.

According to James Robert Parrish and Steven Whitney, *The Abominable Dr. Phibes* grossed $1.5 million (131), making it far more successful with audiences and critics alike than Price's last few vehicles for the studio. Therefore, production on a sequel began within a few months of the film's release. Unfortunately, the resulting picture, *Dr. Phibes Rises Again!* (an exclamation point appears on posters and in other publicity materials, as well as on various video releases, but not on the title card), failed to live up to expectations, bringing plans for a projected series of Phibes films to an abrupt end.

"The incredible legends of the abominable Dr. Phibes began a few short years ago," claims the opening narration by an uncredited Gary Owens (himself a legendary voice performer in cartoons and fondly remembered as the announcer on TV's *Laugh-In*) as the original film is summarized in flashback. According to a subtitle, three years have passed, thus establishing the sequel as taking place in 1928. Specific astronomical configurations cause the apparatus that drained Phibes of his blood to re-activate, resulting in his re-animation. The mad musician announces to Victoria's corpse his plans to head for Egypt, where his pursuit of the legendary River of Life promises "the beginning of [their] greatest adventure," which will result in "resurrection for [Victoria] and eternal life for both of [them]." Phibes summons Vulnavia (this time played by Valli Kemp, replacing Virginia North), who inexplicably is alive and well following the acid bath she took in the previous film.

As he rises on his elevator-cum-organ, however, Phibes is chagrined to discover his house on Maldine Square has been demolished during his long nap. Amid the rubble he finds his safe, but the papyrus containing directions to the River of Life is missing. "What fiend has taken it?" Phibes wonders, immediately realizing that the thief can be "only one who seeks eternal life as I do — Biderbeck!" The film cuts to the fashionable home of Darius Biderbeck (Robert Quarry), who shows off the papyrus as he discusses his own planned expedition to a mysterious mountain in Egypt with his friend Ambrose (Hugh Griffith, returning from the first film, albeit in a different role).

"You're a strange man," Ambrose observes to his friend, noting that Biderbeck "[seems] obsessed with the mystical aspects of life." There's a good reason for Biderbeck to be obsessed with life; unknown to anyone, including his beloved Diana Trowbridge (Fiona Lewis), the wealthy antiquarian has been unnaturally extending his life and vitality for at least a hundred years, and his mysterious elixir is almost exhausted. Biderbeck, Ambrose, and Diana depart for a social engagement, leaving a manservant (Milton Reid) to keep an eye on the house and enjoy his employer's snooker table and liquor cabinet.

Unfortunately for the servant, Phibes and Vulnavia arrive, distracting him with a pair of ingenious mechanical snakes so that a real serpent can strike. When the frightened flunky tries to phone for help, a snake-shaped golden spike Phibes and Vulnavia have rigged up to the telephone punctures his skull. Phibes regains the papyrus, and Biderbeck summons Inspector Trout (Peter Jeffrey) to investigate. Although a bizarre murder has been committed, Biderbeck is more concerned with the theft: "Find the papyrus and doubtless that will lead you the killer," he petulantly points out to Trout, adding, "but find the papyrus first!"

Biderbeck and company continue with their planned voyage to Egypt, completely unaware that Phibes and Vulnavia have booked passage on the same vessel. When a drunken Ambrose stumbles across Victoria's body and some clockwork musicians in the ship's hold, he winds up stuffed in an oversized bottle and tossed overboard thanks to Phibes. During the subsequent search for the missing man, the ship's captain (Peter Cushing) discreetly inquires of Biderbeck, "I don't suppose [Ambrose] ever touched the bottle?" The "drunk in a bottle" washes up on an English beach, and soon Trout and Superintendent Waverley (again played by John Cater) are on the case, interviewing Ambrose's cousin dotty cousin (Beryl Reid) and a chatty shipping agent (Terry-Thomas, who like Hugh Griffith returns from the original, albeit as a new character; evidently these actors were intended to play different roles in each of the Phibes sequels), which leads the police to plan their own trip to Egypt.

Once in the desert, Biderbeck joins the rest of his team, including Hackett (Gerald Sim), Baker (Lewis Fiander), and Stewart (Keith Buckley). Biderbeck is angry because another expedition member, Shavers (John Thaw), has gone off on his own to explore the mountain. Unbeknownst to anyone in the party, Phibes and Vulnavia have already set up camp deep within the mountain, converting a pharaoh's hidden tomb into a makeshift headquarters. Phibes dispatches a hungry eagle to dispatch Shavers, whose mutilated corpse somehow turns up covered in sand in Diana's tent. Meanwhile, Phibes discovers a hidden sarcophagus, within which he finds a secret key. With Vulnavia's help he hides Victoria's body in the sarcophagus until the stars are in proper alignment, at which time the key can be used to unlock the gates to the River of Life.

Phibes passes the time killing off various members of the Biderbeck expedition in outlandish ways. Stewart is stung to death by dozens of scorpions; Baker is crushed in a gigantic vise of Phibes' design. "Whose mind could conceive of such a bizarre way to kill?" asks Biderbeck upon finding Stewart's swollen corpse, at which point the newly arrived Trout and Waverley try to explain the threat and persuade Biderbeck to leave. The explorer consents to send Diana away, accompanied by Hackett, but Biderbeck has discovered the sarcophagus and claimed the key, so he refuses to abandon his quest.

Biderbeck returns to the mountain, losing Trout and Waverley through a secret panel. The antiquarian finally confronts Phibes, who has eliminated Hackett and kidnapped Diana. Phibes explains that Diana will be killed unless the waters beneath her floating deathtrap recede—something that can only happen if the gates to the River of Life are opened, which requires the key now in Biderbeck's possession. Biderbeck parts with the key, muttering, "The devil take you, Phibes" as he does so. "The devil take me? Not for some considerable time, I trust!" is Phibes' sardonic reply.

Phibes opens the gate, accompanied by Vulnavia and Victoria's body as he floats down the river on an elaborate barge. Having freed Diana, Biderbeck attempts to join Phibes. As the gates slam shut in his face, Biderbeck pleads with Phibes to take him along. Diana arrives, accompanied by Trout and Waverley. "Don't worry darling; it's not the end of the world," Diana says comfortingly, even as Biderbeck rapidly ages and dies. Singing a few triumphant (if anachronistic) lyrics from "Over the Rainbow" as his rival perishes, Phibes drifts away, presumably to a new life with a revived Victoria and the faithful Vulnavia.

While a few critics have ranked the sequel higher than the original, such as Ron Pennington in his review for the *Hollywood Reporter* (qtd. in Williams 231), the majority of commentators (and audiences in general) agree that the second Phibes film is inferior to the first. In the rush to get the film made, the screenplay suffered accordingly. While Whiton and Goldstein turned in an initial script, it was soon rejected, leaving the creators of Dr. Phibes with a mere "based on characters created by" credit (although Goldstein at least was chosen to write a second novelization). Having successfully rewritten the first film's script, returning director Fuest took over the new screenplay; however, AIP insisted that veteran TV producer-writer Robert Blees collaborate with Fuest, and the results are uneasy at best. Blees had written several box office hits in the 50s, including *Magnificent Obsession* and *High School Confidential*, but by the early 70s AIP was using him as a sort of all-purpose script doctor, and his ideas never fully meshed with Fuest's approach. Apparently the two writers collaborated almost by long distance, as "Blees wrote his pages in the Hilton hotel, while Fuest wrote at home" (Meikle 180). As a result, enormous plot holes and general confusion reign supreme in *Dr. Phibes Rises Again!*

For example, the exact origins of Darius Biderbeck are never fully revealed. It is never clear exactly how he stumbled across his elixir of life or why he can't get more without going to Egypt — much less precisely how old he is. Sometimes it seems that Biderbeck's elixir might be derived from the River of Life itself, a notion further suggested (though not firmly established) in Goldstein's digressive novelization. Furthermore, Phibes immediately concludes that it is Biderbeck who has taken the papyrus from the safe, indicating that Phibes is fully aware of Biderbeck's pursuit of immortality. However, the film then establishes that Biderbeck keeps his prolonged life a secret from everyone, including Diana; even at the film's climax, neither Diana nor the authorities have learned that Biderbeck's expedition involves the search for immortality. How Phibes knows about Biderbeck and his quest is thus never explained.

Another serious miscalculation is Phibes' verbosity. In the first film, his dialogue is limited, and it appears that even with his artificial voice apparatus speaking is physically difficult for him. However, the protagonist never seems to shut up in *Dr. Phibes Rises Again!* He is constantly explaining himself to Vulnavia, to Victoria, and finally to Biderbeck. Even worse, in many scenes Phibes speaks without being plugged into his voice machine, which ought to be impossible. Apparently much of Price's dialogue was recorded later and edited into the final film as a substitute for scenes that were never shot or to explain a perplexing storyline that should have been less convoluted in the first place.

Perhaps the most serious problem with the script is Phibes' increasingly sadistic and homicidal personality. In the first film, Phibes has a definite (albeit misguided) motive for murder: his quest for vengeance. Nevertheless, he only kills those he holds directly responsible for Victoria's death. In the sequel, however, Phibes often kills unnecessarily; there is no reason whatsoever to kill Stewart and Hackett, for example, and it seems as if the papyrus could be recovered without slaying Biderbeck's servant. "So once more I have been forced to kill for you, Victoria," Phibes tells his dead wife in the aftermath, yet Phibes could have just as easily knocked the servant out as drive a golden spike through his skull! Ultimately Phibes emerges as a far less sympathetic character, which inadvertently makes Biderbeck far more heroic than he ought to be.

In spite of its many shortcomings, though, there is much to admire in *Dr. Phibes Rises Again!* The film is very funny, with a much broader sense of comedy than its predecessor. Phibes' deathtraps are even more outlandish, making the sequel far more blatantly campy than the original. Adding to the silliness is the fact that Phibes always seems to have the equipment available for an impromptu elaborate murder, even in the wilds of the Egyptian desert. There is no effort to explain how Phibes devised the scorpion chair he uses to trap Stewart, nor where he got the hollow dog statue (designed to resemble the RCA Victor mascot Nipper) into which he deposits the key that will release the hapless victim (who winds up breaking the statue and unleashing the live scorpions that kill him). Likewise, the mutilated musician happens to have an oversized industrial fan handy with which he creates an impromptu sandstorm to cover the noise of Baker's murder by vise — during which, incidentally, the title of the book Baker has chosen for bedtime reading can be plainly seen: *The Turn of the Screw!*

Such slapstick, while amusing, is ultimately less effective than the examples of dry British wit that abound. Trout and Waverley are completely ineffectual here, although Trout at least seems more or less competent in the first film (and Goldstein depicts the inspector as quite talented in the novelization). This time around, Trout seems to have completely given up: "Every time we've built a better mousetrap, Phibes has built a better mouse," he observes despairingly. Meanwhile, Superintendent Waverley becomes a complete parody of stuffy and uncomprehending officialdom, chastising Trout for wanting to investigate the mountain. "One needs a warrant to make a search," Waverly tartly points out, adding, "We can't go charging into someone else's mountain! This isn't Hyde Park!"

For all the inconsistencies and unexplained elements of their characterizations, Phibes and Biderbeck do come across as worthy adversaries for one another. Certainly Biderbeck has as much brains and talent as does Phibes and could be as much a boon to society as Phibes was before his accident, as indicated in a passage from the novelization, in which Biderbeck's first name is Jonathan, not Darius:

> No one really knew Jonathan Biderbeck although many sought his acquaintance. His poise, his bearing, the heat of his eyes and the trend of his voice in even the gentlest of conversation held out the hope of arenas of knowledge, vast recollections of delight, and a prescience of all that one questioned, all that one yearned to perceive. In a word, Jonathan Biderbeck was as timeless as all the vast pyramids, temples, and other funereal architecture of an Egypt that had been his obsession for the better part of a lifetime [Goldstein, *Rises*, 24].

Both are brilliant, proud men whose obsessions exemplify their unstable mental conditions. Biderbeck may appear to be sane, but ultimately he shares Phibes' impossible dream: to cheat reality itself by unnaturally prolonging or restoring life. "It is a pity in a way. We have so much in common," Phibes observes to his rival. "You flatter yourself" is Biderbeck's dismissive reply.

In spite of Biderbeck's skepticism, Phibes is correct when he notices that both men are motivated more by women than by their pursuit of eternal life. Like Phibes, Biderbeck is devoted to his beloved. Biderbeck truly loves Diana, telling her, "You're my whole life ... Please, darling, if you know nothing else, you must know that! Every move I make — everything — concerns our future!" When forced to choose between Diana and passage to the River of Life, Biderbeck ultimately chooses the girl, a decision that results in his doom.

Both troubled geniuses revere and adore their women, but both men also share the same sexist attitudes about their lovers. Both Phibes and Biderbeck unconditionally accept a worldview wherein women remain subordinate to men. Both insist on being in control at all times; in Biderbeck's case, this assumption of dominance contributes to his final fate. Over and over again, Biderbeck refuses to explain himself to Diana, thus failing to avail himself of whatever assistance and insight she might be able to provide. In spite of his protestations of love and devotion, Biderbeck does not believe his lover can be trusted with the knowledge of his true nature. Not knowing the true nature of the crisis they face, Diana cannot even adequately defend herself when Biderbeck is absent; her capture makes her a liability, and in trying to save her Biderbeck is destroyed.

The style of both movies lends itself to a "queer" (in both the sexual and alien/Other senses) reading and hints at the sort of gender ambivalence found in the Poe series which indirectly inspired the Phibes films. Harry M. Benshoff identifies *The Abominable Dr. Phibes* (and presumably its sequel) as "a genre-queering opus" intended "to invoke adulation of the clever mad doctor rather than pity for his victims" while implying sexual ambiguity through its elaborate Jazz Age setting and ostentatious Art Deco set and costume designs (210–211). Although Phibes is clearly established as heterosexual, his over-the-top methods of murder, often incorporating ridiculously impractical Rube Goldberg inventions, are certainly exaggerated enough to be campy. Furthermore, Phibes is a sort of late Edwardian cyborg, with much of the tissues and organs destroyed in the accident replaced with prosthetics. As a result, Phibes is "prototypically queer" in that his body is largely artificial (Benshoff 211). Notions of gender ambiguity, therefore, are tied to anxiety about the subversion of physical identity — an anxiety addressed in many of the earlier Poe adaptations, including *The Haunted Palace* (1963).

The elaborate sets are a highlight of both pictures and are a testament to the design sense of Brian Eatwell and the visual style of director Robert Fuest. Designed by Trevor Crole-Rees, the Phibes "skull face" makeup is one of the most memorable in horror film history, even though neither production utilizes it for more than a scene or two. The use of music in both films is noteworthy, with Basil Kirchin's original score in the first picture serving as an appropriate counterpoint to the pop standards that are the film's sonic highlight, particularly the wistful "Vulnavia's Theme." John Gale's score for the sequel makes excellent use of the Bach Singers, a choral group whose voices convey a sense of the ancient majesty and mystery of Egypt and suggest the outsized personalities of the film's protagonists. Interestingly, a soundtrack album resulted from the first film, although the vocal tracks are different (Paul Frees, who sings only "Darktown Strutter's Ball" in the film, provides the lyrics on the album, unwisely singing them in the style of such celebrities as W. C. Fields and Humphrey Bogart) and the title theme, a version of Mendelssohn's "War March of the Priests," is entirely absent. Fortunately, Perseverance Records released acceptable CDs of music from both films in 2003 and 2004.

Both films benefit from strong casts, even in small roles, with Price, of course, taking the lion's share of the credit with his funny, tragic, and frightening performance. It is a pity that the sequel's diminished box office returns, coupled with divisive internal politics at AIP (partners Samuel Z. Arkoff and James H. Nicholson parted company after the Phibes sequel, and Nicholson died of a brain tumor in late 1972) and Price's growing disenchantment with horror roles, ultimately prevented a third Phibes film. Until Price's death in 1993, rumors of a new Phibes picture popped up regularly, with such working titles as *The Brides of Phibes* and *Phibes Resurrectus*. At one point, Forrest J Ackerman, noted science fiction collector and editor of *Famous Monsters of Filmland* magazine, was in discussions to make a cameo appearance in the third film as a "double" for Phibes in one scene. Perhaps the most intriguing of these rumors involved the participation (via his

A new Vulnavia (Valli Kemp) joins Vincent Price for *Dr. Phibes Rises Again!* (1972).

one-time production company Laurel Entertainment) of legendary horror specialist George A. Romero, whose *Night of the Living Dead*, ironically, was one of the major texts that led the horror genre away from the classic Gothic shockers in which Vincent Price made his name (Gagne 194).

In any event, it is lamentable that Price never played his most famous horror role again. However, it seems likely that a remake will surface sooner or later. Given Hollywood's preference for remakes of and sequels to established properties, it's probably inevitable that Dr. Phibes will rise yet again someday, perhaps under the direction of a stylist such as Tim Burton (the notion of Johnny Depp playing his *Edward Scissorhands* co-star's former role for Burton is particularly intriguing). As Inspector Trout prophetically observes, "Oh, it's Phibes, all right, sir ... and he always comes back!"

17

The Temerity to Rewrite Shakespeare
Theater of Blood (1973)

Thanks to the success of the Phibes pictures, Vincent Price found himself enjoying a late career renaissance. Long known as an actor possessed of a broad sense of humor and willing to poke fun at his public persona, Price had been the perfect choice to send up horror films and himself in Robert Fuest's pair of revenge comedies. Playing Dr. Phibes had allowed Price to do something a bit different from the increasingly pedestrian faux-Poe Gothics that had been his bread-and-butter at AIP, but it was obvious that the studio would willingly consign the actor to yet another by-the-numbers horror franchise if given a chance, one that by virtue of already being a parody would deteriorate into formulaic claptrap even more quickly than had the Poe series. Price was experiencing a considerable degree of professional frustration in the early 1970s, a situation that would ameliorate itself only when Price broke with AIP once and for all.

Fortunately for the legendary horror man, an opportunity arose to explore the comedy-horror hybrid in a much more satisfactory way when United Artists agreed to distribute *Much Ado About Murder*, a sly variation on the Phibes formula that owed more to Shakespeare than to Poe. According to Victoria Price, her father had been approached by his "old friend and former agent, Sam Jaffe" (producer of the classic 1966 family film *Born Free*, not the popular character actor) for the starring role in the new film (278), which was directed by Douglas Hickox and written by Anthony Greville-Bell. Finally released under the more exploitative title *Theater of Blood* in 1973, the finished product is one of Vincent Price's best movies — and one of the best combinations of horror and humor ever filmed, period.

Having already added a pun on the Bard — "the Merchant of Menace" — to his various nicknames, and himself a frequent target of unkind reviews, Vincent Price is ideally cast as Edward Kendall Sheridan Lionheart, a barnstorming thespian of the old school whose Shakespearian performances have earned him the undying enmity of London's most acidic theatrical critics. After being humiliated at an award ceremony hosted by the London Critics Circle, Lionheart commits suicide by throwing himself into the Thames. Lionheart survives, however, and with the assistance of his devoted daughter, Edwina (Diana Rigg) and a band of itinerant drunks (the "Methys Drinkers," as they are billed), he proceeds

162

to avenge himself on his tormentors in an appropriately theatrical fashion: he murders them using methods inspired by Shakespeare.

Like Hector in *Troilus and Cressida*, Hector Snipe (Dennis Price, no relation to the star) is impaled on a spear and dragged through the streets tied to a horse's tail, while Oliver Larding (Robert Coote) is drowned in a vat of wine like Clarence in *Richard III* (interestingly, Price himself had played the part of Clarence in one of his first films, 1939's *Tower of London*, in which he met his fate at the hands of Basil Rathbone and Boris Karloff) and so on. One critic, Solomon Psaltrey (Jack Hawkins), is not literally killed; however, Lionheart makes sure Psaltrey is ruined by tricking the jealous critic into strangling his wife (Diana Dors) à la *Othello*. It's all done with a great deal of black humor and a number of withering puns, as when George Maxwell (Michael Hordern), whose stabbing death is based on *Julius Caesar*, uses his dying breath to observe that Lionheart is dead. "Another critical miscalculation on your part," Lionheart replies. "It is *you* who are dead!" Lionheart eventually kidnaps the lead critic, Peregrine "Perry" Devlin (Ian Hendry), whom Lionheart threatens to blind. In all, Lionheart destroys eight of the nine critics before being consumed in a quintessentially Pricean blazing inferno.

Price gives one of his best performances in the role of Edward Lionheart, and he clearly enjoys getting a chance to tackle the Shakespearian roles his status as a specialist in horror movies would otherwise have prohibited. As Britain's *Monthly Film Bulletin* observed, "To cast Vincent Price as a mad Shakespearian actor is to allow him for once to display his deliciously Gothic theatrical style to proper advantage, and Price rises to the challenge superbly, hissing his way throughout the full gamut of Shakespearian characterization...." (qtd. in Parish and Whitney 241–242). Indeed, Price often noted *Theater of Blood* as his favorite among his horror films (Williams 237).

In fact, Price's adept handling of the Bard's monologues is good enough to make viewers wish they could have seen the horror star appear in a legitimate Shakespeare adaptation, which in turn causes a bit of a problem within the context of *Theater of Blood*: the reviewers Price's Lionheart eliminates have all said he is a bad actor, but the scenes Lionheart performs more or less belie this assessment. Also problematic is the fact that the movie strongly suggests that Lionheart was popular with audiences; if not, how else could he have spent decades making a living on the boards? In one scene, police Inspector Boot (Milo O'Shea) comments wryly that Lionheart "was a very *vigorous* actor," a comment that implies Lionheart's lack of talent while simultaneously providing an indication of what audiences might have enjoyed about his performances.

Hickox's direction is restrained, but he makes the most out of the hilariously horrific scenes, successfully encouraging audiences to laugh and scream at the same time. Hickox also concedes the influence of the Bard on popular culture, as when a moving van operated by "Shakespeare's of Fulham" passes by in the background of the opening shot; the opening credits play out against scenes taken from silent versions of Shakespeare. Working from an idea by co-producers John Kohn and Stanley Mann, screenwriter Greville-Bell manages to imbue Lionheart and the other rather exaggerated characters with a pleasing degree of verisimilitude.

One of the most effective elements in the film is Michael J. Lewis' lush score. Lewis avoids traditional "scary movie music." In particular, Lewis makes excellent use of a mournful flute during the main theme and other cues. According to film music expert Jeff Thompson,

> The opening theme combines medievalism and early 1970s pop. At other times, a harpsichord provides a baroque touch, and flutes and piccolos add a shrill overlay of distress to the proceedings. Lewis notably uses percussion to great effect, and he ironically incorporates a tender love theme during the decapitation of Horace Sprout. At the film's fiery climax, Lewis concludes his score with two claps of a church bell, suggesting either a death knell for Lionheart and Edwina or resurrection bells for their possible survival of the blaze.

At first glance, *Theater of Blood* sounds like a blatant rip-off of *The Abominable Dr. Phibes* (1971) and its 1972 sequel, and certainly the formula (madman dispatches victims via a thematic series of ingenious, if improbable, methods) must have initially struck Price as uncomfortably familiar, particularly given the dark humor laced throughout all three films. Yet there is a crucial distinction between the approaches of Douglas Hickox in *Theater* and his counterpart on *Phibes*, Robert Fuest: Hickox imbues his homicidal protagonist with more pathos than does Fuest with his main character. Although the first Phibes film suggests sympathy for its devilish doctor (an element almost wholly absent from the sequel), Hickox's horror-comedy loudly roots for its bloodthirsty actor-manager, providing him with a far more realistic relationship with the woman in his life and portraying his victims as cruel, asinine rotters who truly deserve their horrific fates.

It is important to note that Lionheart's primary assistant — indeed, essentially a full partner in his murderous mission — is not merely a beautiful henchwoman but his own flesh and blood. As such, there is a connection between Lionheart and Edwina that runs far deeper and is much more obvious to the viewer than whatever unexplained association links Dr. Phibes to the mysterious Vulnavia. This connection, in turn, provides many of the most comedic and dramatic moments of *Theater of Blood*, as well as its ultimate suggestion of genuine tragedy.

In an ironic reversal of Elizabethan theatrical tradition, wherein women were not allowed on stage and men in drag essayed female roles, Edwina spends much of the film's running time disguised as Lionheart's male assistant. Evidently this deception was intended to convince audiences that Edwina is an innocent bystander until the shocking revelation of her dual identity at the film's climax, but only the most inattentive viewer could fail to recognize Diana Rigg's distinctive voice, which the actress barely attempts to lower into an identifiably male register. Furthermore, anybody who fails to recognize Rigg decked out as a bimbo actress to lure lascivious Trevor Dickman (Harry Andrews) to his doom is simply clueless. Nevertheless, Edwina's cross-dressing is a crucial signifier of the film's preoccupation with the character's penchant for both upholding and subverting gender roles. The blurring of gender and identity boundaries that is often subtextual in earlier Price horror films is more or less literal in *Theater of Blood*.

Edwina is the definition of a dutiful daughter. She willingly aids her father in the destruction of eight lives, participating in elaborate disguises and deceptions in order to fulfill Lionheart's quest for vengeance. She even conspires to appear hostile towards Devlin and the other critics in order to throw suspicion for the murders on herself; then she

Edwina Lionheart (Diana Rigg) disguises herself as a man to secretly assist her father, Edward (Vincent Price), in *Theater of Blood* (1973). Edwina's crossdressing is just one case of gender subversion in the film.

admits to Devlin that her father is alive but wants to surrender. This falsehood is made manifest when Edwina tricks Devlin into coming with her to meet Lionheart, thus resulting in Devlin's capture and potential blinding. "Don't try to trick me, Devlin," she warns shortly before one of the Methys drinkers clubs the critic into insensibility, adding "He's my father no matter what he's done."

During the restaging of the awards ceremony, Devlin begs Lionheart to consider what his "insane vendetta" has done to Edwina. In response, Lionheart asks, "What have I done to you, my daughter?" At this point Edwina doffs her male wig and moustache, replying to Lionheart's query with some of Cordelia's lines from Act 1, Scene 1 of *King Lear*: "Good my lord, You have begot me, bred me, loved me; I /Return those duties back as are right fit /Obey you, love you, and most honor you." Although these lines are used to represent Edwina's fanatical devotion to her father, it should be remembered that in the context of the original play the lines are from a speech that enrages Lear, leading him to disown Cordelia and thus set in motion the chain of events that results in his ruination. Lionheart's attitude toward Edwina is very different than Lear's reaction to Cordelia, but the result is the same: the fathers' stubborn and unreasonable expectations of their daughters contribute to the destruction of both families.

　　　The most extreme of Lionheart's demands is his daughter's assumption of a male persona. While this disguise protects Edwina from discovery by the police, there are other factors in play. Consider the fact that Lionheart has named his daughter "Edwina"—a feminine derivative of his own given name, Edward—and consider that Edwina is never given a proper name while pretending to be a man (Lionheart refers to this persona as "Stage Manager," substituting a generic title for a proper name). It is clear that Lionheart expects his daughter to "carry on" the family tradition, and it is probable that the aging matinee idol encourages his daughter to cross dress in an effort to alleviate his patriarchal disappointment in not having a male heir.

　　　Edwina's crossdressing opens the door to other instances of gender subversion, including the suggestion of homosexuality. The Stage Manager's disguise consists of a curly wig, dark sunglasses, and a moustache—masculine accouterments, perhaps, yet undermined by the character's effeminacy. Until it is revealed that the Stage Manager and Edwina are one in the same (again assuming that viewers fail to put two and two together earlier), a logical question poses itself: who is the Stage Manager, and why does "he" devote himself to Edward Lionheart? Initially viewers might assume that the Stage Manager is a gay fan of the Shakespearian star, perhaps an overly dedicated theater queen to whom the opportunity to work with Lionheart represents a chance to express his own frustrated performance ambitions. In this context, Lionheart, the Stage Manager, and the Methys drinkers form a "queer" family—social and cultural outcasts who come together under Lionheart's direction to achieve common goals, among which are a sense of purpose (however fiendish that purpose may be) and the appearance of community.

　　　More concrete depictions of "queerness" abound in *Theater of Blood*. The most deliberately over-the-top scene in what is admittedly one of the campiest pictures of Price's career takes place at a beauty salon, where Lionheart, mincing broadly under an outrageous Afro and oversized sunglasses, slays Chloe Moon (Coral Browne), the only distaff member of the Critic's Circle. "Hello, I'm Butch," Lionheart liltingly greets his female victim, the first of many gay references with which he peppers the scene before electrocuting Miss Moon with special (literal) hair curlers of his own design. The execution of Joan of Arc at the stake in *Henry VI Part One* inspires this murder, which Lionheart commits while quoting Warwick's contextually appropriate instructions for Joan's demise: "and hark ye, sirs; because she is a maid, /Spare for no faggots, let there be enow." Given the flamboyant gay stereotypes incorporated in Lionheart's disguise (and the even prissier behavior of Edwina in the Stage Manager costume, who placidly flips through a fashion magazine, oblivious to the searing flesh of the electrified Miss Moon), it is ironic that the killer and the victim became partners in real life. Having met on the set of *Theater of Blood*, Vincent Price and Coral Browne fell in love and eventually married in October 1974 (Price 290).

　　　Almost as flamboyant as Lionheart's Butch disguise is the everyday persona of gay critic Meredith Merridew (Robert Morley). The portly, effeminate Merridew, who is almost always accompanied by a pair of toy poodles he calls his "babies," suffers arguably the most gruesome demise of all. Inspired by the scene in *Titus Andronicus* wherein Queen Tamora is fed a pie made out of her own children, Lionheart and company trick Merridew into thinking he is a guest on a TV cooking show (*This Is Your Dish*), and feed him a pie made out of his beloved dogs. The film's most disturbing sequence occurs as Lionheart, costumed as a chef and sporting an exaggerated French accent, reveals the heads of the two dogs propped up on a second pie, then forces Merridew to continue eating until he chokes to death (the murder of the "queen" takes on additional grotesque irony when it is recalled that Vincent Price was himself a noted gourmet in real life). The inclusion of an actual homosexual victim complements Lionheart's often sexually transgressive plans and the disguises he and Edwina adopt.

Lionheart's over-reliance on Edwina and her excessive devotion to him suggest other questionable aspects of their relationship. In caring for and assisting Lionheart, Edwina has essentially taken the place of Lionheart's wife, who is never mentioned but presumably

A casual shot of Diana Rigg in *Theater of Blood* (1973).

died many years prior to the events in the film. Even before Lionheart's attempted suicide and subsequent murderous rampage, Edwina has evidently never married nor had children; a family of her own might compromise her ability to look after her thespian father, obviously. It is reasonable to assume Lionheart has always been jealous of his daughter's would-be suitors, perhaps including Peregrine Devlin. Something motivates Lionheart to single Devlin out for special treatment, and it seems to go beyond Devlin's chairmanship of the Critics Circle; a conflict over Edwina is therefore quite logical, if subtextual.

At the funeral of Lionheart's first victim, George Maxwell, Devlin is distracted when he notices Edwina visiting her father's grave. The critic's interest in the actor's offspring is further suggested in other scenes; Lionheart certainly uses it near the film's climax to get Devlin away from the supervision of Inspector Boot and Sergeant Dogge (Eric Sykes), the policemen assigned to the case. The familiarity between Edwina and Devlin introduces the possibility that there was at least a one-sided attraction on Devlin's part. Perhaps Lionheart himself thwarted a budding romance, which in turn might contribute to Devlin's incessant critical hostility. "I attacked your father because I thought I could goad him into the 20th century" is Devlin's half-hearted response to Edwina's mocking greeting: "Well, the brilliant Peregrine Devlin. Wielder of the brutal aphorism, master of the killing phrase—my father's murderer!" The possibility that a personal conflict has complicated

Devlin's professional relationship with Lionheart adds an extra degree of vituperation to their interaction.

Whether or not Edwina has any involvement in Lionheart's dislike of Devlin, there is no doubt that Devlin remains one of Lionheart's fiercest critics. "You begin to resent an actor if you always have to give him bad notices," Devlin explains to Inspector Boot at one point, a tacit admission that personal and professional grievances have become intertwined. That Lionheart loathes Devlin in particular is established following the murder of Horace Sprout (Arthur Lowe), whom Lionheart has decapitated in a reference to *Cymbeline*. Devlin is chosen to receive a particularly nasty token of Lionheart's esteem when he finds Sprout's severed headed impaled on a bottle of milk. A similar token comes to Devlin in the form of Trevor Dickman's heart, which is delivered in a fancy gift box. Even this grisly memento cannot prevent the shaken Devlin from making a critical pronouncement; realizing that Dickman's death was inspired by *The Merchant of Venice*, in which no murder occurs, he observes to the police that "only [Lionheart] would have the temerity to rewrite Shakespeare."

In one of the film's most exciting scenes, Devlin attends his weekly fencing lesson, only to find that Lionheart has replaced the regular instructor. An athletic confrontation ensues, with both men parrying and thrusting across the studio (and, briefly, onto matching trampolines) until Lionheart brings Devlin to heel. "Lionheart is immortal! He can never be destroyed!" the crazed performer boasts before taking his critical opponent to task for his failure to appreciate the actor's craft: "How many actors have you destroyed? ... What do you know of the blood, sweat, and toil of a theatrical production? Of the dedication of the men and women of the noblest profession of all?" When Devlin responds by saying he would rather die than listen to more of Lionheart's insane posturing, Lionheart announces that he intends to kill Devlin when it suits him to do so — yet another indication that Devlin has earned an exceptional degree of Lionheart's animosity.

The fact that Lionheart has embroiled his own daughter in his monstrous scheme foreshadows and ultimately underscores the genuine tragedy of the film's conclusion, for Edwina herself dies as a direct result of Lionheart's obsessive need for vengeance. Having captured Perry Devlin and brought him to his lair in the decaying (and quite Gothic) Burbage Theatre, Lionheart demands that Devlin reenact the 1970 Critics Circle ceremony and present the Best Actor award to its "proper" recipient or be blinded by red-hot knives (an allusion to the blinding of Gloucester in *King Lear*). Devlin refuses, Lionheart insists that Edwina present him with the award, and as the police finally close in, the triumphant actor starts a fire to cover his retreat.

However, in the ensuing confusion one of the panicky Methys drinkers smashes Edwina's skull with the Critics Circle statue. Before expiring, Edwina engages in a final exchange of quotes from *King Lear* ("'We are not the first/Who with best meaning have incurred the worst'") with Lionheart; he then carries Edwina's body to the theater's roof, where both father and daughter are finally immolated in the roaring flames. Here Perry Devlin passes final judgment on the actor: "Yes, it was a fascinating performance," he muses to Inspector Boot, "but of course he was madly overacting as usual. But you must admit he knew how to make an exit!"

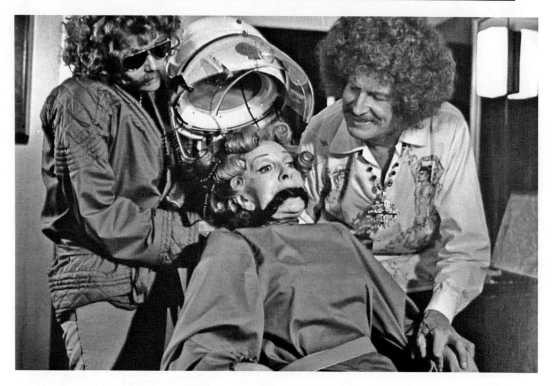

Miss Moon (Coral Browne) suffers a very bad hair day at the hands of the demented Lionheart (Price) while a disguised Edwina (Rigg) looks on the *Theater of Blood* (1973). Interestingly, Browne became Price's third wife after meeting him on the film's graveyard set!

Theater of Blood starts out as a send-up of Shakespearian drama and ends up closely emulating the plays it kids. The film "uses Shakespearean materials abundantly, with style and ingenuity" although with "respect but no reverence" (Pendleton 145). Edward Lionheart becomes a tragic hero, mirroring the characters to whom he has dedicated his professional life — and who, following his "resurrection," have become his entire life. Moreover, Lionheart's last few lines of dialogue are taken entirely from the works of Shakespeare; he speaks no words unique to his character. In a sense, Lionheart the man finally realizes he no longer exists as a distinct being; the revenge tragedy he has plotted has become a scripted drama, perhaps one worthy of the Bard himself.

18

THE COFFIN OF TIME
Madhouse (1974)

On paper, at least, it must have seemed like a good idea at the time. In the waning days of American International Pictures' glory, somebody decided to team up the company's #1 star, Vincent Price, with British bogeyman Peter Cushing. AIP had already hired Cushing to cameo in *Scream and Scream Again* (1970) and *Dr. Phibes Rises Again!* (1972) with Price, although the actors had no scenes together in either picture. Now it was time for Price and Cushing to finally match wits in a thriller based on Angus Hall's *Devilday*, an overheated pulp novel first published in 1969. In collaboration with Amicus, with whom the company collaborated on *Scream and Scream Again*, AIP filmed Hall's novel as *The Revenge of Dr. Death*. By the time of the picture's release, however, the title had been shortened to *Madhouse*. Unfortunately the results are generally considered among the worst efforts on either horror star's resume.

Price essays the role of Paul Toombes, an aging horror star who journeys to England to star in a TV series based on his most famous character, Dr. Death. Twelve years before, Toombes' fiancée, Ellen (Julie Crosthwait), was murdered, and the circumstantial evidence pointed to Paul as the culprit. A nervous breakdown kept the actor out of prison, but the scandal ruined his career. Toombes reluctantly accepts the invitation to recreate Dr. Death out of a sense of obligation to screenwriter Herbert Flay (Cushing), his old friend and co-creator of the skull-faced screen psychopath. Paul also agrees to stay at Herbert's country home, which proves to be an unwise choice of lodgings.

The aging horror star's troubles begin even before he sets foot in England; Paul awakens in his stateroom to find an ambitious starlet, Elizabeth Peters (Linda Hayden), trying to blackmail him into helping her career. Paul is astounded to discover that his new producer is Oliver Quayle (Robert Quarry), a former pornographer who once hired Ellen to perform in his sex films, and that Herbert has a crazed wife, Faye (Adrienne Corri), a horribly scarred former actress who now lives in Herbert's basement and passes the time raising poisonous spiders. Soon Toombes is before the cameras, but a series of murders inspired by his old films casts shadows of doubt on the actor. Elizabeth is the first of many victims. Has playing Dr. Death sent Toombes over the edge — or does somebody else want to ruin Toombes all over again?

Eventually it is revealed that Herbert is the murderer and has lured Paul back to his most famous role in order to kill him, at which point the contract with Quayle stipulates that Flay will get his long-frustrated wish to assume the Dr. Death role. Paul goes mad, setting fire to the set and apparently incinerating himself in the process. However, as a triumphant Flay returns home to celebrate his victory, a badly burned Toombes confronts him. The former friends battle throughout the house, eventually winding up in the base-ment, where Faye stabs Herbert. The dying writer-actor falls into Faye's spider nest, where her hungry babies quickly consume Flay's body. Paul then uses his expertise with makeup to disguise himself as Herbert, assuming his old partner's identity with Faye's cheerful assistance.

Hall's original novel nicely captures the cynicism of television production and the lengths to which some producers will go in order to score high ratings — even if it means hiring scandalous, possibly deranged former movie stars. Not surprisingly, the TV show in the novel is a smash, which doesn't surprise reluctant series director Blount: "Appeal to the lowest common denominator and you can't fail. In this business, nothing succeeds like excretion" (Hall 39). However, only the basic idea — disgraced American horror star Paul Toombs (note there is no "e" in the name in the book) comes to England to recreate his most famous role on British TV — survives the adaptation.

Gone from the novel is the narrator, Barry Lambert, an ambitious young television reporter assigned by his boss to keep an eye on the troublesome Toombs, whose signature character is known as Dr. *Dis*, not *Death*; in Barry's stead we get graying actor-cum-author Flay. Although in the novel Toombs is suspected of being involved in several mur-ders, it's not really his cinematic exploits that make him look bad — it's that he's a fat, hairy, drunken heroin addict and sex fiend who spends every waking moment trying to outrage and horrify everyone around him with his seduction of teenage girls and his par-ticipation in orgies and Satanic rituals. Toombs' favorite greeting is a reference to his Satanic beliefs: "His True Will will always conquer" (Hall 29).

Also jettisoned are most of Hall's supporting characters, although the narrator's sleazy employer, Oliver Quayle, remains as despicable as ever. The cynical producer greedily looks forward to exploiting his star, observing that Toombes' "old movies show all the time on television. There's a whole new cult today for Dr. Death, and I've got him!" Else-where, Quayle delivers one of the film's better lines when he is re-introduced to Paul. Reminded of his blue movie past, Quayle cheerfully responds, "I don't make that cheap crap anymore. I'm in television now!" Quayle even promises bit player Carol Clayton (Jenny Lee Wright) a starring role in the TV show, evidently just to secure her sexual favors.

Other supporting characters from the novel, including Barry's girlfriend, Julia (Natasha Pyne), and the show's director, Blount (Barry Dennen), show up in *Madhouse*, albeit vastly altered from Hall's conceptions. Working as Quayle's publicist, Julia is charm-ing, intelligent, and witty, which endears her to Paul and even suggests she might be in line to someday become the new Mrs. Toombes. Indeed, Julia is developed into the kindest and most likable character in the entire film, making her murder the only one that is truly disturbing. Having pilfered Quayle's files and figured out that Flay is the one with the most to gain by getting rid of Toombes, Julia finds herself confronted by Dr. Death. Cor-nered in an elevator, Julia fights back; however, she winds up with a blade in her neck.

Shortly thereafter, Toombes finds Julia's body propped up in his dressing room, eerily recalling the position of Ellen's body years earlier. Fittingly, it is Julia's death that finally pushes Paul over the edge, inspiring him to torch the set and (apparently) himself as well.

The involvement of Elizabeth in the plot is unnecessary, but the presence of Linda Hayden, a veteran "scream queen" of the early Seventies, distinguishes the character somewhat. Unapologetically ruthless in her pursuit of screen stardom, Elizabeth threatens to accuse Paul of rape if he won't help her. The movie star ignores her threats, but later Elizabeth makes her way to Flay's house in another misguided attempt to secure Paul's assistance, and she winds up impaled on Dr. Death's trusty pitchfork. In the film's most visually poetic scene, the black-cloaked killer places her dead body in a small boat and sets it adrift on the Thames. The body is eventually discovered, the press suggests Paul is involved, and the girl's avaricious foster parents foolishly try to blackmail him, as his watch has been discovered on Elizabeth's body. Not surprisingly, the parents wind up impaled as well — this time on a convenient sword.

Adrienne Corri's turn as Faye is also intriguing, although relatively little is done with the character. In the opening scene it is established that Faye loves Paul from afar. "You're marrying a fine monster," she wistfully remarks to Ellen, adding, "All I ever got was a stake in the heart!" When she becomes reacquainted with Paul in the basement, she suggests her marriage to Herbert was a rash decision made on the rebound. Faye admits that her marriage was unhappy and that she began to sleep with other men, including anonymous pick-ups in bars. Eventually some her "friends" tried to burn her car while she was still inside. "When I came out of it, I wasn't pretty anymore," she confides to Paul, underscoring how her dependence on her beauty and sexuality has lead to her mental and physical breakdown.

That Faye's infatuation with Paul is an integral part of her madness is established when she is depicted prowling around his room and sniffing his clothing in a sensual manner. It is apparent that Faye's insanity stems from her inability to fashion an autonomous identity of her own. The actress couldn't have Paul, so she has settled for the closest replacement, his friend and Dr. Death collaborator — a choice that ultimately destroys her mind and her body. Without the presence of either Paul or Herbert, she is incomplete, as suggested by her mournful reply when Paul asks her name: "I *was* Faye Carstairs." Eventually Faye enjoys a happy ending of sorts when she and Paul settle down as a contentedly demented couple at the film's conclusion, but even here her happiness is dependent on her connection with Paul — who, significantly, now wears the face of Herbert.

It is fascinating to consider the ramifications of the shifting identities represented by Toombes and Flay. *Madhouse* suggests a queer connection between Toombs and Flay in that they are Dr. Death's "parents." Their creation of an alien/Other persona recalls the Frankenstein mythos and its idea of reproduction without the involvement of a female. Both created the Dr. Death character, with Paul playing the role and Herbert writing the adventures. The central conflict lies in the fact that Herbert wants to *be* Dr. Death, and Paul fears that he *is* Dr. Death. "Everybody thinks I'm dead — even myself," Paul muses, acknowledging the way in which his screen identity has replaced his actual identity. Such a state of existence can only be appreciated by a personality in desperate need of expression — and Herbert Flay is such a personality.

Herbert Flay symbolizes the many real-life screenwriters who are frustrated actors, forced to create the characters they cannot play, albeit taken to an extreme. Herbert wishes to replace his personality with that of Dr. Death, and Paul wants to reclaim his own identity from the character that has nearly absorbed him. Ironically, both men lose their individuality: Herbert ceases to exist, but he lives on as Paul's new identity. For his part, Paul assumes Herbert's identity, which also means he must continue to play Dr. Death. In a sense, the Dr. Death persona has triumphed over both creators. These potentially fascinating explorations of gender and identity fluidity, contextualized by the interaction of two major horror personalities, are largely ignored. As with so much else in *Madhouse*, the potential for self-reflexivity is underdeveloped. In the final analysis, the film fails to fully develop "the postmodern urge to conflate reality and the image" (Benshoff 219).

Instead of doing something inventive with the relatively fresh notions and characters provided in the source novel, *Madhouse* scribes Ken Levinson and Greg Morrison fall back on the well-established elements of dark comedies like the Phibes films and *Theater*

Paul Toombes (Vincent Price) shares a friendly moment with Herbert Flay (Peter Cushing), the co-creator of "Dr. Death," in *Madhouse* (1974).

of Blood, wherein Price's character punishes his enemies by killing them in hilariously outlandish ways. Unfortunately this well had pretty much been drained by the time Levinson and Morrison came along, so the murders in *Madhouse* are neither particularly funny nor especially scary. The few humorous lines and sequences that do crop up serve merely to undermine the film's half-hearted attempts to be taken seriously.

The dialogue displays little in the way of caustic wit, although Toombes acidly observes that Quayle reminds him that in the Hollywood of yesteryear, "the monsters didn't need makeup — they just came as themselves." Sadly, too many throwaway lines exist simply to make Paul look crazier than he actually is, such as his remark to the police regarding Elizabeth's blackmailing foster parents: "A lesser man would have strangled them" instead of simply chasing them off. Faye's closing line, in which she offers Paul his favorite dish — "sour cream and red herrings" — is perhaps intended as a sly wink to the audience, a tacit admission of how silly the story must be to contain so many false suspects. However, the ultimate effect of such lines is to suggest the filmmakers lack respect for the material, the cast, and the audience itself.

Even more risible are the many logical gaps in Levinson and Morrison's screenplay. Minutes before Julia is murdered, Quayle is seen leaving a TV studio audience — with Herbert clearly depicted sitting right in front of him. After Julia is killed, Quayle is shown re-entering the same audience — and Herbert has not moved. This business is intended to suggest that it is Quayle who is wearing the Dr. Death disguise — but so blatant is the sequence's execution that only the most gullible viewer would ever think Quayle could be guilty. Even worse, the fact that Flay has obviously not moved a muscle during the murder of Julia means that the screenwriter couldn't possibly slip out, don the necessary costume, and pursue and kill a woman without ever breaking a sweat.

It is also extremely unlikely that a TV set would be decorated with actual weapons, but at one point Dr. Death attacks Toombes with a very sharp axe. Even more implausible is the canopy bed that doubles as a deadly press. To demonstrate, director Blount climbs into the bed, which automatically clamps him in place, and tells Paul to operate the device. Paul finds he can't switch the press off, and Blount is crushed to death. Later still, Paul himself falls onto the bed and narrowly escapes being crushed. The fact that no film crew would allow such a functionally dangerous prop on set makes Blount's demise ridiculous; that such a thing would be allowed to remain on set *and still be operational after it has killed somebody* simply staggers belief. The only explanation is sheer laziness on the part of the screenwriters and a lack of concern on the part of the producers and director.

Jim Clark's direction is competent but nothing special. Clark's main contribution is his method of constructing sequences in which someone in a Dr. Death costume chases pretty girls — sequences which foreshadow Reagan-era slasher flicks by their occasional use of the killer's POV. These scenes are staged briskly but demonstrate neither thematic significance nor a polished style, perhaps because of Clark's limited previous experience as director — although constant rewrites and editorial interference from producer Milton Subotsky certainly didn't help matters (Nutman 83). Ultimately, *Madhouse* was Clark's swan song as a director; having previously established himself as a respected film editor, Clark returned to his Movieola, where he later worked on more prestigious projects like

Marathon Man (1976) and *The World Is Not Enough* (1999) and won an Oscar for editing *The Killing Fields* (1984).

The best word to describe *Madhouse* is "uninspired," though "lethargic" comes close. Even Vincent Price seems uncharacteristically distracted and bored by the proceedings — and indeed the actor was frustrated and disenchanted with AIP, for whom this would be his last project. It is true that Paul Toombes has been in and out of mental institutions for more than a decade and is supposed to be a tired old man. Yet the weariness Price felt in his own life, particularly in regard to the lack of respect afforded him by AIP mogul Samuel Z. Arkoff, seems so great that it smothers the character entirely. The few exceptions occur when Paul discovers the bodies of Ellen and Julia, and then in his climatic rant — but in these scenes Price is completely over the top, demonstrating the campy exaggeration that many critics insisted colored most of his earlier performances. Price's grandly theatrical approach is perhaps the only way to deliver such lines as "there is always room for more in the coffin of time," but it only works well in an otherwise carefully controlled environment, such as the Phibes films.

Sadly, it is impossible to say that the normally dependable Peter Cushing contributes much of value to *Madhouse*. Cushing's turn as Flay is among his least memorable performances; he simply is not believable as a jealous screenwriter who castigates Price for not appreciating the genius of the movie monster they created. "He made you a film star!" Flay observes petulantly during their final struggle, suggesting that Toombes ought to show Dr. Death more respect. Overall, Cushing's histrionics suggest hysteria more than homicidal mania. Granted, the character of Herbert Flay is poorly conceived and underwritten in the first place; better dialogue and more logical motivation would have provided the actor meatier ingredients with which he could have developed a more interesting character.

Yet *Madhouse* is strangely watchable in spite of its many faults. Price and Cushing come alive in an early scene where they grumble about the changing nature of the movie business, and their final battle over the spider pit is exciting. The presence of frequent horror helpers Robert Quarry, Adrienne Corri, and Linda Hayden spices things up, as does the use of clips from Price's earlier efforts for AIP, including *The Haunted Palace* and *The Raven*, as stand-ins for the orig-

Vincent Price as Dr. Death in *Madhouse* (1974). George Blackler's makeup is striking but underused in the film.

inal Dr. Death movies. George Blackler's Dr. Death makeup is quite striking, although it is underused.

In the end, however, the film marks a disappointing finale to Price's long association with AIP and to the Silver Age of Horror Films in general. The story is executed in such a routine, by-the-numbers manner that it is hard to get too excited about the few saving graces. Among all the titles in the Price filmography, this is the most frustrating because of its squandered potential. This production could have been the *Sunset Blvd.* of horror films — a combination of parody and affection for the stars and iconography of an increasingly obsolete cinema aesthetic. At the very least this film should have been the Price-Cushing version of *What Ever Happened to Baby Jane?* and that's why in the final analysis *Madhouse* doesn't quite work.

19

A HIDEOUS THRONG
Miscellaneous AIP Titles

Any discussion of Vincent Price's Poe adaptations must acknowledge a few films that really don't fit into the series in spite of AIP's best efforts to claim otherwise. In addition, a couple of the company's Poe adaptations do not feature Price at all, yet they are interesting to consider because their relative artistic and commercial inferiority provides some perspective on how important are the actor's contributions to the series. Put another way, AIP tried several times to make Price-Poe pictures without either Price or Poe — and each time the results failed to impress either critics or audiences. Some acknowledgment of these projects is necessary to fully appreciate the rest of Price's key horror films.

In 1962, Roger Corman became embroiled in a financial dispute with AIP founders Arkoff and Nicholson. As a result, Corman decided to make his third Poe adaptation for the Pathé film processing lab, which was interested in going into film distribution. However, as Beverly Gray explains,

> When Sam Arkoff got wind of this arrangement, which threatened the AIP monopoly on the highly lucrative Poe films, he warned that AIP would retaliate by withdrawing its business from Pathé's respected film laboratory. [Pathé] capitulated, and Corman was surprised to see Nicholson and Arkoff show up on the set of *The Premature Burial*, cheerfully informing him that he was once again working for them [76].

The Premature Burial (sometimes referred to with the definite article omitted, as Corman left it off in the film's credits) is the only one of Corman's Poe adaptations in which Vincent Price does not appear. In his place, Corman cast another aging former romantic lead, Ray Milland, as Sir Guy Carrell, a British aristocrat who calls off his engagement to the beautiful Emily (Hazel Court in the first of her three Poe appearances for the director) because of his morbid fear of being buried alive. Eventually Emily convinces Guy to marry her after all, but soon a series of terrifying dreams and other phenomena cause Guy to fall into a cataleptic state. Guy is in fact interred, but grave robbers immediately and inadvertently free him. Guy goes on a rampage, electrocuting Emily's anatomist father before subjecting Emily to premature burial. Family physician (and Emily's true love) Miles (Richard Ney) intervenes but is too late to save Emily; Guy's sister, Kate (Heather Angel) shows up and shoots her brother. In the picture's hasty conclusion, Kate explains that Emily married Guy for his money, then played upon his irrational fears to drive him into a cataleptic fit.

Premature Burial is a misfit in the series for many reasons, not the least of which is Price's absence from the proceedings. A capable actor and Oscar winner (for his starring turn in *The Lost Weekend*) who ultimately chalked up enough horror film credits to earn acknowledgment as a minor genre star (Brosnan 278–279), Ray Milland simply doesn't have the screen presence or the voice for Gothic material. His lines are delivered in an almost somnambulistic tone — perhaps appropriate given the character's obsession with catalepsy — and his relationship with Hazel Court seems less likely than the May-December romances Price carried on with young actresses in his films.

Then again, the script by fantasy specialists Charles Beaumont and Ray Russell doesn't give Milland much to work with. *Premature Burial* is talky and slow-moving, featuring less action and fewer shock sequences than the previous Poe adaptations. In perhaps the screenplay's most egregious shortcoming, there is no explanation for Guy's sudden realization that Emily is the actual culprit in the plot. Furthermore, Guy's sister knew the truth "but held her tongue because she was afraid Guy wouldn't believe her unless she had some proof, which is a pretty lame excuse for doing nothing," as Mark Thomas McGee rightly observes (141).

In spite of the film's weaknesses, it is not wholly without interest. Corman's sure directorial sense provides some fascinating camera angles, and the atmosphere of the Carrell estate is unquestionably ominous — once again a testament to Floyd Crosby's cinematography and Daniel Haller's sets. The constantly billowing fog and the desiccated flora contribute to landscape as deathly as the obsessions that motivate Guy. A fine score by Ronald Stein, who provided the music to several Corman productions during this period, is another mood-establishing highlight. Beaumont and Russell make little use of Poe's story, but they do provide Guy with a lengthy monologue that includes Poe's evocative description of the sensations of living burial.

In thematic terms, *Premature Burial* is reasonably successful at conveying the metaphoric connotations of Guy Carrell's obsessions. In a sense, Guy is already "buried alive" as the film opens: his obsession stems from his conviction that his own father was interred prematurely, a particularly morbid notion wholly in keeping with Poe's tradition of unstable protagonists given to similarly bizarre fixations. More significantly, Guy's mania is associated with his family; as in *House of Usher* and *Pit and the Pendulum*, the protagonist of *Premature Burial* wages a losing battle with a long tradition of madness and death within his own bloodline. Similar to Corman's other Gothic works, a protagonist once again leads an apparently innocent younger person (in this case, Emily) on a tour of a subterranean lair, in this case the Carrell catacombs. This symbolic journey into the subconscious — one of Corman's most important acknowledgments of his debt to Freudian theory — concludes with Guy lecturing Emily on the horrific deaths his ancestors have inevitably faced. Guy remarks on the immutability of his fate as an explanation for why he cannot marry and father children to perpetuate the family — another notion borrowed from *House of Usher*.

The idea that the protagonist's way of life is itself outmoded and "dead" that underscores several of Corman's Poe films is present in *Premature Burial* as well. An aristocrat during the rapid socioeconomic changes of the nineteenth century, Guy Carrell mopes around his ancient estate, rarely interacting with the reality beyond his small and obsolete world. The relevance of Guy's "burial" within a changing world beyond his ken or control is personally relevant to Jayne Anne Phillips, who associates this "scion of a dwindling Victorian family" with her own experience growing up and escaping from a dreary West Virginia coal town (43). The suffocation of progress, then, is akin to the suffocation of death.

As for Emily, a product of an apparently respectable but indisputably bourgeois family, it is interesting that she is dedicated to acquiring a fortune by any means necessary. "You always wanted to be a great lady," Miles observes, a reference to her earlier refusal to marry him because he lacked wealth (and a foreshadowing of Emily's real purpose). Emily's greed and ruthlessness in her pursuit of wealth may be evil, but there is also an element of self-preservation inherent in her quest; without an independent source of income, Emily would be entirely as the mercy of a culture in which women are already repressed and limited by numerous factors. Court's turn as Emily foreshadows her role as Lenore in *The Raven*, where once again the actress portrays an ambitious female who plots to use male lovers as tools to overcome female oppression within a patriarchal social system.

In her quest for upward social mobility, Emily herself, it is implied, is as fixed on her obsessions as Guy is with his; the fact that their mutual obsessions lead to their mutual destruction is highly ironic and suggests an inherent and irrepressible conflict between the middle and upper classes. Gary Morris notes that Emily is frequently depicted hovering over her prostrate husband, an image that conveys "a connotation of smothering" (110) akin to the suffocation inevitably following premature burial. In its depiction of a man oppressed by the nature of his decaying status and unbreakable bonds to family and social traditions firmly rooted in the past, *The Premature Burial* does succeed in making the horror of live burial — itself a virtual impossibility by 1962 due to modern medical practices — an effective metaphor for the burial of the individual under the weight of both past and present anxieties. Indeed, the film might be a classic — if only Vincent Price were in it!

In the wake of Roger Corman's departure from the Poe franchise, AIP elected to continue the Poe series with another director. Director Jacques Tourneur was brought in based on his success both within the company (his 1964 effort, *The Comedy of Terrors*) and without (his horror films for legendary producer Val Lewton in the 1940s). Tourneur's most important horror film, *Night of the Demon* (called *Curse of the Demon* in America, 1957), boasted a script by Charles Bennett, whose previous credits included work for Alfred Hitchcock; logically enough, Bennett was brought in to develop a new script with Tourneur. However, the resulting film enjoys a far less sparkling reputation than the previous Tourneur-Bennett collaboration.

War-Gods of the Deep, as the film became known in the United States, was shot in England as *The City Under the Sea*, which remained its British title. The original title is a derivation of "The City in the Sea," itself an 1845 revision of Poe's "The Doomed City" (1831). Set in 1903, the film concerns the efforts of intrepid American scientist Ben Harris (Tab Hunter) and cowardly English Artist Harold Tufnell-Jones (David Tomlinson) to rescue pretty Jill Tregillis (Susan Hart) from the clutches of underwater tyrant Sir Hugh Tregathion (Price), an eighteenth century smuggler who has conquered the sunken city of Lyonesse. Now generally called "the Captain," Sir Hugh believes Jill is the reincarnation of his late wife; he and his fellow pirates no longer age thanks to some idiosyncrasy in the sunken city's climate, and Sir Hugh intends to share this virtual immortality with Jill. Eventually Lyonesse is consumed by the volcano, the protagonists escape to the surface, and Sir Hugh dies when he leaves the protective atmosphere of his ruined kingdom.

Nothing in Poe's output remotely resembles this storyline; indeed, the plot of *War-Gods of the Deep* is more akin to the science-fiction adventures of Jules Verne, whose *Master of the World* (1961) had been previously lensed by AIP, also with Price in the title role. Nevertheless, *War-Gods of the Deep* does feature some distinctly Poesque touches and certainly evidences a stronger association with the author than some of the movies that followed it. The film opens with a voice-over of Price reciting a few lines from Poe's poem. While this device may at first appear to be a desperate attempt to connect to Poe, it is one of several allusions to the American author sprinkled throughout the production.

Lines and ideas from the poem abound, such as a terrified fisherman's observation of "red in the sea, like blood-color," which recalls Poe's line, "The waves have now a redder glow" (964). Elsewhere, Sir Hugh refers to himself as "Death looking gigantically down" on his underwater subjects, a paraphrase of Poe's couplet, "While from a proud tower in the town/Death looks gigantically down" (964). Sir Hugh also refers to his underwater world as a "maelstrom," which alludes to Poe's story "A Descent into the Maelstrom," itself announced as one of the dozen productions being considered at the same time Tourneur's film went before the cameras (Meikle 134).

The film's set design incorporates many elements inspired by the artwork of antiquity, including hieroglyphics, friezes, and statuary clearly intended to suggest the artifacts of ancient Egypt. Although the poem itself contains no direct reference to the Egyptians, it does contain descriptions of domes, spires, "kingly halls" and "Babylon-like walls" (964). Thus, the film is designed with the ancient appearance of Poe's underwater city in mind, a design choice every bit as valid as the art direction incorporated into previous AIP Poe adaptations.

Beyond quotations from the poem, Tourneur's film incorporates thematic references to Poe's output and previous entries in the AIP series. Sir Hugh follows in the tradition of Nicholas Medina, Erasmus Craven, and other Price characters by mourning his long-dead wife. Unlike the haunted protagonists of *Pit and the Pendulum* et al, Sir Hugh's mourning is not suffused with dread; there is no evidence that his dead Beatrice was evil or unfaithful. As a result, Sir Hugh's fascination with Jill becomes subtly pathetic, not horrific; the cruel irony that he can live forever but his wife cannot is the sort of dark romantic tragedy that Poe includes in such poems of loss as "The Raven" and "Lenore." Interestingly, Charles Bennett's script (doctored by Louis M. Heyward) includes a scene in which Ben and Harold discover a "first English edition" of Poe's poetry among Sir Hugh's treasures; the undying smuggler, of course, has dog-eared the page upon which "The City in the Sea" is printed. This bit of business is an early example of postmodern self-reference in the series, an element that becomes increasingly prevalent in the films that follow.

On yet another level does *War-Gods of the Deep* append itself to Poe thematically, although so subtly that the filmmakers themselves probably did not fully appreciate it. Like Roderick Usher, M. Valdemar, and others, Sir Hugh is a relic of sorts. He represents a bygone era, a time in which men of aristocratic heritage assumed dominion over others as a matter of course. Again and again in Poe's stories and especially in the cinematic adaptations, men

Vincent Price in a late 60s publicity still.

of wealth and influence live on, the hegemony of their class still extant within the boundaries of tiny, self-determined kingdoms that do not reflect the transformations in society at large. That these characters do not adapt to the social and psychological changes afoot in the real world is the ultimate wellspring of conflict, of madness, of horror, and ultimately of the destruction of the characters themselves.

Sir Hugh Tregathion used his status as an aristocrat to cover his smuggling at the dawn of the nineteenth century; when he and his men fled to Lyonesse, he assumed tyrannical control over that realm by virtue of his standing as an aristocrat. By the time the events of the film unfold in 1903, Sir Hugh has no doubt that it is perfectly acceptable to kidnap Jill because she reminds him of his departed beloved. His survival over the course of three centuries is only possible because the station to which he was born has been preserved by a freakish aberration of nature. It is significant that this aberration takes place not only far from the "real" world, but also among the ruins of a lost city — itself a relic by the time Sir Hugh stumbled upon it in 1803.

War-Gods of the Deep/ The City Under the Sea does not enjoy the critical and popular affection reserved for so many of Vincent Price's Poe adaptations. Michael Weldon, for example, calls it a "dull and unconvincing adventure film" (761). It is perhaps improperly catalogued as a horror film, although the appearance of the "fish men" Sir Hugh includes among his subjects adds an element of the monstrous to the plot. Certainly the wooden acting of co-star Tab Hunter and the annoying comic relief provided by David Tomlinson (at the time quite a catch for AIP thanks to his recent co-starring turn in *Mary Poppins* for Disney) and his pet chicken, Herbert, undermine the serious atmosphere that Tourneur and Bennett establish in the film's opening scenes.

Two somewhat misfit titles require acknowledgment, if not extensive discussion:

Spirits of the Dead (1969) and *Murders in the Rue Morgue* (1971). Originally lensed two years before its American release, *Spirits of the Dead* (original title: *Histoires Extraordinaires*) is a French-Italian co-production boasting the participation of three leading European directors (Roger Vadim, Louis Malle, Federico Fellini) and an internationally renowned cast (Jane and Peter Fonda, Brigitte Bardot, Terence Stamp) in an upscale arthouse interpretation of three lesser Poe tales ("Metzengerstein," "William Wilson," and "Never Bet the Devil Your Head"). Yet in spite of its impressive pedigree, it is neither particularly engaging nor especially entertaining; talky, ponderous, and dull, *Spirits of the Dead* "lacks the polish, style, and solid terror of the best Roger Corman contributions to the Edgar Allan Poe series," as John Mahoney rightly observed (qtd. in Lucy Chase Williams 220).

To bridge the gap between "legitimate" AIP Poe productions and this strange European effort, Vincent Price was brought in to recite a few verses from "Spirits of the Dead," an early poem that first appeared as "Visit of the Dead" in *Tamerlane and Other Poems* (1827), Poe's first collection, to justify the American title. Price's narration includes the first and last verses of the poem, including the memorable couplet "Thy soul shall find itself alone/'Mid dark thoughts of the gray tombstone" (Poe 1016). In all, Price's contribution to the film lasts exactly 27 seconds, according to Lucy Chase Williams (220). Although the American version, dubbed into English, still circulates as a TV print, the version of *Spirits of the Dead* easily accessed on video is the subtitled European cut — without Price's recitations.

The final AIP Poe feature, *Murders in the Rue Morgue*, represents a concentrated but ultimately vain attempt to till new ground. Once again director Gordon Hessler and screenwriter Christopher Wicking (writing in collaboration with veteran mystery and soap opera specialist Henry Slesar) were assigned the task of adapting a Poe classic for the screen, but for the first time Vincent Price was not part of the deal. The actor was exhausted with the series, with AIP, and with the direction of his career in general. Jason Robards signed on to play Charron, the leader of a French acting troupe that specializes in recreations of Poe's most famous mystery. Members of the troupe fall prey to a mysterious killer, apparently one of their fellows who allegedly died years earlier.

Murders in the Rue Morgue benefits from particularly fine costume and set designs and a stronger than usual (for AIP) cast. Veteran thespians Herbert Lom, Lilli Palmer, Michael Dunn, and Adolfo Celi lend credible support to Robards, and several visual and thematic references to the 1932 version of the tale featuring Bela Lugosi indicate a desire to foreground the film within a rich and comparatively obscure offshoot of cinematic horror tradition. The allusions to the earlier version, coupled with the use of "Murders in the Rue Morgue" as a plot device rather than the movie's actual storyline, further develop the self-reflexivity and postmodern tendencies that inform the series beginning at least as far back as *War-Gods of the Deep*. Certainly *Murders* has its admirers: Phil Hardy concludes that it is "... Hessler's finest achievement to date" and enthusiastically defends the story's "intriguingly layered form which ultimately comes to represent the movement of fantasy itself.... In this way the boundaries between fantasy and reality are totally blurred.... the film's final sequences [are] lifted to the level of surrealist poetry" (237).

A number of slow-motion dream sequences seem to inform Hardy's assessment of the film, but in actuality these elements merely erode the glacier-like pace. Like *Cry of the Banshee, Murders in the Rue Morgue* is talky and seems much longer than its 87-minute running time; the plot twists are so unlikely as to expose the film to charges of absurdism more easily than surrealism. Most damning of all is a singularly ineffectual leading performance by Robards. Hailed as one of the finest stage actors of his generation, Robards seems absolutely incapable of delivering his lines with anything approaching conviction, and his wooden performance cannot help but inspire comparisons to Vincent Price, whose tendency to overplay silly parts would at least enliven the Charron character. Robards cannot imbue his character with either verisimilitude or a camp aesthetic; for all his talent, like Ray Milland in *Premature Burial,* Robards cannot "do" Vincent Price. *Murders in the Rue Morgue* is in the final analysis an interesting failure and a disappointing end to one of the most intriguing horror franchises in cinematic history.

Finally, any discussion of the Poe-Price series must note *An Evening of Edgar Allan Poe* (1972), a TV special produced by AIP and starring Vincent Price. Running less than an hour, the special serves as a one-man show for the star, who acts out a quartet of Poe's stories: "The Tell-Tale Heart," "The Sphinx," "The Cask of Amontillado," and "The Pit and the Pendulum." Although a low-budget affair shot on video, *An Evening of Edgar Allan Poe* is noteworthy as the most "pure" cinematic adaptation of the author's work, if only because writer-director-producer Kenneth Johnson — later to specialize in TV science fiction projects such as *The Incredible Hulk* (1977–1982) and *V* (1983–1984) — merely edits the stories so the star can perform them as a series of vignettes. What results is an appropriate farewell to Poe from the star. Interestingly, this project was for many years rarely broadcast and difficult to see — at least one fan magazine has claimed it was a "lost" film — but upon its DVD release in 2003, it became widely available and is frequently screened in literature classes for its faithful treatment of the source material.

CONCLUSION
A Play of Hopes and Fears: Final Thoughts

Although the tales of Edgar Allan Poe have been adapted for the cinema since the medium's infancy, it is the series of films produced by American International Pictures between 1960 and 1972 that represent the only significant effort to establish a franchise of Poe movies. As such, the series is a significant representation of the author's influence on popular culture and evidence of his relevance and recognition among modern audiences. Furthermore, the films constitute a major portion of the films made by AIP and directed by Roger Corman; they are also numbered among the key films that star Vincent Price and contribute substantially to his reputation as one of the most important horror stars in cinematic history.

In his influential survey, *American Horrors*, Gregory Waller claims that the early 1960s were

> dominated by horror films much safer and more formulaic ... like [the AIP] adaptations of Edgar Allan Poe stories ... peopled by inspired, grandly theatrical, often middle-aged villains; well-meaning, innocuous, young male heroes; and buxom young women waiting to be ravished or rescued. Blending an unambiguous style with easily decoded themes and "messages," these films are often small-scale social fables that reveal certain correctable flaws in the ... worlds they depict [257].

Waller's description of the iconography of these films may be accurate, but his reading of their significance is off the mark. As this study has suggested, there are far more complicated and conflicting messages about sexuality, the family unit, and sociopolitical cultural constructions here than Waller admits. Granted, a considerable number of themes and motifs are reiterated throughout the series, perhaps enough to make the series seem "formulaic." Nevertheless, there seems little justification for the claim that these films are "safer" just because they are not as explicit as Waller's primary concerns, the graphic and more obviously transgressive films that appeared in the wake of *Rosemary's Baby* and *Night of the Living Dead* (both 1968). There is more to Price's horror films than is apparent from cursory viewing. Perhaps it is their derivation from classic literature that makes the Poe series seem "tame" to Waller, but clearly the subversive commentary on class and gender encoded within the films is transgressive and provides insight into the sexual and social politics of the era in which the films were made.

Nevertheless, the most surprising realization that a close reading of the AIP Poe series offers is how faithful the entries are to the spirit, if not the letter, of Poe. Walter Kendrick is simply wrong when he dismisses the Poe cycle by asserting that Corman "turned Poe's stories back into the run-of-the-mill pulp they sprang from" and is concerned only with "the look, not the logic" of the source material (237). Certainly the first couple of efforts most resemble the sources, taking into account the modifications necessary to craft feature-length productions based on brief stories written long before the concept of motion picture adaptation emerged. Yet even films of later vintage, such as *The Oblong Box*, which seem to borrow a title and nothing else from Poe, are nevertheless informed by an awareness of the thematic and iconographic underpinnings of the author's work. It may well be that this awareness is derived more from the earlier entries in the AIP series than by anything specifically described in Poe's fiction and poetry, but even this theory admits the influence of the source material, even at a distant remove, on each of the movies discussed in this study.

Even when a film is made by different personnel from the usual AIP crew and originated with absolutely no idea of referencing Poe, as in the case of *Witchfinder General/The Conqueror Worm*, there *is* a thematic association with the author. The notion that Sam Arkoff and Jim Nicholson simply affixed a Poe title to the Michael Reeves film with no other consideration in mind other than profit has been disproved by Arkoff's own testimony and an examination of how Reeves' worldview neatly corresponds to Poe's *Weltanschauung*. It is true that AIP *forced* a Poe connection onto *Witchfinder General*—but it is also true that the device used to forge the connection is *appropriate*.

Each of the entries is foregrounded in an awareness of Poe's thematic concerns. Premature burial is an obvious dramatic element in the film of that title, but the concept is also more or less crucial to the plots of *House of Usher*, *Pit and the Pendulum*, *Tales of Terror* ("The Black Cat" episode), and *The Oblong Box*. The significance of will power and its relationship to hypnosis is contemplated in the "Case of M. Valdemar" episode of *Tales of Terror*, *The Haunted Palace*, and *The Tomb of Ligeia*. The pursuit of revenge against a perceived wrongdoer is crucial to the storylines of *Pit and the Pendulum*, the "Black Cat" episode of *Tales of Terror*, *The Conqueror Worm*, *The Oblong Box*, and *Cry of the Banshee*; the theme emerges to a lesser degree in most of the other films as well. Most significantly, all of the films are concerned with death, and all concern themselves to a greater or lesser extent with female characters.

Stephen Neale identifies "an intimate relationship [that] seems to exist among the filmic presentation of the horror monster, the castration anxiety it evokes, and the cinematic representation of the female form" (qtd. in Hollinger 296), and this theory is apparent in the Poe films where the attractive but deadly women are the monsters, challenging male hegemony and threatening to subvert rigidly defined gender roles. In turn, the subversion of masculine gender saps the male characters of intellectual, social, and sexual authority, further contributing to the collapse of performatively male identity. These subversive tendencies exist even when women are depicted as protagonists, as in the case of Rowena in *The Tomb of Ligeia*.

Interestingly, comparatively few of Poe's major female characters are clearly identified as victims; the narrator's wife in "The Black Cat" is unnamed and is a comparatively

Roderick Usher (Vincent Price) is master of his domain in Roger Corman's *House of Usher* (1960).

minor contributor to the action, other than through her association with the feline of the title. Therefore, the AIP films often create or modify females for Price to menace. Madeline Usher, Elizabeth Medina, and Emily Gault are the only female leads in the films clearly vilified, victimized, and venerated in relatively equal measure. Ligeia and Rowena, Elizabeth Shepherd's dual characters in *The Tomb of Ligeia*, are more difficult to identify because they are two different women who ultimately merge into one being. Thus the Ligeia persona is vilified and venerated, but never victimized; Rowena is certainly a victim and is venerated, more or less, by the male characters, but she is never identified as a villain. Only a few leading female characters are portrayed unambiguously; even victims like Francesca in *The Masque of the Red Death* and Sarah Lowes in *The Conqueror Worm* are portrayed as women to be venerated, for they are held up as idealized women by Prospero and Richard Marshall, respectively. Significantly, the less ambiguous female leads, such as Elizabeth Markham in *The Oblong Box*, are less complex and therefore less memorable.

As Steven Thornton has noted, women in the Poe series demonstrate a gradual growth as individuals:

> Pathetic Madeline Usher is the doormat of the bunch, failing to exhibit any personal initiative until her options have been restricted by a closed coffin lid. Both Elizabeth Medina and Lenore Craven improve on this approach somewhat by taking their affairs into their own hands.... Francesca and Juliana demonstrate even further progress by using the powers of their higher consciousness to influence the people around them. Finally, Lady Rowena ... becomes a virtual role model for today's generation of post-liberated women [241].

Thornton's survey ends with Corman's last contribution to the series; perhaps as a result of this change in creative direction, the developmental trend that Thornton describes is not continued in the films helmed by Gordon Hessler. Neither Elizabeth Markham nor Maureen Whitman demonstrates any measurable growth; Elizabeth is a totally static character, and Maureen becomes even more embroiled in the perverse dynamics of her dysfunctional family before dying unredeemed. Hilary Dwyer's first and foremost characterization, as Sarah in *The Conqueror Worm*, is unique in that she regresses from innocent country girl to ostensible willing victim before ultimately disintegrating into madness, destroyed along with her family, her fiancée, and her conceptions of justice and injustice — the intellectual and emotional components of her innocence.

The fate of Sarah Lowes is perhaps the most tragic example of the cultural horror experienced by the women in the Poe series. Even when the Price characters treat their distaff associates with kindness and love, these women remain oppressed by the patriarchal societies around them. Barbara Creed describes

> the concept of a border [that] is central to the construction of the monstrous in the horror film; that which crosses or threatens to cross the "border" is abject. Although the specific nature of the border changes from film to film, the function of the monstrous remains the same: to bring about an encounter between the symbolic order and that which threatens its stability [40].

The women in the Poe series dwell on this threshold between order and chaos, often inspiring or setting into motion the sequence of events that inevitably end in death and madness because they deliberately or inadvertently challenge the assumptions or expectations placed on them by their environments. Poe's women, and hence the women in these films, are frequently depicted in catatonic or hypnotized states. Sometimes they are controlled from beyond the grave, as in the case of Helene Valdemar. Annabel Herringbone is brutally murdered for cuckolding her dissipated husband even after years of patient and loving acquiescence to his cruel tyranny; her terrible death is an "acceptable" punishment for daring to transgress against Montresor's "rights" as a man and head of the household.

The least sympathetic of the female characters are still victimized by the repressive sociopolitical constructs in which they exist. Elizabeth Medina is possessed by the sexual insanity that haunts Castillo Medina, itself the product of a rigid patriarchal code established and enforced by her late father-in-law and his fellow members of the Inquisition. Lenore Craven seduces Erasmus and later Scarabus because it is her only means to gain a measure of power and independence in either the real or the magical realms, as both societies are dominated by male hegemony. It is only through marital or sexual alliance to older, aristocratic men — Sir Guy Carrell and Prince Prospero, respectively — that Emily Gault and Juliana can be assured of continual financial and personal security; it is their quest for hegemonic equality or supremacy that results in their destruction at the hands of their partners, men who cannot and will not tolerate any significant transgression against the codes of the patriarchy. Interestingly, these four women are portrayed by Barbara Steele (Elizabeth) and Hazel Court (the others), actresses already associated with horror films whose status as iconic "scream queens" would be solidified by their contributions to the Poe franchise. As a result, Steele and Court are almost as emblematic of the series as is Vincent Price; their personas are iconographic signifiers almost as familiar as the legendary horror star's image, even though they appear in far fewer entries than Price.

It is interesting to note that children are almost unheard of in the AIP series, even though most of the protagonists have apparently been married to their wives for several years. Of the 16 characters portrayed by Vincent Price over the course of the Poe series (including *Twice-Told Tales*), only four — Locke, Rappuccini, Erasmus Craven, and Lord Edward Whitman — are definitely established as being fathers. This is a strange statistic to discover considering that only four characters — Roderick Usher, Fortunato, Prospero, and Matthew Hopkins — are unmarried, although all are clearly sexually active except for Roderick (who may or may not have engaged in incestuous behavior with Madeline). Yet it is tendency reiterated throughout the horror films of Vincent Price that his characters remain childless; outside of the Poe series, Price's protagonists father children only in *The Last Man on Earth* (in which the child has died, as revealed in flashback) and in *Theatre of Blood*, in which the character's daughter (Edwina) is his enthusiastic assistant in mayhem.

Why there are no more children present is never definitely stated, but the emphasis on alternative sexuality, such as sadomasochism, in several films posits scenarios in which the characters do not practice conventional sexual intercourse. In some cases, such as in *Pit and the Pendulum* and *The Raven*, the wives in question are held up as romantic ideals, women so pure (at first glance) that they apparently cannot be "sullied" by coitus. In one instance, the "Case of M. Valdemar" episode of *Tales of Terror*, age and illness may explain the inability of a Price character to perform sexually. Furthermore, it is odd that when Price's characters do have children, the offspring are almost always female — both in the Poe series and in Price's other horror movies. This tendency further underscores the emphasis on women as objects of veneration — when wives do get pregnant, they can best be honored by bringing females in their image into the world. The lack of male children can be construed several ways; on one hand, there is a suggestion of incest, or at least a degree of unhealthy symbiosis between Price's characters and their daughters; on the other hand, the lack of sons foreshadows the inevitable end of the family lines that the Price characters represent. In yet another context, the absence of children suggests the queer nature of Price's characters, either in the sexual sense or in the broader sense of being "unsuccessful" heterosexual males.

If they die without a male heir, Price's characters will preside over the extinction of the family itself. Whatever wealth and prestige that remains will ultimately be subsumed by another family if daughters survive and marry; if the daughters do not reproduce, the family name dies anyway. In *House of Usher*, Roderick's greatest fear is that his line will continue — tellingly, under another name. In *Cry of the Banshee*, Price does have male children — two sons — yet they and their sister are portrayed as violent, wicked, incestuous people with little regard for their wealth or responsibilities. *Cry of the Banshee* is the only horror film — within the series or without — that depicts Vincent Price's character as having sons — and they are among the most despicable characters portrayed in any of the actor's projects. The lack of descendants, especially males, in the series symbolizes the decay of the aristocratic and patriarchal social order that the Price characters embody. The decay of the patriarchy in the series ultimately mirrors the social upheaval associated with sex and gender roles during the era in which the films were produced, in effect becoming pop culture commentaries on the transformations taking place within society at large.

Mark Neimeyer praises the efforts of Roger Corman and Vincent Price as "one of the high points in the commodification of Poe," although he undercuts his praise by attributing their popularity to "a semi-cult status that allows viewers to appreciate, and indeed revel in, the cheap special effects, campy dialogue, and kitschy atmosphere" (223). Crediting the survival of the Poe series to an enduring interest in "camp" and "kitsch" fails to take into consideration the millions of fans who have embraced the films out of a legitimate interest in horror, Poe, or Price himself. While undoubtedly some viewers approach the Poe films intending to laugh at them, the retrospectives of Corman's work and the many books about Price reveal a widespread affection and respect for the series essentially free of irony on the part of critics and fans alike.

Perhaps it is the presence of Vincent Price that makes associations with "camp" and "kitsch" so easy to make. While the actor does have a reputation for kidding the material in many of his acting assignments, his contributions to the AIP series demonstrate that the actor took them seriously, at least in regard to the first and best developed entries, such as *House of Usher*, *The Tomb of Ligeia*, and *The Conqueror Worm*. Roger Corman sums up the actor's importance best: "The keynote of his art lies, I believe, in his uncanny ability to embody and project the effects of mental aberration. He is rightly noted for his speaking voice and suave, polished presence through which he can convey eerie graduations of a sinister motivating force" (qtd. in Wiater 136).

In most cases, Price comes across as "campy" when he is performing a comic role, such as in the obviously farcical "Black Cat" episode of *The Raven*. Among the straight horror films, Price is unquestionably over the top and suggests an embrace of blurred or unstable sexuality in the early scenes of *Pit and the Pendulum*. However, once the simpering, confused Nicholas Medina is fully possessed by the spirit of his murderous father, Price's characterization is totally serious and aggressively heterosexual. Granted, the irony and malice inherent in some of Price's line readings throughout the series might inspire a grim chuckle among audiences, but such a reaction could well reflect viewers' relief that Price's depredations are not directed at them. By the time the Revenge Cycle films were made, Price's screen persona was so firmly established that the movies made self-reflexive acknowledgment a major justification for their creation in the first place.

Price's movies have promoted interest in and awareness of Poe's place, not just as a figure in horror literature, but among the most influential writers in American literature and popular culture. As this study demonstrates, the star's major horror films contain pointed (though often subtextual) observations about gender and sex roles. Although intended as commercial products intended to make a profit from the amusement of a largely youthful and presumably uncritical audience, the films are rich with symbols and subtle allusions to the volatile issues associated with the social and sexual revolution of the Sixties. Such symbolic and thematic richness helps explain the films' continuing appeal. In the final analysis, however, the series' initial success and source of enduring interest is primarily attributed to the charismatic, energetic, and (more often than not) controlled performances of Vincent Price.

Virginia North as Vulnavia enjoys the Phibes ballroom in *The Abominable Dr. Phibes* (1971).

FILMOGRAPHY

The Abominable Dr. Phibes. Dir. Robert Fuest. Scr. James Whiton, William Goldstein. Perf. Vincent Price, Joseph Cotten, Virginia North, Caroline Munro. AIP, 1971.

The Bat. Dir. Crane Wilbur. Scr. Crane Wilbur. Perf. Vincent Price, Agnes Moorehead, Gavin Gordon, Lenita Lane, Darla Hood, John Sutton. Allied Artists, 1959.

The Comedy of Terrors. Dir. Jaques Tourneur. Scr. Richard Matheson. Perf. Vincent Price, Peter Lorre, Boris Karloff, Basil Rathbone, Joyce Jameson, Joe. E. Brown. AIP, 1963.

The Conqueror Worm. Dir. Michael Reeves. Scr. Michael Reeves, Tom Baker. Perf. Vincent Price, Ian Ogilvy, Hilary Dwyer, Rupert Davies, Robert Russell, Patrick Wymark. AIP, 1968.

Cry of the Banshee. Dir. Gordon Hessler. Scr. Tim Kelly, Christopher Wicking. Perf. Vincent Price, Essy Persson, Hilary Dwyer, Hugh Griffith, Elizabeth Bergner. AIP, 1970.

Diary of a Madman. Dir. Reginald LeBorg. Scr. Robert E. Kent. Perf. Vincent Price, Nancy Kovack, Joseph Ruskin. United Artists, 1963.

Dr. Phibes Rises Again! Dir. Robert Fuest. Scr. Robert Blees, Robert Fuest. Perf. Vincent Price, Robert Quarry, Valli Kemp, Caroline Munro, Peter Cushing. AIP, 1972.

Dragonwyck. Dir. Joseph L. Mankiewicz. Scr. Joseph L. Mankiewwicz. Perf. Gene Tierney, Walter Huston, Vincent Price. 20th Century–Fox, 1946.

An Evening of Edgar Allan Poe. Dir./Scr. Kenneth Johnson. Perf. Vincent Price. AIP, 1972.

The Fly. Dir. Kurt Neumann. Scr. James

Poster artwork for *Dr. Phibes Rises Again!* (1972).

Clavell. Perf. Al Hedison, Patricia Owens, Vincent Price, Herbert Marshall. 20th Century–Fox, 1958.

The Haunted Palace. Dir. Roger Corman. Scr. Charles Beaumont. Perf. Vincent Price, Lon Chaney, Debra Paget. AIP, 1963.

House of Usher. Dir. Roger Corman. Scr. Richard Matheson. Perf. Vincent Price, Mark Damon, Myrna Fahey. AIP, 1960.

House of Wax. Dir. Andre de Toth. Scr. Crane Wilbur. Perf. Vincent Price, Phyllis Kirk, Frank Lovejoy, Carolyn Jones, Paul Picerni. Warner Bros., 1953.

House on Haunted Hill. Dir. William Castle. Scr. Robb White. Perf. Vincent Price, Richard Long, Carol Ohmart, Elisha Cook. Allied Artists, 1958.

The Last Man on Earth. Dir. Sidney Salkow, Ubaldo Ragona. Scr. Richard Matheson (as Logan Swanson), William P. Leicester. Perf. Vincent Price, Franca Bettoia, Emma Danieli, Giacomo Rossi-Stuart. AIP, 1964.

The Mad Magician. Dir. John Brahm. Scr. Crane Wilbur. Perf. Vincent Price, Eva Gabor, Donald Randolph, Mary Murphy, Patrick O'Neal. Columbia, 1954.

Madhouse. Dir. Jim Clark. Scr. Greg Morrison, Ken Levison. Perf. Vincent Price, Peter Cushing, Adrienne Corri, Robert Quarry, Natasha Pyne, Linda Hayden. AIP, 1974.

The Masque of the Red Death. Dir. Roger Corman. Scr. Charles Beaumont, R. Wright Campbell. Perf. Vincent Price, Hazel Court, Jane Asher. AIP, 1964.

Murders in the Rue Morgue. Dir. Gordon Hessler. Scr. Christopher Wicking. Perf. Jason Robards, Herbert Lom, Adolfo Celi. AIP, 1971.

The Oblong Box. Dir. Gordon Hessler. Scr. Lawrence Huntington. Perf. Vincent Price, Christopher Lee, Hilary Dwyer, Rupert Davies. AIP, 1969.

Pit and the Pendulum. Dir. Roger Corman. Scr. Richard Matheson. Perf. Vincent Price, Barbara Steele, John Kerr, Luana Anders. AIP, 1961.

Premature Burial. Dir. Roger Corman. Scr. Charles Beaumont and Ray Russell. Perf. Ray Milland, Hazel Court, Richard Ney, Heather Angel, Alan Napier. AIP, 1962.

The Raven. Dir. Roger Corman. Scr. Richard Matheson. Perf. Vincent Price, Peter Lorre, Boris Karloff, Hazel Court, Jack Nicholson. AIP, 1963.

Return of the Fly. Dir. Edward L. Bernds. Scr. Edward L. Bernds. Perf. Vincent Price, Brett Halsey, David Frankham, John Sutton, Danielle De Metz. 20th Century–Fox, 1959.

Scream and Scream Again. Dir. Gordon Hessler. Scr. Christopher Wicking. Perf. Vincent Price, Christopher Lee, Peter Cushing, Judy

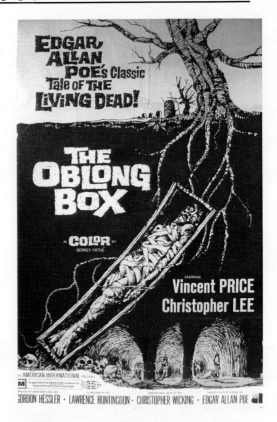

One-sheet for *The Oblong Box* (1969).

Huxtable, Alfred Marks, Michael Gothard. AIP, 1970.

Shock. Dir. Alfred Werker. Scr. Eugene Ling. Perf. Vincent Price, Lynn Bari, Anabel Shaw. 20th Century–Fox, 1946.

Spirits of the Dead. Dirs. Roger Vadim, Louis Malle, Federico Fellini. Scr. Roger Vadim, et al. Perf. Jane Fonda, Peter Fonda, Alain Delon, Brigitte Bardot, Terence Stamp, Vincent Price (narration). AIP, 1969.

Tales of Terror. Dir. Roger Corman. Scr. Richard Matheson. Perf. Vincent Price, Peter Lorre, Basil Rathbone, Joyce Jameson, Debra Paget, Leona Gage, Maggie Pierce. AIP, 1962.

Theatre of Blood. Dir. Douglas Hickox. Scr. Anthony Greville-Bell. Perf. Vincent Price, Diana Rigg, Ian Hendry, Coral Browne. United Artists, 1973.

The Tingler. Dir. William Castle. Scr. Robb White. Perf. Vincent Price, Judith Evelyn,

Darryl Hickman, Patricia Cutts, Philip Coolidge. Columbia, 1959.

The Tomb of Ligeia. Dir. Roger Corman. Scr. Robert Towne. Perf. Vincent Price, Elizabeth Shepherd, Oliver Johnson. AIP, 1965.

Tower of London. Dir. Roger Corman. Scr. Leo V. Gordon, Amos Powell, and James B. Gordon. Perf. Vincent Price, Michael Pate, Joan Freeman, Robert Brown, Charles Macaulay, Sandra Knight, Bruce Gordon. United Artists, 1962.

Twice-Told Tales. Dir. Sidney Salkow. Scr. Robert E. Kent. Perf. Vincent Price, Sebastian Cabot, Mari Blanchard, Brett Halsey, Joyce Taylor, Beverly Garland. United Artists, 1963.

War-Gods of the Deep. Dir. Jacques Tourneur. Scr. Charles Bennett and Louis M. Heyward. Perf. Vincent Price, Tab Hunter, David Tomlinson. AIP, 1965.

WORKS CITED

Benshoff, Harry M. *Monsters in the Closet: Homosexuality and the Horror Film*. Manchester: Manchester University Press, 1997.

Berenstein, Rhonda J. *Attack of the Leading Ladies: Gender, Sexuality, and Spectatorship in Classic Horror Cinema*. New York: Columbia University Press, 1996.

Bloom, Harold, ed. *Edgar Allan Poe*. Broomall, PA: Chelsea House, 1999.

Boot, Andy. *Fragments of Fear: An Illustrated History of British Horror Films*. London: Creation, 1996.

Brosnan, John. *The Horror People*. New York: St. Martin's, 1976.

Butler, Judith. *Gender Trouble: Feminism and the Subversion of Identity*. 1990. Rpt. In *The Norton Anthology of Theory and Criticism*. Ed. Vincent B. Leitch. New York: Norton, 2001. 2485–2501.

Castiliga, Paul. "*Tales of Terror* (1962), *The Raven* (1963), and *The Comedy of Terrors* (1963)." Svelha and Svelha 185–197.

Castle, William. *Step Right Up! I'm Gonna Scare the Pants Off America*. New York: Putnam, 1976.

Clark, Mark. *Smirk, Sneer and Scream: Great Acting in Horror Cinema*. Jefferson, NC: McFarland, 2004.

Clover, Carol. *Men, Women, and Chain Saws: Gender in the Modern Horror Film*. Princeton, NJ: Princeton University Press, 1992.

Corman, Roger, and Jim Jerome. *How I Made a Hundred Movies in Hollywood and Never Lost a Dime*. 1990. New York: Da Capo, 1998.

Creed, Barbara. "The Monstrous-Feminine: An Imaginary Abjection." *Screen* 29.1 (Jan.–Feb. 1986) Rpt. in Grant 35–65.

Fisher, Benjamin, Franklin Fisher. "Poe and the Gothic Tradition." Hayes 72–91.

French, Karl, and Phillip French. *Cult Movies*. London: Pavilion, 1999.

Gagne, Paul R. *The Zombies That Ate Pittsburgh*. New York: Dodd, Mead, 1987.

Gelder, Ken, ed. *The Horror Film Reader*. London: Routledge, 2000.

Goldstein, William. *Dr. Phibes*. New York: Award, 1971.

_____. *Dr. Phibes Rises Again!* New York: Award, 1972.

Grant, Barry Keith, ed. *The Dread of Difference: Gender and the Horror Film*. Austin: University of Texas Press, 1996.

Gray, Beverly. *Roger Corman: Blood-Sucking Vampires, Flesh-Eating Cockroaches, and Driller Killers*. New York: Thunder's Mouth, 2004.

Hall, Angus. *Devilday*. 1969. Rpt as *Madhouse*. London: Sphere, 1974.

Hawthorne, Nathaniel. "Dr. Heidegger's Experiment." *Young Goodman Brown and Other Short Stories*. 1–9.

_____. *The House of the Seven Gables*. 1851. Mineola, NY: Dover, 1999.

_____. "Rappaccini's Daughter." *Young Goodman Brown*, 35–59.

_____. *Young Goodman Brown and Other Short Stories*. New York: Dover, 1992.

Halligan, Benjamin. *Michael Reeves*. Manchester: Manchester University Press, 2003.

Hardy, Phil, ed. *The Encyclopedia of Horror Movies*. New York: Harper, 1986.

Harrison, William N. "The Curses of Dr. Phibes." *Monsterscene* 10 (1997): 4–13.

Hayes, Kevin J., ed. *The Cambridge Companion*

to *Edgar Allan Poe*. Cambridge and New York: Cambridge University Press, 2002.

Hollinger, Karen. "The Monster as Woman: Two Generations of Cat People." *Film Criticism* 13.2 (Winter 1989): 36–46. Rpt. in Grant 296–308.

Hutchinson, Tom, and Roy Pickard. *Horrors: A History of Horror Movies*. Secaucus, NJ: Chartwell, 1984.

Janis, James J. J. "150 Years of Women and Horror: She Has Always Lived In the Castle." *Midnight Marquee* 71/72 (Summer 2004): 50–63.

Kendrick, Walter. *The Thrill of Fear: 250 Years of Scary Entertainment*. New York: Grove, 1991.

King, Stephen. *Stephen King's Danse Macabre*. New York: Berkley, 1983.

Lampley, Jonathan Malcolm. "*The Tomb of Ligeia* (1964)." Svehla and Svehla 216–221.

_____, Ken Beck, and Jim Clark. *The Amazing, Colossal Book of Horror Trivia: Everything You Ever Wanted to Know About Scary Movies but Were Afraid to Ask*. Nashville: Cumberland House, 1999.

Levitch, Vincent B. *The Norton Anthology of Literary Criticism*. New York: Norton, 2001.

Lovecraft, H. P. *The Case of Charles Dexter Ward*. 1941. New York: Beagle, 1971.

Maltin, Leonard, ed. *Leonard Maltin's 2007 Movie Guide*. New York: Signet, 2006.

Matheson, Richard. *I Am Legend*. 1954. New York: Orb, 1997.

McCarty, John. *The Modern Horror Film: 50 Contemporary Classics*. New York: Citadel, 1990.

McGee, Mark Thomas. *Roger Corman: The Best of the Cheap Acts*. 1988. Jefferson, NC: McFarland, 1997.

Meikle, Denis. *Vincent Price: The Art of Fear*. London: Reynolds and Hearn, 2003.

Miller, Mark A. "*Pit and the Pendulum* (1961)." Svehla and Svehla 159–171.

Morris, Gary. *Roger Corman*. Boston: Twayne, 1985.

Mulvey, Laura. "Visual Pleasure and Narrative Cinema." *Visual and Other Pleasures*. Rpt. in Leitch, et al., 2179–2192.

Murray, John B. *The Remarkable Michael Reeves: His Short and Tragic Life*. 2002. Baltimore: Luminary, 2004.

Neimeyer, Mark. "Poe and Popular Culture." Hayes 205–225.

Nollen, Scott Allen. "*The Fall of the House of Usher* (1960)." Svehla and Svehla 139–145.

Nutman, Philip. "Scream and Scream Again: The Uncensored History of Amicus Productions." *Little Shoppe of Horrors* 20 (2008): 5–98.

Parish, James Robert, and Steven Whitney. *Vincent Price Unmasked*. New York: Drake, 1974.

Peary, Danny. *Cult Movies: The Classics, the Sleepers, the Weird, and the Wonderful*. New York: Gramercy, 1981.

Pendleton, Thomas A. "What Price Shakespeare?" *Literature Film Quarterly* 29.2 (2001): 135–146.

Phillips, Jayne Anne. "*Premature Burial*." *The Movie That Changed My Life*. Ed. David Rosenberg. New York: Viking, 1991. 37–49.

Pirie, David. *A Heritage of Horror: The English Gothic Cinema, 1946–1972*. New York: Equinox/Avon, 1974.

Pitts, Michael R. *Horror Film Stars*. 3d ed. Jefferson, NC: McFarland, 2002.

Poe, Edgar Allan. *The Complete Tales and Poems of Edgar Allan Poe*. New York: Vintage, 1975.

_____. "The Black Cat." Poe, 223–230.

_____. "The Cask of Amontillado." Poe, 274–279.

_____. "The Conqueror Worm." Poe, 960–961.

_____. "The Facts in the Case of M. Valdemar." Poe, 96–103.

_____. "The Fall of the House of Usher." Poe, 231–245.

_____. "The Haunted Palace." Poe, 959–960.

_____. "Ligeia." Poe, 654–666.

_____. "The Masque of the Red Death." Poe, 269–273.

_____. "Morella." Poe, 667–671.

_____. "The Pit and the Pendulum." Poe, 246–257.

_____. "The Poetic Principle." Poe, 889–907.

_____. "The Premature Burial." Poe, 258–268.

_____. "The Raven." Poe, 943–945.

_____. "Spirits of the Dead." Poe, 1016–1017.

Prawer, S. S. *Caligari's Children: The Film as Tale of Terror.* New York: Oxford University Press, 1980.

Price, Victoria. *Vincent Price: A Daughter's Biography.* New York: St. Martin's, 1999.

Rigby, Jonathan. *English Gothic: A Century of Horror Cinema.* London: Reynolds and Hearn, 2000.

Saxon, Peter. *The Disorientated Man.* 1966. Rpt. as *Scream and Scream Again.* New York: Paperback Library, 1970.

Senn, Bryan. "*Witchfinder General* (1968)." Svehla and Svehla 223–233.

Silver, Alain, and James Ursini. *More Things Than Are Dreamt Of: Masterpieces of Supernatural Horror, From Mary Shelley to Stephen King, In Literature and Film.* New York: Limelight, 1994.

_____, and _____. *Roger Corman: Metaphysics on a Shoestring.* Los Angeles: Sillman-James, 1996.

Skal, David J. *Hollywood Gothic: The Tangled Web of Dracula from Novel to Stage to Screen.* Rev. ed. New York: Faber and Faber, 2004.

_____. *The Monster Show: A Cultural History of Horror.* Rev. ed. New York: Faber and Faber, 2001.

Smith, Don G. *The Poe Cinema: A Critical Filmography.* Jefferson, NC: McFarland, 1999.

Svehla, Gary, and Susan Svehla, eds. *Vincent Price.* Baltimore: Midnight Marquee, 1998.

Thompson, Jeff. Personal Interview. July 30, 2009.

Thornton, Steven. "The Women of American International Pictures." *Bitches, Bimbos, and Virgins: Women in the Horror Film.* Ed. Gary J. Svehla and Susan Svehla. Baltimore: Midnight Marquee, 1996. 206–245.

Todorov, Tzvetan. "Definition of the Fantastic." *The Fantastic.* Ithaca: Cornell University Press, 1975. Rpt. in Gelder 15–19.

Waller, Gregory A. "Introduction." *American Horrors.* Urbana and Chicago: University of Illinois Press, 1987. Rpt. in Gelder 256–264.

Weldon, Michael. *The Psychotronic Encyclopedia of Film.* New York: Ballantine, 1983.

Wiater, Stanley. *Dark Visions: Conversations with the Masters of the Horror Film.* New York: Avon, 1992.

Williams, Linda. "When the Woman Looks." *Re-Vision: Essays in Feminist Film Criticism.* Frederick, MD: University Publications/ American Film Institute, 1983. 83–99. Rpt. in Grant 15–34.

Williams, Lucy Chase. *The Complete Films of Vincent Price.* New York: Citadel, 1995.

Worland, Rick. "Faces Behind the Mask: Vincent Price, Dr. Phibes, and the Horror Genre in Transition." *Post Script: Essays in Film and the Humanities* 22.2 (2003): 20–33.

Worrall, Dave, and Lee Pfeiffer. "*Witchfinder General.*" *Cinema Retro* 2.5 (2006): 26+.

Wright, Bruce Lanier. *Nightwalkers: Gothic Horror Movies: The Modern Era.* Dallas: Taylor, 1995.

INDEX

Numbers in **_bold italics_** indicate pages with photographs.